Viajes fantásticos

The Storyteller's Series

*To Tracy David Terrell,
who loved storytelling.*

Viajes fantásticos

Elías Miguel Muñoz

McGraw-Hill, Inc.

New York   St. Louis   San Francisco   Auckland   Bogotá
Caracas   Lisbon   London   Madrid   Mexico City
Milan   Montreal   New Delhi   San Juan
Singapore   Sydney   Tokyo   Toronto

Viajes fantásticos

This book is printed on acid-free paper.

8 9 0   FGR   FGR   9 0 9 8

ISBN 0-07-044311-4

This book was set in Bauer Bodoni by Clarinda Typesetting.
The editors were Thalia Dorwick and Richard Mason.
The text consultant was Polly Hodge.
The production supervisor was Diane Renda.
The text and cover designer was Juan Vargas.
The cover illustrator was Don Baker.
The photo researcher was Stephen Forsling.
This book was printed and bound by Fairfield Graphics.

Library of Congress Cataloging-in-Publication Data
Muñoz, Elías Miguel.
    Viajes fantásticos / Elías Miguel Muñoz.
        p.   cm. — (The Storyteller's Series)
    ISBN 0-07-044311-4
    1. Spanish language—Readers. I. Title. II. Series:
Storyteller's Series (San Francisco, Calif.)
PC4117.M86   1994
428.6'4—dc20   93-42280
                                                               CIP

Grateful acknowledgment is made for use of the following photographs:

Page 1 © Polly Hodge; *3* © Robert Frerck/Odyssey Productions; *4* © Polly
Hodge; *8* Chip and Rosa María de la Cueva Peterson; *23* The Bettmann
Archive; *25* © Robert Frerck/Odyssey Productions; *27* From the Codex
Mendoza, courtesy of The Bodleian Library, Oxford, ms. Arch. Selden A. 1.
folio 67r; *28* courtesy of the Trustees of The British Museum; *29* The
Bettmann Archive; *31* © Nigel Atherton/Tony Stone Images; *36* © Robert
Frerck/Odyssey Productions; *39* © Robert Frerck/Odyssey Productions;
47 Neg. no. 326597, courtesy of the Department of Library Services,
American Museum of Natural History; *54* From the Codex Mendoza, courtesy
of The Bodleian Library, Oxford, ms. Arch. Selden A. 1. folio 60r; *62* The
Bettmann Archive; *69* Mary Evans Picture Library; *76* Mary Evans Picture
Library; *81* courtesy of the Biblioteca Nazionale Centrale, Florence, photo by
M. Schioppetto, La Photographie; *83* © Stuart Cohen/Comstock.

Contents

Preface

Pleasure Reading

Pleasure reading is without a doubt one of the most effective means for helping students improve in a second language. There is overwhelming evidence that reading for pleasure is highly beneficial for language acquisition and literacy development. Research studies have shown that those who read more read better, write with a more sophisticated style, have larger vocabularies, spell more accurately, and have a deeper understanding of complex grammatical structures. In fact, research strongly suggests that time spent pleasure reading is more beneficial for language development than time spent in direct instruction.[1]

Pleasure reading has numerous other benefits. It is an important source of knowledge and ideas. Studies show

---

[1] For a review of the research on the benefits of reading, *see* Krashen (1993), *The Power of Reading*. Englewood, Colorado: Libraries Unlimited.

that those who read more know more.[2] By definition, pleasure reading is also very enjoyable. According to Mihaly Csikszentmihalyi, a researcher in psychology at the University of Chicago, this type of reading induces a state of "flow," deep but effortless involvement, in which the concerns of everyday life disappear. Flow, in turn, induces "enjoyment" which, Csikszentmihalyi argues, is different from physical or biological pleasure. Although flow can result from a number of activities, reading "is currently perhaps the most often mentioned flow activity in the world."[3]

For those concerned about the relationship between reading for pleasure and the study of literature, we have good news: Reading for pleasure may lay the foundation for the appreciation of literature. A group of researchers (Davis, Kline, Gorell, and Hsieh) recently investigated predictors of positive attitudes toward literature among students enrolled in sixth-semester foreign-language literature classes. Leisure reading was one of the strongest predictors. Those who had done more leisure reading in a foreign language reported more positive attitudes toward the study of literature.[4]

Pleasure reading may be part of the bridge that the foreign language teaching profession has been looking for

---

[2] Research reviewed in Krashen (1990). *How Reading and Writing Make You Smarter, or, How Smart People Read and Write*, J. Alatis (Ed.), Georgetown University Round Table on Languages and Linguistics, 1990 (364–376). Washington, D.C.: Georgetown University Press.

[3] Csikszentmihalyi, M. (1990). *Flow: The Psychology of Optimal Experience.* New York: Harper Perennial.

[4] Davis, J., Kline, R., Gorell, L., and Hsieh, G. (1992). "Readers and Foreign Languages: A Survey of Undergraduate Attitudes Toward the Study of Literature." Modern Language Journal, 76, 320–332.

between beginning language courses and the study of literature. A student who has read extensively for pleasure will be much better prepared for more difficult input.

Our challenge is to provide beginning language students with reading that is both pleasurable and comprehensible. It is fairly easy to satisfy one of the two requirements of pleasure and comprehension, but not both. Interesting readings are readily available; the real world is full of good books. Comprehensible readings are also easy to find; beginning language textbooks, for example, are full of accessible practice materials. But *authentic* readings are usually not comprehensible to language students, and the comprehensible readings we usually find in textbooks are not always interesting.

The Storyteller's Series provides students of Spanish with comprehensible reading material and hopes to inspire in them the desire to read more. The stories in this series take advantage of the principle of *narrow input*, the idea that comprehension and thus language acquisition increase when the reader reads a great deal in one area, on one topic, or reads works by a single author. Instead of short passages or brief excerpts, these readers provide students with full-length novellas. Because of the familiar context provided by the novellas, such long texts are much more comprehensible, and therefore result in more language acquisition.

How to Use *The Storyteller's Series*

The best way to use this series is as leisure reading. No pre-reading activities are necessary; pre-reading activities are only needed when the text facing the student is too difficult or when he/she lacks necessary background information. But readers don't need special background knowledge in order to follow the stories in *The Storyteller's Series.* Also, because these texts are designed to be read for *pleasure*, students should not feel "forced" to read them. If the story a student is reading is too difficult, if there are too many unknown words *(see below)*, then the student should not be reading that story. We recommend that he/she first read something easier and try the story later.

Activities are provided for each story at the back of the book and are meant to be done after students have read the entire piece. These activities were not designed as comprehension-checking exercises, nor were they supposed to reinforce grammar or vocabulary; rather, they were written to help stimulate interesting discussion of the meaning of the story and to relate its themes to the students' lives. In other words, these **Actividades** treat the texts as literature, not as pedagogical exercises. Through classroom discussion, students will get additional comprehensible input and deepen their appreciation for what they have read.

No comprehension checking is necessary. When reading is meaningful, the act of reading itself provides its own comprehension check. If the story makes sense, the reader is clearly understanding it.

Nor are there vocabulary exercises in *Viajes fantásticos* or the other *Storyteller* books. Research has shown that pre-teaching vocabulary before reading is of doubtful value, and we expect students to *acquire* vocabulary as they read. Studies indicate that each time we see an unfamiliar word in print, we acquire a small portion of its meaning, eventually building up to the full meaning of the word.

We recommend that when students encounter an unfamiliar word, they first try to skip it. Ironically, this practice will result in more vocabulary acquisition, not less. If readers skip unknown words they will read more, and acquire more words from context; if they stop to look up every new word they will read less, and, of course, reading will then become a tedious activity devoid of the pleasure we are trying to induce.

When a word cannot be skipped because it is truly essential to the meaning of the passage, we encourage students to *guess* at the word's meaning. If the student guesses correctly, the text will make sense. If the student guesses incorrectly, the text will probably not make sense and the student will guess again. In those cases where guessing doesn't work and a word is essential, the student can look it up in the glossary provided or in a dictionary. We anticipate that this will not happen very often in our series.[5]

Reading can be done in class or as homework. Some instructors prefer to set aside five to ten minutes per period for "sustained silent reading" and/or read the initial portions of the stories out loud to students in class. This in-class reading helps to get the students involved in the text and to whet their appetites for reading at home.

Our hope is that readers of *The Storyteller's Series* will be reading for pleasure in Spanish long after their courses end. If they continue to read, they will continue to improve their language abilities, whether native speakers are available to them or not. In addition, they will gradually gain a deep appreciation for another culture while engaging in an activity that is profoundly enjoyable.

---

[5] The strategy recommended here is for use in extensive reading, not intensive reading. In intensive reading, readers cannot risk skipping words. The strategy of skipping words, then guessing, is ideal, however, for extensive pleasure reading; it explains why leisure reading is such a good way of building vocabulary knowledge and developing other aspects of language and literacy competence.

Mi querida cuñada

1

 Aquel mes que pasé en San Juan fue estupendo:
playa, sol, bailes. Me divertí mucho y conocí a
gente chévere.[1] Pero las vacaciones de verano
llegaban a su fin. Ya no tenía dinero y, la verdad,
estaba cansado de tantas fiestas. Era hora de volver a Quebradillas, mi pueblo.

Vista aérea de San Juan, capital de Puerto Rico. La ciudad se encuentra en una península al nordeste de la isla.

---

[1] *super, cool* (*coll. P. R.*)

Una mañana muy temprano me fui a las afueras de la ciudad. Tendría que pedir pon[2] hasta Quebradillas: ochenta millas, más o menos. «¡Ojalá que no tenga que esperar mucho tiempo!», pensé. Tenía hambre y me dolía un poco la cabeza. Por suerte, después de media hora de espera, me recogió el conductor de un camión de carga; era un hombre mayor de aspecto amistoso. El interior del vehículo tenía un fuerte olor a sudor. Una estampa de la Virgen colgaba del espejo retrovisor y en la guantera[3] estaba pegada la foto de dos mujeres. El camionero se dio cuenta de que yo estaba observando la foto.

EL OCÉANO ATLÁNTICO

San Juan

Quebradillas

Puerto Rico

EL MAR CARIBE

—Son mis hijas— comentó, sonriendo.

—Qué bonitas son —le

Puerto Rico.

dije. Pero eso no era cierto, sólo una de ellas era bonita.

Le pregunté sobre la carga que llevaba, y me respondió que normalmente transportaba un poco de todo. En este viaje cargaba productos para un supermercado. Me explicó que no podía llevarme muy lejos; iba a recoger a dos amigos en un pueblito a unos treinta kilómetros de San

---

[2] pedir... *to hitch a ride* (*coll. P.R.*)   [3] *glove compartment*

Juan. En su camión, obviamente, no había espacio para cuatro personas.

Aquel camionero me inspiraba confianza. ¡Qué lástima que no iba a poder continuar mi viaje con él! Yo tenía deseos de conversar con alguien y, además, no quería seguir pidiendo pon. De pronto me sentía enfermo, con una sensación muy extraña. Todas las cosas a mi alrededor⁴ se veían desenfocadas,⁵ como a través de un cristal opaco. El único objeto que podía distinguir con claridad era la foto de aquellas dos muchachas. Una era hermosa, de pelo castaño y mirada tierna; la otra llevaba demasiado maquillaje.

Cerré los ojos por unos segundos y traté de calmarme. Cuando los abrí, el mareo⁶ había pasado y me sentía un poco mejor. Noté que estábamos acercándonos al pueblito. Vi a dos hombres que nos hacían señas.⁷ El camionero los recogió y me dejó a mí allí, a la entrada del pueblo.

—Buena suerte —me dijo. Y vi desaparecer el camión en la distancia.

Yo conocía todos los pueblos entre San Juan y Quebradillas, pero no recordaba esta villa⁸ tan desolada. No se veía a nadie en las calles. ¿Qué lugar era éste? ¡Hacía tanto calor!

Caminé hasta llegar a la pequeña plaza y me senté a descansar. Estaba a punto de quedarme dormido cuando un enorme monstruo se detuvo ante mí. Al principio creí que era una alucinación causada por el hambre y el calor.

---

⁴ a... *around me* ⁵ *out of focus* ⁶ *nausea, dizziness* ⁷ nos... *were waving to us* ⁸ *village*

Me levanté, di unos pasos, y entonces comprendí que aquel monstruo era un Cadillac. Lo conducía una extraña mujer. Tenía la cara delgada, muy maquillada, y su cabello rubio parecía una peluca.[9] Llevaba puestos unos guantes azules. Saludé a la señora secamente. Subí al carro y tiré mi mochila en el asiento de atrás. Luego salimos de allí.

—¿Va usted muy lejos? —me preguntó la mujer, sonriendo.

—Voy a Quebradillas —le contesté.

—¡Perfecto! Para allá voy yo también. Y me alegro mucho, porque no me gusta viajar sola. ¿Es usted de Quebradillas?

—Sí.

—¿Cómo se llama usted?

— Vicente —le dije sin mirarla.

—Mi nombre es Marie; se pronuncia *Marí*, como en francés, con acento en la *í*.

La observé detenidamente.[10] Nunca antes había visto a esta señora y, sin embargo, su cara me era familiar. Había algo en ella, su mirada quizás, que me daba la impresión de conocerla.

—Dígame, Vicente, ¿le gusta San Juan?

—Sí. Bastante. Voy cada vez que puedo.

—A mí también me gusta, aunque prefiero Nueva York; los rascacielos, los teatros.... Viví los mejores años de mi vida en la Gran Manzana. Desde que murió mi esposo, resido en San Juan. Le voy a ser sincera: si no fuera[11] por mi hermana, nunca saldría de la capital.

—¿Dónde vive su hermana?

—En Quebradillas, claro. Por eso voy para allá... Ella es muy buena, una mujer muy fuerte. La pobre, desde que

---

[9] *wig*   [10] *intently*   [11] si... *if it weren't*

se casó con Vicente... ¡Ay! ¡Qué casualidad! Mi cuñado se llama Vicente, como usted... En fin, como le decía, desde que se casó con él, no ha podido salir de ese pequeño infierno. Ella dice que le gusta vivir en el campo...

—Pero Quebradillas no es campo —comenté, defensivo—. Es casi una ciudad.

—¡Por Dios, Vicente! Ese lugar es más pueblo que ciudad y más campo que pueblo.

—Si usted lo dice...

—Sé muy bien lo que digo, Vicente. Yo nací en Quebradillas, y mi hermana también...

—¿Cómo puede hablar tan mal del lugar donde nació? —le reproché.

—No hablo mal —contestó ella, muy calmada—. Sólo digo la verdad. Es cierto que por estar en la costa, Quebradillas tiene el atractivo del mar y un clima ideal, aire limpio. Pero toda la gente de allí es tan provinciana. ¿No cree usted?

—No. No creo.

—Perdone, Vicente. A veces hablo sin pensar. Usted es de Quebradillas y entiendo que se sienta ofendido...

—No me importa lo que usted piense de mi pueblo. Yo estoy orgulloso de ser de ese «pequeño infierno».

—Bueno, debo admitir que los niños de mi hermana se han criado muy saludables en Quebradillas. ¡Ay, quiero tanto a esos niños! Yo no pude tener hijos; mi hermana y mis dos sobrinos son toda mi familia. Por supuesto que excluyo al inútil de mi cuñado.[12] Vicente es muy buen padre, pero es tan tonto ese hombre, tan mediocre...

Marie no paraba de hablar. Para aliviarme de su voz, me concentré en el paisaje. Por la ventanilla veía pasar

---

[12] al... *my good-for-nothing brother-in-law*

Los flamboyanes son una presencia constante en la flora de Puerto Rico. En los paisajes de la isla abundan estos árboles de flores rojas.

palmeras y colinas verdes. Los flamboyanes[13] a lo largo de[14] la carretera —altos, hermosos— daban la impresión de ser el techo de un túnel. Y nosotros íbamos a través de aquel túnel que era de un color rojo, intenso, lleno de luz.

—Mi difunto esposo —continuó Marie— me acostumbró a las comodidades de la metrópolis. Yo no podría vivir, como mi hermana, en esos laberintos rurales. Sólo

---

[13] árboles de hermosas flores rojas que crecen en los países del Caribe
[14] a... *alongside*

espero que un día mis sobrinos puedan salir de allí. ¡Qué graciosos son esos niños! ¡Y muy inteligentes! Mire, le muestro una foto...

Marie sacó de su cartera la foto de un niño y una niña que tendrían de seis a siete años. Tuve que admitir que en verdad eran muy hermosos.

Me sorprendió la confianza que la mujer ponía en mí. Allí estaba yo, un desconocido que fácilmente podría ser un delincuente; y allí estaba ella con su cartera y sus billetes adentro. «Qué fácil sería agarrar todo el dinero, volver a San Juan y continuar mis vacaciones», pensé. «Pero no, yo no soy un ladrón», me dije a mí mismo, reprochándome aquella fantasía.

—¿Qué le parece si paramos a comer algo? —me preguntó Marie.

—Me parece muy bien —le respondí.

—¿A usted qué tipo de comida le gusta, Vicente?

—La que hace mi madre.

—¡Oh! Pues a mí me gusta la *cuisine française*.[15] ¡Qué salsas tan deliciosas! La comida francesa es muy bella, con mucho adorno, ¿no cree usted? Es para ser admirada y saboreada poco a poco, con placer. Cuando como a la francesa me siento, ¿cómo diría yo?, con un *je ne sais quoi*,[16] me siento *chic*... ¡Ay, espero no estar aburriéndolo, Vicente!

Nos detuvimos a comer en un cafetín de esos que abundan a lo largo del camino. Me pareció raro no ver a nadie aden-

---

[15] *cuisine... French cuisine (Fr.)*   [16] un... *a certain something* (Fr.)

tro; era la hora del almuerzo y las cinco o seis mesas del lugar estaban vacías. Marie y yo nos sentamos en una que estaba junto a la ventana.

—Señora... —le dije.

—¡Por favor! —me interrumpió—. ¡Llámeme Marie! Con acento en la *í*.

—Bueno, Marie... le agradezco el pon que me está dando. Es usted muy amable.

—No me gusta viajar sola, Vicente, ya se lo dije. Para mí es un placer llevarlo a su pueblo.

—¿No le da miedo levantar a un tipo como yo?

—¿Un tipo como usted? ¿Qué quiere decir con eso?

—Míreme bien: tengo aspecto de vagabundo.

—¡No! Usted es simplemente un joven que quiere regresar a casa de sus padres. ¿Por qué iba a tenerle miedo?

—Es que, hoy en día no se puede confiar mucho...

—Vicente, cuando yo miro a alguien, sé inmediatamente qué tipo de persona es. Usted, la verdad, me inspira confianza.

—Qué bueno, Marie... Y ahora, quiero pedirle un gran favor.

—Sí, ¿qué se le ofrece?

—Es que... no tengo dinero para la comida.

—Pida lo que quiera. Yo lo invito.

—Gracias. Cuando lleguemos a Quebradillas, le devuelvo el dinero.

—¡Nada de eso! No tiene que devolverme nada.

La mesera apareció por fin. Era una mujer gruesa,[17] de unos cincuenta años. Su aspecto era amistoso y su sonrisa espontánea. Al verla me sentí a gusto en aquel lugar vacío.

---

[17] gorda

—Bienvenidos —dijo—. ¿Qué van a pedir?

—¿No nos trae el menú? —le preguntó Marie.

—Señora, el menú lo traigo yo aquí adentro —dijo, tocándose la frente—. ¡Soy la dueña y también la cocinera! Puedo servirle sopa de pollo, ensalada de lechuga y tomate, arroz con gandules,[18] tostones,[19] pan, arepas,[20] café, cerveza y agua. Es todo lo que tengo. ¿Qué le gustaría pedir?

—A mí... no sé —dijo Marie, un poco indecisa, mientras se quitaba los guantes—. A mí tráigame la sopa y un café.

—¿Nada más? ¿No quiere probar el arroz con gandules? ¡Es mi especialidad!

—No, gracias. Prefiero algo ligero.

—Muy bien. ¿Y usted, señor?

—Tráigame un poco de todo.

—¡¿Un poco de todo?! —exclamó la mesera, sorprendida.

—Sí. Tengo mucha hambre —dije, mirando a Marie—. Y la señora invita.

—¡Claro que sí! —contestó mi compañera de viaje.

La comida resultó muy sabrosa; me gustaron especialmente las arepas y el café. Después de comer, continuamos nuestro viaje. Marie quería seguir hablando, pero yo tenía sueño y muy pocas ganas de escucharla. Le dije que quería dormir un rato y ella pareció desilusionada. Recuerdo lo último que le oí decir:

— Si gusta, venga a visitarnos. Le va a caer muy bien

---

[18] arroz... *rice with pigeon peas*   [19] *fried green plantain slices*
[20] *fried, flat cornmeal cakes*

mi hermana. ¡Y los niños! Voy a quedarme con ellos una semana. Venga a vernos, Vicente.

Dormí durante el resto del viaje y Marie me despertó cuando llegamos a Quebradillas. Miré a mi alrededor. No estábamos muy lejos de mi casa.

—Déjeme aquí mismo, por favor —le pedí.

—¿Está seguro? Puedo llevarlo a su casa...

—Aquí está bien.

Le di las gracias y ella extendió su mano de guante azul. Yo tuve el impulso de besarle la mano como todo un caballero y así lo hice. Ella se mostró halagada[21] y un poco sorprendida.

—¡Venga a visitarnos! —me dijo al despedirse.

—¡Lo haré! —contesté, mintiéndole. Porque yo no tenía el menor deseo ni intención de ver a aquella señora otra vez.

---

[21] *flattered*

2

 Mis padres se alarmaron mucho cuando me vieron tan delgado y con una barba de dos días.

—¡Vicentico! —exclamó mamá, besándome—. ¡No te reconozco! ¿Estás enfermo, mijo[22]? ¿Qué te pasa?

—No me pasa nada, mamá. Sólo estoy un poco cansado.

Papá cargó[23] mi enorme mochila y la llevó a mi cuarto. El viejo tenía esa sonrisa de felicidad que brilla en su cara cada vez que vuelvo de un viaje.

—Bienvenido, muchacho— me dijo, y me abrazó.

¡Qué raro se sentía estar allí! Siempre que pasaba algún tiempo en San Juan, olvidaba cómo era aquella casa. Y en cada regreso experimentaba el mismo choque. Me ponía a observar los cuadros de vivos colores, los adornos, el papel floreado de las paredes, las lámparas de cristal, las flores en la mesa del centro...

A pesar del choque, esta vez sentí que la casa me daba la bienvenida, que me recibía como lo hacían mis padres, con los brazos abiertos.

---

[22] mi hijo (*coll.*)   [23] *carried*

Después de una noche de sueño tranquilo, me desperté con la primera luz del día y fui a la cocina. Allí encontré a mi madre, quien me ofreció un cafecito fuerte y un abrazo.

—Qué alegría me da tenerte aquí, muchacho.

—Y yo me alegro de haber vuelto, mamá.

—¡Te extrañé tanto!

—¡Pero si sólo estuve fuera un mes!

—Y parece que no comiste nada en todo ese tiempo —observó mamá, mientras me preparaba el desayuno.

—¿Dónde está papá? —le pregunté.

—En el campo. El trabajo del campesino empieza antes que el día, ya tú lo sabes.

—Esto está delicioso —le dije, saboreando el café.

—Y espera que pruebes las arepas que te estoy haciendo. ¡Están para chuparse los dedos![24]

Recordé en ese momento lo que le había dicho a Marie, que la comida que más me gustaba era la de mi madre. Era verdad. Estando allí con ella, en la cocina, no me podía imaginar un mejor lugar en todo el mundo. El olor dulce a plátano frito, el aroma del pan recién hecho, el sonido de las arepas cuando caen a la sartén[25] con grasa caliente, la voz de mamá... Aquella cocina era el hogar.[26] La realidad. Quebradillas.

—A ver si esta noche estás de ánimo[27] para recibir a don Manuel —me dijo mi madre.

—¿Don Manuel?

—Sí, hijo. Ese hombre se portó tan bien contigo.

---

[24] ¡Están... *They're finger-licking good!*   [25] *frying pan*   [26] casa
[27] de... *in the mood*

Vendrá a visitarnos esta noche con su esposa y su hija, Laurita.

—¿De qué don Manuel me hablas?

—Del camionero, hijo. Te recogió en las afueras de San Juan y te trajo hasta la misma puerta de la casa. ¡Dice que durante el camino tuviste un desmayo!

—Yo no recuerdo haberme desmayado...

—Normalmente cuando uno se desmaya luego no recuerda que se desmayó, Vicentico.

—No entiendo...

—Es que el hambre y el cansancio te han afectado la cabeza. Yo te lo dije: No vayas otra vez a San Juan. ¡La capital corrompe a los jóvenes!

—No exageres, mamá.

—¿Que no exagere? ¡Mira en qué condiciones te encuentras! Si no fuera por don Manuel, quién sabe dónde estarías ahora.

—Sigues hablando de ese hombre que yo no conozco.

—Vas a reconocerlo cuando lo veas, estoy segura... Tiene un corazón de oro ese don Manuel. Te llevó a un restaurante del camino y te hizo comer y descansar. Y no siguió su viaje hasta que te vio recuperado.

—¡Pero eso no es cierto, mamá! Yo volví a esta casa gracias a Marie, una señora que me recogió en su Cadillac, me invitó a almorzar y me dejó cerca de aquí...

—¿Quién dices que te trajo?

—¡Marí! —casi le grité, pronunciando el nombre con una erre francesa muy marcada.

—Ay, bendito.[28] ¿Pero estuviste... con una mujer, Vicentico? ¡Y con una que tiene un nombre tan ridículo!

—Esa mujer sólo me dio pon, mamá. Viajé con ella.

---

[28] *good God!* (*coll. P. R.*)

—No, hijo —dijo Mamá, preocupada—. Aquí no llegó ninguna mujer contigo.

Le describí a mi madre en detalle mi viaje con Marie. Se lo describí varias veces tratando de convencerla. Ella sólo me miraba incrédula, me acariciaba[29] la frente y me decía que yo todavía necesitaba mucho descanso y buena comida...

---

[29] *caressed*

3

 Estaba ansioso por descifrar aquel misterio. Le pedí prestado el auto a un amigo para recorrer otra vez el camino que había recorrido con Marie. Tenía que encontrar pruebas. Iría a ver a la dueña de aquel café donde almorzamos. Ella seguramente recordaría a mi compañera de viaje. Esa mujer me sacaría de dudas.[30] ¡Yo estaba seguro!

A mis padres el plan les pareció una locura. Mamá hizo todo lo posible por calmarme y trató de comprender mi ansiedad. Papá me escuchó con paciencia. Pero ninguno de los dos entendía la razón de mi búsqueda.[31] ¿Para qué tenía yo que regresar a San Juan? ¿Qué «verdad» tenía yo que buscar en ese camino?

—Por favor, Vicentico —me imploró mamá—. Olvídate ya de esa tal «Ma-rrí». ¿Qué necesidad tienes tú de ir otra vez a ese lugar que te trastornó la cabeza[32]?

—San Juan no me trastornó la cabeza, mamá.

—No, ya lo sé, fue esa mujer la que lo hizo. ¿Por qué no tratas de olvidarla, hijo?

—No puedo. Porque aquí todos piensan que estoy loco. Y yo tengo que probarles que no lo estoy.

---

[30] me... *would clear up my doubts*   [31] *quest, search*   [32] te... *drove you crazy*

—Nadie dice que estás loco, Vicentico. Lo que sí dice la gente... y es lo que yo creo también, es que cuando te desmayaste en el camión de don Manuel, probablemente tuviste un sueño. Y ahora piensas que ese sueño fue la realidad, pero...

—¡Yo no me he inventado ese viaje, mamá!

—Bueno, bueno —intervino mi padre—. ¡Anda! Busca las pruebas que necesitas para convencernos. Pero... déjame que vaya contigo.

—No, papá. Tengo que ir yo solo.

Recorrí en el auto de mi amigo aquella ruta misteriosa. Casi podía escuchar otra vez la voz de Marie. Por la ventanilla veía pasar un paisaje conocido. El túnel rojo de flamboyanes refrescaba en mi memoria la presencia de aquella señora: sus guantes azules, su voz insoportable, su peluca rubia...

Llegué por fin al cafetín donde Marie y yo paramos a comer. Había mucha gente. Miré por todos lados, pero no encontré a la mujer que nos había servido. Una mesera joven se movía rápidamente entre las mesas, atendiendo ella sola a tantas personas. Me le acerqué y le dije que necesitaba hablar con la dueña.

—Ahora la llamo —me dijo—. Pero está en la cocina, y muy ocupada, así que va a tener que esperar.

—No me importa esperar.

—Está bien. Siéntese y tome algo, si quiere.

Me senté y pedí un café con leche. Pasaron veinte minutos y por fin apareció la dueña y cocinera, la mujer que nos había servido a Marie y a mí. ¡Era la misma! Gruesa, de sonrisa amable. Sentí un gran alivio al verla.

Después de saludarla, le expliqué por qué quería hablar con ella.

—Hace unos días yo estuve aquí. ¿Se acuerda de mí?

—Sí... —respondió la mujer.

—¿Y recuerda usted a la señora que vino conmigo? Fue ella quien pagó la comida, ¿recuerda? Tenía el pelo rubio y llevaba guantes azules...

La dueña se quedó pensando unos minutos y luego dijo:

—A usted sí lo recuerdo, pero a esa señora no. Usted llegó a este restaurante con un camionero. El hombre venía muy preocupado porque usted se había desmayado en su camión. Yo le puse compresas[33] en la frente y lo reviví con una sopa de pollo y con mi buen café...

—¿Está segura, señora? —dije, exasperado—. Piénselo bien.

—Por aquí pasa mucha gente, señor. Pero muy poca llega desmayada. A usted lo recuerdo perfectamente porque cuando entró aquí tenía cara de muerto. ¡Estaba tan pálido!

—¿Y con quién llegué? ¿Quién me trajo?

—¡Ya se lo dije! Un camionero...

—¡Todos quieren hacerme creer que estoy loco! —grité—. ¡Todos se han puesto de acuerdo! ¡Todos!

—¡No sé de qué me habla! —exclamó la mujer.

—Se lo repito, señora: yo entré aquí con una mujer. Nos sentamos y ella le pidió el menú. Usted le dijo que el menú lo tenía memorizado y entonces recitó todo lo que nos podía servir. ¿Recuerda? Sopa de pollo, arroz con gandules, tostones, arepas, café...

---

[33] *cold packs*

—¡Pero aquí servimos mucho más que eso! —contestó la dueña, ofendida—. ¡Y mire usted! —agarró uno de los menús que había en una mesa—. Aquí sí tenemos menú. ¡Y es muy bonito! Lo diseñó mi hija...

—¡Escúcheme, señora! —grité otra vez—. Aquel día no había menús. Mi compañera de viaje pidió la sopa y yo pedí un poco de todo. Y usted se sorprendió. ¿No se acuerda? ¡Dígame que sí se acuerda!

La pobre mujer empezó a temblar. Debo haber parecido un verdadero loco. Me amenazó con llamar a la policía si no me iba inmediatamente. Algunos de los hombres que comían allí se me acercaron; uno me agarró por el cuello[34] y me ordenó:

—¡Fuera de aquí!

Confundido, me fui de aquel lugar. Al parecer mis padres tenían razón. Todos tenían razón. El hambre, el cansancio y el calor me habían causado el desmayo y luego aquel absurdo sueño: mi viaje con Marie.

«El camionero que me recogió en las afueras de San Juan», pensé, «aquel señor de aspecto amistoso, era don Manuel. Este amable conductor nunca me dejó en aquel pueblito desolado y tampoco recogió a sus dos amigos. Yo seguí mi trayecto con él hasta Quebradillas y nunca me encontré con Marie. Nunca.»

Me sentí más calmado después de aceptar, por fin, la verdad de aquella pesadilla. Regresé a casa con el propósito de olvidar a Marie, de borrarla[35] para siempre de mi memoria.

---

[34] me... *grabbed me by the neck*   [35] *erase her*

4

 Don Manuel tenía el corazón de oro, según mi madre. Y era cierto: el hombre era generoso y noble; todo el mundo lo quería en Quebradillas.

Don Manuel tenía dos hijas. La mayor se había ido desde muy joven a Nueva York y allí se había casado con un comerciante norteamericano. Nadie se acordaba de ella en el pueblo. La otra hija, Laura, era soltera y se parecía mucho al padre en el carácter. Laura era, además, una mujer muy bella.

Poco tiempo después de aquel extraño viaje, empecé a salir mucho con Laura. Nos gustaba estar juntos, conversar, dar largas caminatas por la playa, abrazados. No exagero al decir que nos enamoramos locamente. Al cabo de unos meses de noviazgo, le propuse matrimonio y ella aceptó. Pedí su mano, nos comprometimos y tuvimos una modesta pero memorable boda en la iglesia del pueblo.

He tenido varios trabajos; entre ellos, ayudando a mi padre en las faenas[36] del campo y manejando el camión de don

---

[36] trabajos

Manuel. Hace dos años encontré el empleo que tengo ahora. Soy cajero de un banco. Me gusta mucho este trabajo porque me permite usar mi talento para las matemáticas.

Laura y yo somos los orgullosos padres de un niño y una niña. Confieso que soy feliz, aunque hemos tenido nuestros altos y bajos; cosas típicas de todos los matrimonios.

Nuestra pelea[37] más grande, hasta ahora, fue por causa de la hermana de Laura. Es una señora extravagante de peluca rubia y guantes azules que viene a visitarnos con frecuencia. Se llama Marie, con acento en la í, y habla constantemente. ¡Nunca se calla!

Tolero a mi «querida» cuñada porque adora a mis hijos; además, quiero evitarle sufrimientos a mi esposa. Pero tengo razones suficientes para detestar a esta señora. Aunque ella trate de ser amable conmigo, siempre, desde aquel viaje en Cadillac, he sabido lo que opina de mí.

---

[37] *fight*

El último sol

Prólogo

Tenochtitlán

Según el mito azteca, los antiguos mexicanos o *mexica* vinieron de Aztlán, una región árida y fría del norte. Un día su dios jefe les habló de una zona fértil que se encontraba al sur. «¡Búsquenla!», les dijo. «Deben detenerse al encontrar un *nopalli*[1] y un águila real en su nido».

Entonces todos los mexica —llamados también az-

El emblema mexicano del águila sobre el nopal y la serpiente.

---

[1] nopal

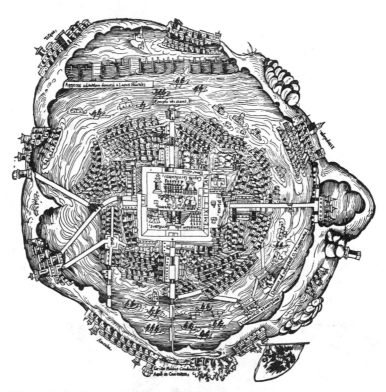

Plano de la ciudad de México-Tenochtitlán.

tecas por venir de Aztlán— salieron hacia el sur. El
trayecto duró años. Llegaron por fin a un valle donde había
un lago, y en el centro de ese lago descubrieron una isla
deshabitada. Allí estaba el águila sobre el nopal. En esa isla
fundaron su ciudad, Tenochtitlán.

Mientras construían su ciudad, los aztecas podían ver
cada noche a «Metzli», la luna, reflejada en las aguas del
lago. Por eso empezaron a llamar a su tierra Metzli-Xictly,
«en medio de la luna». Con el tiempo, el nombre se abrevió
a Mexitli, y después a México. Desde que fundaron su
ciudad, los mexica tuvieron como signo y emblema el águila

sobre el nopal. En el pico,[2] el águila sostiene una serpiente, símbolo de guerra.

Los mexica, o aztecas, extendieron su dominio y llegaron a tener una civilización poderosa. Ellos consideraban que México-Tenochtitlán estaba en el centro del universo, *In Cem-Anahuac Yoyotli*, y que Tenochtitlán era el corazón del mundo.

La guerra florida y el sacrificio humano

El imperio de los aztecas fue muy vasto. El emperador sometía[3] a los pueblos vecinos y les pedía tributos excesivos. En batallas que los aztecas llamaban «guerras floridas», capturaban a sus adversarios para sacrificarlos a Tonatiuh, dios del sol.

Guerreros aztecas con sus trajes militares.

---

[2] *beak* [3] *subdued, mastered*

Cuchillo de obsidiana que se usaba en el sacrificio humano.

El sacrificio consistía en atar[4] al prisionero sobre una piedra. Luego un sacerdote le abría el pecho con un cuchillo y le sacaba el corazón. Este corazón era presentado como ofrenda[5] a los dioses, para calmar su hambre y conseguir su protección.

Las cinco eras del mundo

Los aztecas tenían un calendario al cual llamaban la Piedra del Sol. Este calendario era una piedra plana[6] de forma redonda.[7] En su superficie estaban grabadas todas las eras anteriores en la historia sagrada.

La primera era —o sol —fue destruida por tigres, la segunda por vientos, la tercera por lluvia ardiente y la cuarta por agua. El quinto sol, la era bajo la cual vivieron los aztecas, nació en la fecha ceremonial de 13-Caña.[8] Los aztecas creían que cada 52 años ocurriría una catástrofe que daría fin a la quinta era, pero ellos posponían su destrucción por medio de sacrificios.

La catástrofe llegó finalmente, y ellos no pudieron evi-

---

[4] *tying up* [5] *offering* [6] *flat* [7] *round* [8] *13-Reed*

tarla. El quinto sol quedó extinto al llegar los españoles al «centro y corazón» del mundo.

El calendario, la hermosa Piedra del Sol, dejó de funcionar en 1519, año en que Hernán Cortés[9] entró en Tenochtitlán.

El calendario azteca, también conocido como la Piedra del Sol. En el centro está la figura de Tonatiuh, dios del sol, quien recibía simbólicamente el corazón de los soldados sacrificados. Alrededor de Tonatiuh se ven los cuatro períodos cósmicos del mundo y, en el próximo círculo, los 20 símbolos del día. Abajo se juntan las colas de dos serpientes en la fecha sagrada de la creación.

---

[9] conquistador español (1485–1547)

Parte I

Paseo de la Reforma en la Ciudad de
México.

Uno

Daniel Flores tuvo suerte cuando llegó a la Ciudad de México. Consiguió un trabajo de botones[10] en el Hotel del Prado. Trabajaba seis horas en la mañana y por la tarde recibía clases de agronomía en la UNAM.[11] Su trabajo era aburrido y monótono; más que nada cargaba[12] maletas. Pero de vez en cuando conocía a personas interesantes. Y siempre podía admirar el mural de Diego Rivera que había en el hotel, el cual mostraba numerosos eventos de la historia mexicana.

Daniel sentía pasión por la historia; quería dedicarse a su estudio, pero ésa no era una carrera práctica. Inevitablemente, sus estudios tenían que estar relacionados con el campo y la agricultura. Su deber era ayudar a su padre a mejorar los medios de cultivo en su finca.

Fue su padre quien lo convenció de venir al Distrito Federal[13] para hacer una carrera. Un día le dijo:

—Daniel, hijo, ya tienes dieciocho años. Es hora de que salgas de aquí y estudies. Nosotros vamos a ayudarte. Podemos vender parte de la tierra y algunos animales. Tu

---

[10] *bellhop*   [11] Universidad Nacional Autónoma de México   [12] *he carried*   [13] Distrito... la capital del país; comparable con el Distrito de Columbia

madre y yo necesitamos poco para vivir. No tenemos otros hijos que mantener. Te ayudaremos.

Agradecido, Daniel aceptó la oferta de su padre. Se propuso aprovechar al máximo su tiempo en la capital y terminar pronto su carrera. El dinero que sus padres le facilitaban con sacrificios no era suficiente. Por eso tenía que trabajar para comprar sus libros y pagar su alojamiento.[14] Pero tarde o temprano Daniel iba a realizar su sueño. Su objectivo era estudiar mucho hasta llegar a ser ingeniero agrónomo. Después de finalizar sus estudios, iba a regresar a Ayapango, su pueblo, para ayudar a su familia en el trabajo de su finca. Y, quizás, para casarse con su novia, Chalchi.

Los primeros meses en la capital fueron difíciles. Daniel extrañaba su casa y el enorme nogal[15] del patio con sus nueces que caían como lluvia. Extrañaba el olor a humo de la cocina, la lucha diaria con las ardillas[16] que querían comerse el maíz almacenado.[17] Y extrañaba sobre todo la vista fantástica de los volcanes Iztaccíhuatl y Popocatépetl.

Cuando Daniel era niño, se levantaba muy temprano casi todos los días y se sentaba debajo del nogal. Los volcanes iban apareciendo lentamente, con la luz del día. Él los saludaba desde el patio de su casa. Después, de adolescente, todos los domingos hacía el viaje en tren desde Ayapango hasta el pueblo de Amecameca, que está casi a los pies del «Izta» y del «Popo». El paisaje lo llenaba de ánimo:

---

[14] *lodging*   [15] *walnut tree*   [16] *squirrels*   [17] *stored*

los campos abiertos, el verde de la tierra, las humildes casitas de teja roja.[18]

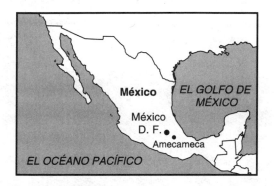

Allí, tan cerca de los volcanes, Daniel se dejaba llevar por su imaginación, recordando todas las leyendas sobre esas dos montañas. En todos los relatos, los protagonistas eran dos amantes separados por la muerte y unidos por los dioses. La unión eterna de un hombre y una mujer convertidos en volcanes...

Allí, junto a Popo e Izta, Daniel pensaba en Chalchi, su noviecita de la infancia.

Después de un año en la Ciudad de México, Daniel todavía visitaba con frecuencia el Museo de Antropología. Las visitas al museo eran su premio[19] por todo el estudio y el trabajo. En la Sala Mexica estaba la exhibición que más le interesaba. Le gustaba observar detenidamente los diferentes instrumentos de obsidiana, reliquias de la an-

---

[18] teja... *red tile*   [19] *reward, prize*

El Museo de Antropología en la Ciudad de México.
Después de vivir un año en la capital, Daniel todavía
visitaba este museo con frecuencia. Sus visitas eran un
premio por todo el estudio y el trabajo.

tigua cultura que él ahora podía describir como todo un
experto.

Una estatua pequeña de barro negro: Tezcatlipoca,
dios de la noche. Otra figurilla con un falo[20] enorme:
Quetzalcóatl, el dios de la creación. Otra con plumas:
Huitzilopochtli, dios de la guerra. La diosa del maíz, Chi-
comecóatl, era una figura sencilla de piedra caliza.[21] Y una
figura de mujer, pequeña, con pechos[22] exuberantes era
Xochiquétzal, diosa del amor y la fertilidad.

El objeto más impresionante del museo era sin duda la
Piedra del Sol, el calendario azteca. A primera vista parecía
un objeto arqueológico más. Era grande, redonda, y en el
centro llevaba la cara de Tonatiuh, dios del sol; su mirada

---

[20] *phallus*   [21] piedra... *limestone*   [22] *breasts*

fija en el vacío, la boca abierta, dispuesta a devorar corazones. Alrededor de Tonatiuh estaban representadas las cuatro eras del mundo que precedieron al quinto y último sol; con esa piedra se podía estudiar el comienzo y el fin de una de las civilizaciones más poderosas que ha existido en el mundo.

Daniel salía a veces con compañeros de la universidad. Iba al parque, a fiestas. Pero nadie podía ocupar el lugar que él tenía guardado para su novia. Después de un año de separación, la extrañaba como el primer día. De aquella muchacha le gustó primero su nombre, Chalchiunenetl, que en el idioma náhuatl[23] quería decir «muñeca[24] de jade».

Chalchi, como la llamaban todos, tenía los ojos muy verdes; ella era mucho más que una simple muñeca de jade para Daniel. Chalchi vibraba, se movía segura de sí misma; era industriosa y expresiva. Ayudaba a su madre en los quehaceres de la casa y en la crianza[25] de sus hermanos menores. Pero también conocía los secretos del maíz y le gustaba conversar con su padre sobre los detalles de su cultivo.

Chalchi escuchaba, fascinada, los pasajes de la historia mexicana que Daniel compartía con ella. Él le regalaba libros — novelas en ediciones baratas que compraba en la Ciudad de México— porque a Chalchi le apasionaba la lectura. Ella soñaba con hacer una carrera, pero no se animaba a abandonar a su familia. Sus padres, que ya esta-

---

[23] idioma de los aztecas   [24] *doll*   [25] *upbringing*

ban viejos, la necesitaban; como también la necesitaban sus hermanos.

Daniel quería ser amigo y compañero de Chalchi. La extrañaba mucho. Sólo le consolaba pensar que, al concluir sus estudios, volvería a Ayapango para casarse con ella. ¡Pero faltaba tanto tiempo! Tardaría casi cuatro años en[26] terminar su carrera. Mientras tanto, podía comprometerse formalmente[27] con ella. Sí, eso es lo que iba a hacer muy pronto: proponerle matrimonio a Chalchi; iba a pedir su mano y fijar la fecha de la boda. Todavía no podía darle un anillo de compromiso;[28] tendría que ahorrar mucho para comprarlo.

Vivirían en Ayapango y tendrían hijos, una casa, una finca pequeña...

«¡Qué típico!», pensaba Daniel. Típicos eran los dos. O quizás no. Quizás eran dos seres únicos, fieles el uno al otro, unidos desde siempre como los dos volcanes.

---

[26] Tardaría... *It would take him almost four years*   [27] *formally*
[28] anillo... *engagement ring*

Dos

Hoy Daniel trabajó más de lo acostumbrado. No tiene deseos de estudiar; tampoco quiere quedarse en este cuarto que alquila en una casa de familia, a escuchar música en su pequeño radio. Este verano, por suerte, no toma ninguna clase y le queda más tiempo para estar con sus amigos, y para leer sus libros de historia y mitología mexicanas.

Después de quitarse el uniforme de botones y ponerse

Detalle de un mosaico de Diego Rivera en el Parque de Chapultepec.

otra ropa, Daniel trata de hacer algún plan. Por lo general, en un día largo de verano, le gusta caminar por el Parque de Chapultepec y sentarse a la sombra[29] de un árbol. A veces se encuentra con algún amigo en la explanada de la UNAM y van a tomar algo en el Café de Filosofía y Letras.[30]

Daniel camina largo rato por la Avenida Juárez,[31] donde está el Hotel del Prado. Toma el metro en la primera parada que tiene delante, y se baja en la Avenida Insurgentes. Llega al café, que está repleto de gente.

Hoy, por primera vez, le molesta el ruido y la compañía de los demás. Se queda allí, tomando cerveza y conversando con sus cuates [32] por una hora, y luego se despide. Tiene deseos de estar solo. Esta noche quiere leer hasta muy tarde.

Daniel piensa en sus padres. Hace tiempo que no los visita. ¿Un mes? Al principio, cuando llegó a la capital, iba a verlos con frecuencia. Ahora tiene tanto que estudiar y demasiado trabajo en el hotel. Pero ya es hora de volver a Ayapango. Esta vez tiene una razón especial: ¡va a proponerle matrimonio a Chalchi!

Le ha pedido unos días libres a su jefe, sus primeras vacaciones desde que empezó a trabajar en el Prado. Al irse, corre el riesgo[33] de perder su empleo. «No importa», piensa él. «Si pierdo éste, ya conseguiré otro.»

Sube a su habitación, que está en la azotea,[34] y se

---

[29] *shade* [30] Café... en el edificio de la Facultad de Filosofía y Letras de la Universidad Autónoma [31] Avenida... avenida nombrada por Benito Juárez (1806–1872), presidente de México de 1857 a 1872 [32] amigos, compañeros (*coll. Mex.*) [33] corre... *he runs the risk* [34] *attic*

alegra de poder vivir aquí arriba. Le gusta contemplar el paisaje de luces de neón, el movimiento constante que enciende las venas de la ciudad. Transportado por su imaginación, se pregunta cómo habrá sido[35] realmente este lugar cuando un día de 1519, Cortés lo tuvo ante sus ojos.

Daniel trata de recordar uno de los poemas del libro que ha estado leyendo últimamente, *Los Metzli;* es una antología de un grupo de jóvenes poetas que trata de rescatar[36] y actualizar la poesía náhuatl. Daniel ha conocido a algunos de aquellos escritores en el Café de Filosofía y Letras, y los admira mucho. Él quisiera escribir, como ellos, sobre los mitos aztecas: dioses, flores, las cuatro épocas del mundo. Quisiera, pero no puede. «Yo no soy poeta», piensa Daniel. Prefiere aprenderse los poemas de memoria...

Entre flores de luz naciste un día
Tenochtitlán
para brillar en todo el universo
tu corazón
el corazón de todo ser viviente
tu voz
la voz del sol
la voz del viento

De las aguas brotaste[37]
Tenochtitlán
como el águila azul
volaste al cielo
y regresaste para ser el Centro
In Cem-Anahuac Yoyotli
El corazón de todo el universo...

---

[35] cómo... *what it must have been like*   [36] *recover, rescue*
[37] *you sprang forth*

La mañana siguiente, Daniel se levanta muy temprano y hace la maleta. Llama a su jefe y le recuerda que va a estar ausente por unos días. Su jefe le repite que siempre hay mucho trabajo en el hotel, que regrese lo antes posible.

Esa misma mañana, Daniel Flores toma el tren en la estación San Lázaro, rumbo a su pueblo natal, Ayapango.

Tres

A través de la ventanilla del tren, Daniel disfruta del paisaje. El cielo nunca le pareció tan azul, ni el verde de la hierba tan verde. Daniel nota el contraste entre aquellos hogares provincianos y los rascacielos del Distrito Federal. En la capital: tráfico incesante y aire contaminado. En la provincia: campos de maíz, el silencio de las noches interrumpido a veces por una guitarra campesina.

«La capital tiene un poder extraño sobre la gente», —piensa Daniel—. «La estimula con mil distracciones y le impide momentos de reflexión».

Daniel siente que necesita la tranquilidad de Ayapango, la calma de las mañanas. Mientras recorre a pie el corto camino de la estación de tren a su casa, Daniel recuerda con alegría el sabor a humo y a agua fresca de los platos de su madre, las tortillas calentitas que ella amasa.

Y recuerda a Chalchi.

Luvina, su madre, dio gritos de alegría cuando lo vio parado en la puerta. Lo abrazó. Lo besó. Empezó a hablar, sin descanso, de lo último que ocurría en el pueblo. Daniel la escuchaba y la observaba. Siempre la misma sonrisa, los mismos pasos lentos y la mirada baja, el mismo rebozo[38] y la falda larga, limpia a pesar del duro trabajo de la casa.

Su padre, Juan, también lo abrazó. Le dijo que se alegraba de verlo. Le preguntó cómo estaba y que cuánto tiempo pensaba quedarse.

—Unos días —le respondió Daniel.

—¿Y tus estudios? —preguntó Juan, preocupado.

—No tengo ninguna clase este verano, papá.

—¿Y el trabajo en el hotel? —le preguntó su madre.

—Pedí vacaciones.

Luvina notó algo diferente en su hijo. Lo encontraba más callado,[39] pensativo. Se dio cuenta de que Daniel observaba la casa, la ropa que ella llevaba, el fogón de leña,[40] las cazuelas.[41] Lo miraba todo como por primera vez.

Ella se le acercó y le pasó la mano por la frente, por el cabello.

—Daniel, ¿te sientes bien? —le preguntó—. ¿Te pasa algo?

—No, mamá, no me pasa nada. Es que... tenía muchos deseos de verlos, de estar aquí con ustedes.

Luvina y Juan intercambiaron[42] una mirada. Estaban felices. Ella se dirigió al fogón y empezó a mover cazuelas, entusiasmada.

—Voy a ponerme a cocinar —dijo—. Juan nos trajo un cabrito[43] y voy a prepararlo con mole picosito,[44] una cazuela grande de arroz y tortillas calentitas acabadas de amasar.[45]

—Allá en la capital extraño mucho tu comida, mamá.

---

[38] *shawl*   [39] *silent*   [40] fogón... *wood stove*   [41] *pots*   [42] *exchanged*
[43] *young goat, kid*   [44] mole... salsa picante hecha de chocolate, cacahuates, chiles y otras especias   [45] acabadas... *just kneaded*

—Lo sé, mijo.[46] Lástima que esa universidad esté tan lejos.

Daniel se puso unos guaraches[47] cómodos, una camisa y un pantalón de trabajo. Salió al patio. Recorrió los alrededores de la casa, con calma, y luego se sentó debajo del nogal.

La llegada de Daniel fue para Chalchi una tremenda sorpresa. Él no le había anunciado la visita, como lo hacía normalmente, por carta. Se abrazaron; fue un abrazo largo, apasionado. Se besaron y después dieron una larga caminata por el pueblo, visitando los viejos rincones de su infancia. Tomaron el tren y llegaron hasta Amecameca, hasta el pie de los volcanes...

—Tenía muchos deseos de estar contigo, Chalchi.

—Abrázame, Daniel. Así, fuerte.

—Sí, Chalchi... Chalchiunenetl. Me gusta tanto tu nombre.

—¿Es todo lo que te gusta de mí?

—Y tus ojos, que parecen esmeraldas brillantes y me iluminan la vida. A veces, cuando miro tus ojos, creo ver una luz que viene de tu corazón. Esa luz tiene una voz rítmica, melodiosa; me dice suavemente «te quiero»...

—Mis ojos no mienten, Daniel... Te quiero.

Hablaron del futuro. Ella le contó que había decidido estudiar en la universidad. Quería realizar su sueño de ser profesora. Por suerte, sus padres apoyaban su decisión. Sí, ése era su deseo: estudiar literatura, tener frente a ella

---

[46] mi hijo *(coll.)*   [47] *huaraches, sandals (Mex.)*

jóvenes estudiantes para hablarles de las grandes obras mexicanas, para ayudarlos a leerlas y apreciarlas.

Daniel recibió contento la noticia. Se ofreció para ayudarla a empezar sus estudios en la UNAM. La apoyaría[48] en todo. Vivirían juntos en la capital, como esposos.

—Porque algún día—dijo él—, muy pronto, quiero casarme contigo.

—¿Casarnos?— preguntó Chalchi, un tanto sorprendida.

—Sí, Chalchi. Quiero ser tu compañero.

Daniel notó las lágrimas de alegría en los ojos de su novia.

—Yo también quiero unir mi vida a la tuya, Daniel— dijo ella.

Esa noche Daniel se acostó pensando en Chalchi, en lo felices que serían los dos juntos, casados. Se quedó dormido hacia la medianoche y soñó repetidas veces con la Piedra del Sol y los volcanes. En sus sueños podía penetrar la piedra; podía ver su propio rostro grabado en la superficie de la roca, junto a Tonatiuh, dios del sol. Sentía un calor intenso, como un fuego que lo consumía, mientras viajaba al mismo centro y corazón de una montaña...

---

[48] La... *He would support her*

Parte II

El Templo Mayor en Tenochtitlán reconstruido por Ignacio Marquin.

Uno

«¡Tozani!» Escucho una voz de mujer que viene de lejos. «¡Tozani!» Trato de despertar, pero me pesan los párpados.[1] Siento mucho frío. «¡Tozani!» La voz se hace más fuerte. Abro por fin los ojos y veo mi cuerpo, casi desnudo. Sólo llevo un taparrabo[2] y estoy acostado en una cama que no es la mía; es un petate.[3] Busco a la dueña de la voz y por fin la veo, parada frente a mí.

—Despierta ya —me dice ella.

Habla un idioma extraño que yo, de una manera también muy extraña, puedo comprender. Sus palabras llegan a mí como filtradas por el aire frío de este cuarto.

—Despierta —repite—. Es hora de ir al lago.

La observo. Es una muchacha joven, hermosa. Tiene el cabello atado atrás,[4] con dos trenzas[5] sobre la frente. Lleva un vestido largo, blanco; en la cintura, un amplio cincho bordado.[6] Sus ojos son de un verde intenso. Se parece tanto a Chalchi que la llamo por ese nombre, Chalchiunenetl, y ella responde...

—Sí. Has dormido mucho, Tozani.

---

[1] *eyelids* [2] *loincloth* [3] *sleeping mat* [4] atado... *tied back*
[5] *braids* [6] cincho... *embroidered belt*

—¿Tozani? Yo no me llamo Tozani —le digo, confundido. Y ella me mira sonriendo.

—Levántate ya, esposo.

¡Me ha llamado *esposo*! Miro a mi alrededor y descubro que no estoy en casa de mis padres. Este lugar es mucho más grande; las paredes son blancas y a lo largo de cada una hay tiestos[7] enormes con flores de varios tipos y colores. Los muebles son escasos pero hermosos, de madera densa: un pequeño armario, una mesa baja y dos sillas. Hay una armonía total en este sitio. La puerta que da a[8] la calle está inundada de luz.

¿Dónde estoy?

Trato de ordenar mis pensamientos. Debo estar soñando. Cierro los ojos. Me golpeo la cara para despertar, ¡una, dos, tres veces! Y escucho la voz asustada de Chalchi; sus manos sujetan las mías.

—¡Tozani! —exclama—. ¡¿Qué haces?! ¿Por qué te golpeas?

No puedo contestarle. Algo en la garganta me impide hablar.

—Estabas soñando, esposo —me dice ella, mientras me acaricia.

—¿Soñando? —le pregunto, incrédulo.

—Sí. Pero ya, por fin, empiezas a despertar.

Me muevo. Respiro. Tengo los ojos muy abiertos. Sí. Estoy despierto.

---

[7] *flower pots*   [8] da... *leads to*

—Cuando regreses del lago, comeremos —me dice Chalchi. Y se va a otro cuarto.

El lago. ¿Qué tendré que hacer en el lago? Me acuesto otra vez en el petate incómodo. ¿Cómo explicar todo esto?

—¡Chalchi! —la llamo, y ella aparece ante mí.

—Estoy amasando *tlaxcalli*,[9] preparando tu *atolli*.[10] ¿Por qué no te has ido al lago?

—¡Porque no sé para qué diablos tengo que ir al lago!

—¿Estás soñando otra vez, querido mío? —ella me dice, sonriendo—. Tienes que ir al lago para bañarte, claro. Luego te vestirás de guerra para asistir al Templo Mayor. No olvides que el Reverendo Padre quiere verte.

—¿El Reverendo Padre?

—Sí. El señor emperador, Moctezuma.

—¡¿Quién?!

—Pobre de ti. Ese sueño de anoche te obsesiona.

—¿En qué año estamos, Chalchi?

—Acatl. El año 1-Caña,[11] el día de 2-Casas.

Trato de recordar el calendario azteca. Un escalofrío[12] me invade el cuerpo cuando por fin descifro el significado de aquella fecha. *Acatl,* equivalente al año 1519 del calendario cristiano. El día 2-Casas, o sea, el 29, probablemente del mes de junio. Un mes antes de la entrada de Hernán Cortés en Tenochtitlán.

---

[9] tortillas   [10] atole *(creamy, corn-based drink)*   [11] *1-Reed*
[12] *chill*

Dos

 Hay un aroma exquisito que impregna el aire; es un perfume de flores y tierra fresca. Observo la variedad impresionante de plantas que hay en este lugar, y salgo por la puerta que da a la calle. Si soy víctima de una comedia, de una broma de mal gusto,[13] será fácil darle fin. Sólo tengo que salir y buscar la verdad...

El mundo que descubro aquí afuera es aún más extraño que el del interior de la casa. Veo una calle muy amplia, y a lo largo de toda la calle está el agua, el hermoso lago que encontraron los antiguos aztecas. Hay hombres en canoas, hombres vestidos como yo: taparrabo y manto. Veo gente que camina, gente que sonríe y conversa. Hombres cubiertos de plumas, vestidos con pieles de tigre. Algunos, los que llevan lanzas,[14] hacen ante mí un gesto de reverencia, y siguen su camino.

Si me alejo mucho[15] voy a perderme. Necesito a Chalchi; necesito su guía, sus explicaciones. Regreso a la casa —¿mi casa?— y le pido a mi «esposa» que me acompañe. Ella se limpia las manos, obediente, y abandona sus quehaceres. Yo la sigo.

---

[13] broma... *nasty joke*   [14] *spears*   [15] Si... *If I go very far away*

Los edificios blancos brillan con la primera luz del día.
Muchos tienen en sus fachadas frescos[16] de diseños diferentes, mosaicos trabajados en detalle, todos de varios colores.
En los techos de cada templo y cada palacio flotan ban-
deras[17] de plumas doradas. Algunas muestran insignias de
los dioses y los emperadores de la antigua historia mexicana. ¿Mi historia?

Chalchi señala hacia los volcanes, que se ven en la
distancia, bajo el azul intenso del cielo; sus cimas[18] cubier-
tas de nieve.

¡Estoy en México-Tenochtitlán!

Llegamos a un mercado repleto de gente y vende-
dores. Hay comerciantes de legumbres y condimentos; ar-
tesanos de las plumas. Hay carnes y animales vivos, perros
y changos,[19] telas, pieles. Continuamos a paso lento y
aparece ante nosotros una plaza enorme. Chalchi dice algo
que no comprendo. Lo repite:

—*Tenochtitlán, Cem-Anahuac Tlali Yoloco.*

Y por fin entiendo lo que me está diciendo en náhuatl:
«Éste es el verdadero corazón y centro del único mundo».

Chalchi se detiene frente a una pirámide gigantesca.

—¿Es esa la Gran Pirámide? —le pregunto. Ella res-
ponde que sí. Yo continúo: —Ahí dentro está el Templo de
Tláloc, y el Templo de Huitzilopochtli, lugar de sacrificios.
¿No es cierto?

—La Gran Pirámide, sí —responde ella, sorpren-

---

[16] *frescos*   [17] *flags*   [18] *tops*   [19] *monkeys* (*Mex.*)

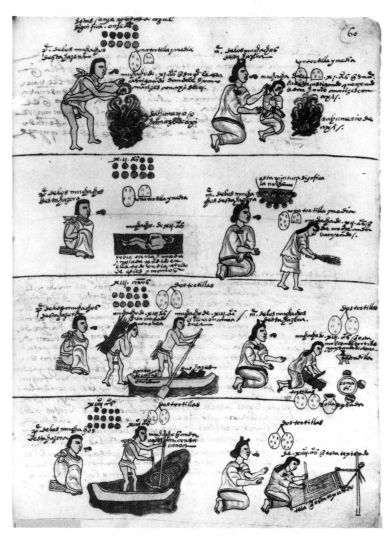

Página del Códice Mendoza que muestra la crianza de los niños aztecas. Las niñas, que se ven al lado derecho, tenían que aprender a cocinar y a tejer desde temprana edad. Al lado izquierdo se ven los varones, quienes aprendían desde pequeños a pescar. Para ambos, la disciplina y el duro trabajo eran parte de su rutina diaria.

dida por tantas preguntas—. Ahí han sacrificado a muchos de tus prisioneros de las guerras floridas.[20]

Le pido a mi «esposa» que me lleve a la Piedra del Sol. Ella cambia de dirección. Y nos acercamos a un templo de mármol: el palacio de Moctezuma. Seguimos caminando, ahora de prisa.

—¿Por qué vamos tan rápido, Chalchi?

—Porque pronto comenzará la ceremonia —me explica—. Y no tenemos tiempo para presenciarla. ¡Te espera el Reverendo Padre!

—¿De qué ceremonia estás hablando? —le pregunto.

—La dedicación diaria de Tonatiuh —Chalchi responde.

Y ahora veo por fin la Piedra del Sol, una escultura espléndida. Es como la del museo, sólo que aquí la piedra brilla al aire libre. La imagen de Tonatiuh, dios del sol, es la misma: su mirada fija en el vacío, la boca abierta, con hambre de corazones humanos. Abajo se ven las colas[21] de dos serpientes, que se juntan en la fecha sagrada de la creación.

—Se acabará este mundo, Chalchi, esta civilización —le digo.

Chalchi me toma la mano; busca en mis ojos una aclaración. ¿Pero qué puedo decirle? ¿Cómo puedo compartir con ella mi verdad? Simplemente le explico que estamos viviendo en la última era, la del quinto sol.

---

[20] guerras... guerras organizadas por los aztecas con el fin de obtener víctimas para el sacrificio   [21] *tails*

—Es verdad, Tozani —comenta ella—. Lo sé. Todos lo sabemos. Esta era terminará con una catástrofe. Y se acabará el mundo.

—Pero vendrá otro mundo muy distinto a éste, Chalchi. Reinará otro rey y adoraremos a un solo dios.

—¿Un solo dios? ¡No es posible!

—Nada podrá evitar el fin...

—¿Ni siquiera los sacrificios?

—¡Nada, Chalchi!

—¿Viste la catástrofe en tus sueños anoche, Tozani? ¿Te hablaron los dioses?

—Sí, Chalchi.

—Fue un sueño que te hizo sufrir mucho, Tozani, y que te atormenta todavía. Debes tratar de olvidarlo.

—No, Chalchi. Los sueños del futuro no se olvidan.

Aparece un hombre vestido con un largo traje de plumas blancas, las piernas pintadas de azul, sandalias doradas. En el brazo derecho carga un escudo[22] con el símbolo del águila y una bandera de plumas amarillas. Se queda de pie ante la Piedra del Sol. Levanta los brazos. La multitud que nos rodea grita, «*¡Yyyo Ayyo!*», y todos se echan al suelo.[23] Chalchi me empuja para que yo también haga el acto de reverencia.

—¿Quién es? —le pregunto cuando nos levantamos.

—Es el sacerdote de Tonatiuh —ella responde, muy seria.

—¿Qué hace?

---

[22] *shield* [23] todos... *everyone falls face downward on the ground*

—La dedicación diaria de Tonatiuh. Le pide protección. Esta vez para ti, Tozani, para tu misión...

El sacerdote dice unas palabras que no comprendo y luego se va. La gente se dispersa.[24] Chalchi me lleva a lo largo del lago, hasta llegar a una zona rodeada por un muro de barro. Hay una entrada circular como la boca de una cueva, por donde entran soldados y jóvenes y hombres de diferente edad.

—¡Anda! Te espero —me dice Chalchi.

—¿Qué debo hacer? —le pregunto, con aprensión.

—Debes bañarte en el lago. Dame tu manto; yo lo guardo.

Después de darme un baño incómodo en el agua fría del lago, regresamos a casa. Chalchi prepara nuestro almuerzo: una porción de *atolli* y dos tortillas. Nos sentamos y comemos en silencio. Saboreo la tortilla tibia, hecha por ella esta mañana; la crema de maíz, *atolli*, que sabe a miel y a limón, deliciosa.

—Conseguí un poco de *octli*, ¿no quieres? —me pregunta. Le digo que sí y lo pruebo. Es como un vino blanco, un poco amargo.[25]

Chalchi se levanta sin haber terminado su comida.

—Se hace tarde —me dice, señalando un traje de plumas que está sobre la mesa—. Te ayudaré a vestirte.

—Chalchi, ¿por qué quiere verme Moctezuma?

Ella me mira como diciéndome, «despierta ya, querido esposo». Exasperada y sin comprender mi pregunta, me explica:

—El reverendo señor Moctezuma, *Huey-Tlatoani* de los aztecas, quiere encomendarte una misión muy importante...

---

[24] se... *scatters*   [25] *bitter*

—¿Qué misión es?

—¿Tampoco lo recuerdas? ¡Ese sueño de anoche te ha convertido en otro hombre, Tozani!

—Mi misión tiene que ver con los «dioses blancos», ¿verdad?

—Sí. En la última reunión del consejo gobernante,[26] nuestro emperador decidió enviar una comisión para recibir a los seres blancos, para llevarles regalos y guiarlos hasta nuestra ciudad. El consejo te escogió a ti para encabezar[27] la comisión.

—Esos seres no son dioses, Chalchi.

—¿Cómo lo sabes?

—Lo sé. Simplemente lo sé.

Chalchi se queda pensativa unos minutos. Luego me dice, agitada:

—Los mensajeros de Moctezuma que han visto a esos seres, cuentan que son grandes de estatura, que tienen la cara cubierta de cabello. Y algunos de ellos tienen cuatro patas[28] enormes y dos cabezas, una de animal y otra de hombre...

—Son los españoles, Chalchi —le digo, sabiendo que no me entenderá. Repito: —Son los soldados de Cortés.

—Los soldados... ¿de quién?

—De Cortés, un hombre que viene a destruirnos.

—¡No! Moctezuma dice que son dioses. Dice que nuestro creador, Quetzalcóatl, ha regresado para recuperar su reino.

—¡Está loco el emperador!

—¡Tozani! ¿Cómo te atreves a hablar así de nuestro *Huey-Tlatoani*?

La abrazo y la beso.

---

[26] consejo... *governing council*   [27] *head up, lead*   [28] *lcgs*

—Debes creerme, Chalchi. El Reverendo Padre está equivocado. Y yo voy a hacerle ver la realidad... ¿Sabes cuántos soldados estarán a mi disposición?

—Todos nuestros guerreros están bajo tus órdenes, Tozani.

—¿Por qué, Chalchi?

—Tozani, querido, ¿también quieres que te hable de tus triunfos? ¿Del honor que has recibido?

—Sí, háblame de todo eso, Chalchi, por favor.

—Eres el comandante del ejercito. Tienes el título honorable de *Quahtli-Yaoyotl*, Águila de Guerra. Has estado al frente de dos guerras floridas y has ampliado las fronteras de nuestro imperio. Eres el orgullo de tu pueblo, Tozani Quahtli-Yaoyotl.

—¿Y tú, Chalchi? ¿Estás orgullosa de mí?

—Más que nadie, porque soy tu esposa.

Honores de guerra. Prisioneros sacrificados por mí. ¿Cómo voy a poder asumir esta vida que no es la mía? ¿Cómo voy a poder vivirla, si no la conozco? Trato de recordar todo lo que he leído, las leyendas de Ayapango, los relatos orales, la poesía, pero en ningún sitio encuentro a Tozani, este personaje en quien me he convertido. ¿Existió de verdad? ¿Por qué no recuerdo una sola prueba de su existencia?

Chalchi me quita el manto. Lo coloca encima del petate. Luego me acaricia las piernas suavemente. Beso su rostro, sus pechos. La cubro con mis brazos. Ella me murmura algo al oído...

«Tu corazón, el corazón de todo ser viviente... »

Hacemos el amor bañados por el aroma de las flores. Estar así con ella es habitar el mismo sol: fuego,

energía. Entre caricias me murmura palabras que yo recuerdo...

«Tu voz, la voz del sol, la voz del viento... »

Chalchi me trae un pañuelo[29] blanco bordado, mi taparrabo.

—Vístete, Tozani —me pide—. El Reverendo Padre
te espera.

Con la ayuda de Chalchi, en poco tiempo estoy uni-
formado. Llevo un traje que se ajusta a mi cuerpo, y pantalones de una sola pieza que me llegan a los tobillos, sandalias doradas, una armadura acolchonada[30] por dentro y
un casco[31] de plumas amarillas con un pico de águila.

—¡Qué hermoso te ves, Tozani Águila de Guerra! ¡Estoy tan orgullosa de ser tu sirviente!

—Eres mi esposa, Chalchi, mi compañera. No mi «sirviente».

Antes de partir, le doy un beso y un abrazo. Y le
prometo que regresaré con noticias de los blancos, esos
misteriosos seres de otro mundo.

---

[29] *cloth*   [30] armadura... *padded armor*   [31] *helmet*

Tres

Recorro el mismo camino que recorrí con Chalchi, hasta llegar al palacio de Moctezuma. Los dos guardias a la entrada me saludan con una reverencia, haciendo el gesto de besar la tierra. Entro y otro soldado me guía. Lo sigo. Nos detenemos[32] delante de una puerta enorme que muestra el símbolo del águila y la serpiente. El soldado la abre y me invita a pasar.

Entro y observo, sorprendido, la simplicidad del salón real.[33] El emperador está sentado en una silla de piedra. Lo acompañan dos hombres vestidos de manto, los consejeros. Me acerco, con temor, y hago el gesto de besar la tierra, como lo han hecho todos los soldados ante mí.

—¡*Yyyo Ayyo*! —me saluda, y me pide con la mano que me acerque—. He estado esperándote, Tozani.

—Perdona mi tardanza, Reverendo Padre. Quise presenciar la ceremonia de Tonatiuh...

—Entonces, ya sabes que el sacerdote le pidió a Tonatiuh luz para tu misión.

—Sí, Señor. Lo sé. Y le estoy agradecido.

—Los seres blancos se acercan a nuestra ciudad, Tozani. Y todavía no sabemos quiénes son, qué es lo que

---

[32] Nos... *We stop*   [33] salón... *royal hall*

Moctezuma II (1480–1520), emperador de los aztecas
(1502–1520) durante la conquista y colonización de
México.

quieren, por qué están aquí. Mis consejeros y yo pensamos que son dioses enviados por Quetzalcóatl. Yo sospecho que se trata del mismo Quetzalcóatl, que ha regresado a recuperar su imperio.

—¿Cómo puedes estar seguro que son dioses, Señor?

—No estoy seguro. Por eso te envío a ti para recibirlos. Debes ayudarme a entender, a explicar su presencia.

—Trataré de hacerlo, Reverendo Padre.

—Esos seres se detuvieron al pie de los volcanes. Debes llegar hasta ellos y hacer que te entiendan. Explícales que estás allí para darles la bienvenida. Les ofrecerás regalos y los invitarás a nuestra ciudad. No debes pelear. Recuérdalo: no vas en misión de guerra.

—Entendido, Gran Señor.

Uno de los consejeros habla con el emperador en secreto. Conversan durante largo rato. Luego Moctezuma me dice:

—Vas a quedarte en mi palacio esta noche, Tozani. Mañana a la primera luz de Tonatiuh partirás. Te acompañará el guerrero Ollín, como segundo en comando. Tendrás trece soldados a tu disposición.

—¿Por qué tan pocos soldados, Gran Señor?

—Porque no vas a hacer la guerra. Además, el número trece te traerá suerte.

¡Claro! El quinto sol, la era bajo la cual vivieron los aztecas, nació en la fecha ceremonial de 13-Caña. ¿Un número de suerte? ¡Qué ironía!

—Esta noche —continúa el emperador— escogeré yo mismo los regalos que vas a llevar. Te presentarás a los seres blancos y les dirás que eres un noble de mi corte.

Hace una pausa. Me mira y mira a sus consejeros.

—Es todo, Tozani —me dice—. Vete ya.

Hago una reverencia y salgo del salón real.

Viene hacia mí una muchacha, casi una niña. Me saluda y me guía a través de salones y pasillos. Nos detenemos en una sala con muchas ventanas y flores.

—Este es tu lugar de descanso, señor —me informa. Y luego me muestra las comodidades[34] de mi alojamiento: dos mesas, varias sillas, un enorme armario de madera, candelabros rústicos con una infinidad de velas,[35] y una chimenea.

Pasamos a otra sala. La muchacha señala una plataforma grandísima, cubierta de mantas y cobijas;[36] es mi cama. Por último, el baño, que es increíblemente moderno: una bañera de azulejos,[37] un inodoro[38] y varios tubos de barro por donde corre el agua.

—Pronto te traigo la comida, señor —me dice la muchacha, mientras jala una cuerda que cuelga del techo, en la sala principal—. Si necesitas algo, llámame con esta cuerda.

Después de irse la jovencita, me acerco a una de las ventanas y admiro el patio de canales y jardines. La luz del día lo invade todo. Todavía no estoy seguro de lo que estoy haciendo aquí, ni de cómo llegué. No me explico cómo es que entiendo y puedo hablar este idioma antiguo, el náhuatl; cómo he aprendido a comportarme entre esta gente, a ser uno de ellos.

Hago un esfuerzo[39] otra vez por recordar todo lo que sé de este mundo. Pero es inútil; en ningún lugar de mi

---

[34] *comforts, amenities*   [35] *candles*   [36] *blankets*   [37] *tiles*
[38] *toilet*   [39] Hago... *I try*

Cuatro

 Ollín es un hombre de gran estatura, musculoso. Le pido que nos sirva de guía. El me mira confundido; se supone que Tozani conoce mejor que nadie estas tierras. Tozani es —¿yo soy? —el valiente jefe del ejército azteca. Mi mandato no tiene sentido, pero Ollín me obedece. Y seguimos sus pasos.

Soportamos[40] el frío intenso de las noches, el calor de los días. El paisaje es el mismo del México que dejé atrás. Veo los volcanes en la distancia y el cielo de un azul intenso.

Pasamos por varios pueblos, casi todos muy pobres. Gente medio desnuda, sucia, hambrienta.

—¡Qué injusticia! —digo en voz alta. Ollín me mira y calla. Sigue adelante, con paso firme.

Una noche, Ollín señala por fin las luces que aparecen a lo lejos.

—¡Ayyo! —exclama—. Nos acercamos al campamento de los blancos.

---

[40] *We endure, put up with*

Doy órdenes de acampar. Les explico a mis soldados que deben esperar aquí. Les digo que Ollín y yo tenemos que llegar al campamento de los seres extraños. Mis soldados me obedecen, silenciosos.

Me acompañan Ollín y tres hombres que cargan los regalos. Vamos guiados por la luz de nuestras antorchas. Puedo reconocer cada árbol, cada vuelta del camino, cada pedazo de cielo. Esta es la ruta de los volcanes.

Descubrimos primero los cañones[41] en el campamento de los blancos. Vienen a nuestro encuentro cinco soldados españoles, vestidos de guerra: sus trajes gastados,[42] sus cascos oxidados por las lluvias. Dos de ellos me ponen la boca de sus armas en el pecho.

—¡Alto! —me dicen—. ¿Qué queréis?[43]

Yo no digo una sola palabra. No quiero que sepan que hablo su idioma. Les muestro los regalos, las pieles, las plumas, el cacao, las piedras preciosas y, sobre todo, el oro. Hago gestos de ofrecimiento. Les digo, con las manos, que quiero ver a su jefe para entregarle los regalos. Ellos sonríen, y nos guían hasta donde está su líder.

Entramos en una de las carpas.[44] Nos recibe un hombre grueso de pelo y barba muy rojos. Debe de ser Alvarado. Lo acompaña una mujer que no es blanca. Alvarado me mira, nos inspecciona.

---

[41] *cannons*   [42] *worn out*   [43] *¿Qué... ¿Qué quieren? (Spain)*
[44] *tents*   [45] Pedro de Alvarado (1495–1541), segundo en mando bajo Cortés en la conquista de México

Hernán Cortés (1485–1547). El capitán español llegó a
Tenochtitlán el 8 de noviembre de 1519.

soy un asesino. Y no puedo culparlo a él solo de todo lo que
ocurrió en México. Su llegada fue parte de un plan mayor,
típicamente imperialista, de los reyes de España.

Quizás la muerte de Cortés podría posponer —¿evitar?— la colonización de Tenochtitlán.

¡Quién sabe!

Después del encuentro con los blancos, regresamos a nuestro campamento. El frío de la noche es más intenso, pero los hombres lo resisten sin quejarse.[49] Algunos tienden[50] sus mantos y se duermen junto a sus lanzas, sus arcos y sus flechas.[51] Otros hacen hogueras[52] y se sientan a mirar el fuego. Ollín y yo también hacemos una hoguera y nos acomodamos para recibir su calor.

Tengo que tomar una decisión. ¿Guío a Cortés hasta la capital, haciéndome cómplice de su invasión, o lo destruyo? Sé que él está aquí porque desobedeció las órdenes del rey Carlos; llegó hasta estas tierras por intereses personales. Si destruyo a Cortés, el rey mandará de España a otro explorador, pero ya para entonces estaremos preparados.

El ejercito español es grande. Ellos tienen sus cañones y sus caballos. Pero no conocen este terreno como nosotros; no saben que podemos arrastrarnos[53] por el suelo como serpientes, llegar hasta ellos y asfixiarlos. Cortés y sus soldados no esperan agresión de nuestra parte. Quedaron convencidos de que Moctezuma va a abrirles las puertas de la ciudad. La situación es ideal. El plan de ataque: llegar hasta su campamento y sorprenderlos mientras duermen.

¡Imposible! Tengo muy pocos soldados. Y esos pocos no van a comprender la razón de mi desobediencia. Van a temer la ira de Huitzilopochtli, la ira del Reverendo Padre. Además, antes de combatir con sus enemigos, ellos querrán seguir el ritual de la guerra florida y hacer sus ofrendas.

---

[49] *complaining* [50] *spread out* [51] *arrows* [52] *bonfires* [53] *drag ourselves*

Pero, ¿cómo explicarles que estos hombres con armas que vomitan fuego no conocen nuestros ritos? ¿Cómo convencerlos, primero, de que estos hombres blancos son nuestros enemigos, y luego hacerles entender que la única manera de ganar es con un ataque secreto, sin ritos que anuncien la guerra?

Lo que yo propongo es pelear a traición. Mi plan va en contra de las reglas ancestrales de esta gente. Es deshonroso.[54] Y sin embargo, sólo con un ataque de sorpresa podríamos vencer. Nuestros *maquahuime*[55] de obsidiana se harían pedazos contra las armas españolas. Mis soldados se quedarían paralizados con sólo mirar a los conquistadores. Los que para mí son caballos para los aztecas son seres monstruosos, mitad hombre y mitad animal.

Yo no soy un asesino. Soy un estudiante de agronomía, Daniel Flores. Vengo de un tiempo futuro, del año 1992. ¿Estoy aquí para terminar con Cortés? ¿Para evitar la destrucción de México-Tenochtitlán? Sí, quizás. No me queda alternativa. Debo ir yo. Yo solo. Introducirme en la carpa de Cortés y matarlo. Esa es mi verdadera misión en este viaje de regreso al año 1-Caña. *Acatl*, 1519.

El menor ruido puede descubrirme.[56] Ya casi llego a la carpa de Cortés. Hay un soldado a la entrada. Le doy un golpe con mi cuchillo de obsidiana y queda inconsciente.

Encuentro a Cortés despierto, sentado. Está solo.

—¡Buenas noches! —lo saludo.

---

[54] *dishonorable*   [55] arma de madera con cuchillos de obsidiana
[56] *give me away*

Cortés mira el arma que está sobre su cama. Da unos pasos.

—¡Un paso más y te apuñalo![57] —le advierto.

—Hablas muy bien nuestra lengua, noble azteca —dice, y se me acerca.

—Me alegra encontrarte solo —digo—. Así no habrá testigos de tu muerte, Hernán Cortés.

—¡Qué estúpido eres! —me grita el capitán—. En cualquier momento estarán aquí mis hombres. No vas a escapar con vida.

El conquistador me da una patada y mi cuchillo cae al suelo, lejos de mí.

—Cuerpo a cuerpo[58] —me invita a pelear—. Sin armas, indio. ¡Defiéndete!

Me golpea el estómago y me deja sin aire. Me recupero. Lo golpeo con todas las fuerzas que puedo sacar de mis brazos. El español cae, vencido. Sin darle tiempo a incorporarse, me tiro sobre él.[59]

¡Qué increíble es ver así a Cortés, totalmente indefenso! ¿Cómo pudo esta persona afectar el destino de tanta gente? Hernán Cortés: un navegante con grandes ambiciones y sueños. Debajo de su grueso traje de guerra, es sólo un hombre pálido y delgado; un hombre que en estos momentos me mira y me pide con los ojos que no lo mate.

Agarro[60] mi cuchillo mientras Cortés trata de ponerse de pie. Voy a asesinarlo. *Tengo que hacerlo.* Pero... no puedo. ¡No puedo! Yo no soy un asesino.

Escucho los pasos de alguien; miro afuera y veo a Malinche, que se acerca a la carpa. Al entrar, corre inmediatamente a ayudar a Cortés. Cuando me ve, da un grito.

Afuera, muy cerca, se escuchan las voces de los sol-

---

[57] te... *I'll stab you*   [58] Cuerpo... *Hand-to-hand*   [59] me... *I throw myself on him*   [60] l grab

dados españoles. No hay escapatoria. ¿Moriré así, en el cuerpo de Tozani? ¡No! ¡Yo tengo que salvarme! Sigo un impulso y agarro a Malinche, envolviéndole el cuello con mi brazo. El capitán ya está de pie. Me rodean sus soldados.

—Si muero yo —le digo a Cortés —¡también muere tu amante!

Él observa a la indígena, quien tiembla bajo el filo de mi obsidiana. Quizás al conquistador no le importe la vida de esta mujer. ¿Dará la orden a sus hombres de destruirnos a los dos?

Aprovecho los segundos que pasan, largos y densos, y camino hacia la salida de la carpa. Salgo, sujetando fuertemente a Malinche. Parece que Cortés ha decidido dejarme escapar. Oigo su voz que me habla...

—Anda, noble azteca. ¡Corre! Y dile a tu emperador que pronto recibirá nuestra visita.

—¡Estaremos preparados! —respondo.

—Tarde o temprano este mundo será mío —dice él—. ¡Y del rey don Carlos!

—¡Viviré para impedirlo! —le grito.

—¡Viviré yo para conseguirlo! —agrega él, finalmente.

Me subo a un caballo, levantando a Malinche y situándola delante de mí. Y galopamos. Galopamos en la profunda oscuridad de la noche mexicana hasta llegar lejos del campamento español. Allí, en medio del campo, abandono a la silenciosa Malinche. Ella conoce bien estas tierras; podrá encontrar el camino de regreso a su amante y señor.

Galopo, desesperado, al campamento de mis hombres. Y voy pensando en otro plan. No pude matar a Cortés, pero quizás todavía sea posible reescribir este pasado. ¡Si sólo tuviera una idea de quién fue Tozani! Lo único que puedo hacer ahora es hablar con Moctezuma, tratar de convencerlo de que está equivocado. ¡Tengo que hacerle ver la realidad!

Cinco

Hago el gesto acostumbrado de besar la tierra, y me quedo de pie ante el trono del gran Moctezuma. Está inquieto, nervioso. No lo acompañan sus consejeros. Me observa fijamente.[61]

—¿Por qué tardaste tanto en venir? —me pregunta—. Sé que llegaste anoche.

—Llegué exhausto, Gran Señor. Estuvimos caminando dos días con dos noches, sin parar. Quise descansar un poco antes de venir, para tener fresca la memoria. Tengo que informarte de muchas cosas.

—¡Habla ya! —me ordena, impaciente.

—Señor, hace veinte años que los primeros barcos salieron de la tierra lejana de España para explorar el océano hacia el oeste de sus costas. Los soldados que iban en esos barcos encontraron muchas islas y subyugaron a todos sus habitantes.

Hago una pausa, esperando la reacción del emperador. Me ordena seguir.

—Durante los últimos veinte años, los hombres blancos han estado colonizando esas islas, haciendo a sus habitantes esclavos del rey de España. Han estado mandando

---

[61] Me... *He stares at me.*

piedras preciosas y metales y semillas aromáticas a su país. La sed de riqueza[62] de estos hombres es insaciable. Su búsqueda[63] los trajo a estas tierras, y ya se acercan a Tenochtitlán. Vienen dispuestos a tomar posesión de nuestro imperio.

Moctezuma se levanta. Da unos pasos, sin mirarme.

—Tienes mucha imaginación, Tozani, demasiada para un soldado.

—¡Debes creerme, Gran Señor! Me pediste información. Me pediste ayuda para aclarar este misterio. Pues bien, ¡te estoy diciendo la verdad! El jefe de los blancos no es un dios. Se llama Cortés y se emborracha[64] como los hombres. Se acuesta con mujeres como los hombres...

—¡Ayyo! —me interrumpe el emperador—. Las historias sagradas cuentan que Quetzalcóatl sucumbió a la intoxicación y al deseo carnal; por eso, avergonzado,[65] se marchó. Parece que este dios nuestro sigue siendo el mismo de antes...

—¡El jefe de los blancos no es Quetzalcóatl!

Moctezuma se queda pensando unos minutos. Luego me informa que estamos en el décimosegundo[66] mes de nuestro año, *Teotleco*.

—Es el mes del regreso de los dioses —afirma.

—No, Señor. ¡Escúchame, por favor!

—Ha regresado Quetzalcóatl —anuncia el emperador—. Debemos preparar el recibimiento.

—¡Gran Señor! —le grito, frustrado—. Vas a cometer un grave error. ¡La invasión de los blancos se acerca!

Moctezuma camina de un lado a otro, enfurecido.

---

[62] *wealth* [63] *search, quest* [64] *se... he gets drunk* [65] *ashamed*
[66] *twelfth*

—¡Ayyo Ouiya Ayyo! —exclama—. ¡¿Cómo te atreves a decir que estoy equivocado?!

—Lo que te estoy diciendo es la verdad, Señor.

—Quetzalcóatl dijo que un día iba a regresar, en paz y amor, a recuperar su reino, y tú lo has ofendido con tus dudas y tus cuentos. Sólo con sangre se puede limpiar esta ofensa, Tozani, sangre del sagrado sacrificio.

—¡Reverendo Padre!

—Yo sé que Quetzalcóatl y sus soldados blancos van a entrar en esta ciudad muy pronto...

—Más pronto de lo que tú imaginas, Señor.

—¡Silencio! El día de su llegada va a recibir una bienvenida grandiosa. Le abriremos nuestras puertas. Y le ofreceremos un regalo: ¡tu corazón!

El primer encuentro entre Cortés y Moctezuma en Tenochtitlán.

Los mismos soldados que antes me obedecían, ahora me encierran[67] en una celda[68] oscura. Moctezuma lo ha decidido: voy a ser sacrificado. Su sentencia:

—No vamos a esperar la llegada de los dioses blancos. Tu sacrificio será mañana mismo, con la primera luz de Tonatiuh.

Tengo frío... y hambre. Un guardia me trae comida y la devoro. Pido más; no me hacen caso. Me acomodo en un rincón.

Voy a morir en este mundo extraño, una muerte que no me pertenece.[69] En este momento, torturado por el frío y la soledad, yo sólo sé que quiero vivir.

Escucho una voz conocida, suave a mis oídos: «¡Tozani!» Y veo luego a Chalchi, que corre hacia mí. La abrazo desesperadamente.

—¡¿Qué haces aquí, Chalchi?!

—El Reverendo Padre me permitió unos segundos a tu lado.

—Van a sacrificarme, Chalchi.

—¡Lo sé, Tozani! Y yo quiero irme contigo, morir junto a ti.

---

[67] *they lock me up*   [68] *cell*   [69] *que... that isn't mine (doesn't belong to me)*

Nos besamos, llorando.

—No. No puedes acompañarme.

—Mi vida no vale nada sin tu amor, Tozani.

—No digas eso. Tu vida vale mucho.

—¡Déjame ofrecer mi corazón también a Quetzal-cóatl!

—Chalchi, querida mía, no sé cómo explicarte. Tienes que escucharme muy bien... y creerme.

—Te escucho y te creo.

—Yo... llegué aquí de otro mundo, de un tiempo futuro...

—¿La era de los dioses blancos?

—Sí. En el mundo del que yo vengo, soy estudiante y me llamo Daniel. Allí tengo una novia que se llama como tú, Chalchiunenetl; es una mujer buena y hermosa, de ojos muy verdes, como los tuyos.

—Esa mujer que se llama igual que yo... ¿es tu esposa?

—No, Chalchi. Todavía no...

—Cuando regreses a tu mundo, ¿te casarás con ella?

—Sí. Porque de una manera misteriosa, tú eres ella... Y ella eres tú.

Chalchi deja de llorar. Me mira con ternura[70] y tristeza.

—¡Llévame contigo, Tozani!

—Eso no es posible, amada mía. No sé cómo ni por qué llegué aquí. Y tampoco sé cómo voy a volver.

—Habla con el dios-creador de tu futuro. ¡Pídele a él una respuesta, Tozani!

---

[70] *tenderness*

—¿A mi Dios? Sería en vano, Chalchi. Porque aquí, en la ciudad de los aztecas, el dios de los blancos no existe.

—Si es verdad que te llamas Daniel y vienes de otra era, dime, entonces, por qué estás aquí, en mi mundo. ¡¿Por qué tienes el cuerpo y la voz de mi esposo?!

—No sé. Al principio pensé que la razón de mi viaje era matar al jefe de los blancos, impedir la destrucción del quinto sol. Pero no pude realizar ese objetivo. Y tampoco voy a poder evitar mi sacrificio. Quizás... quizás regresé a este mundo sólo para impedir tu muerte junto a mí, Chalchi.

—Te escucho, y quiero creerte. Pero todo es tan extraño.

—¡Chalchi! ¡Chalchiunenetl! —le grito—. Prométeme que vas a vivir. ¡Júralo![71] ¡Júrame que no vas a ofrecer tu corazón a Quetzalcóatl!

—¡Lo juro! Porque mi corazón te pertenece sólo a ti, Tozani. Viviré para adorar tu recuerdo.

Cinco soldados me sujetan fuertemente. Me llevan a lo largo de la plaza, hasta la Gran Pirámide. Escucho los gritos de la gente, «¡Ayyo Ouiyya!» Se despiden del bravo guerrero Águila de Guerra.

Entramos en el templo de Huitzilopochtli. Está oscuro y apesta a sangre seca. Encienden varias antorchas y me

---

[71] *Swear it!*

atan[72] a la piedra de los sacrificios. Cierro los ojos, exhausto, vencido. Me desnudan con violencia. Sobre el suelo, a mi lado, colocan mis armas.

Los soldados se van. Y aparece entonces un hombre vestido de plumas, maquillado de blanco. Es el sacerdote. En la mano derecha sujeta el cuchillo de obsidiana. Detrás de él viene Moctezuma. El emperador hace un gesto con la mano.

—¡Yya Ayya Ouiya! —grita el sacerdote, mirando hacia el cielo—. Para ti, Huitzilopochtli. El corazón de este guerrero va a saciar tu hambre...

El sacerdote me mira y me dice:

—Estamos preparados para concederte un último deseo, Tozani. ¡Habla, guerrero!

Sé que debo pedir el honor de esta muerte. Eso es lo que esperan de mí. Ir en contra del ritual es condenarme a la oscuridad eterna. Debo decir que mi último deseo es recibir el honor de la muerte florida. Debo decir que me alegro de vivir y morir en este momento, en esta era gloriosa iniciada en el año 13-Caña, era del Quinto Sol. Debo recibir, sin gritar, sin llorar, el puñal de obsidiana en mi pecho. Pero no puedo. Porque yo no soy Tozani.

—Sí, tengo un último deseo —digo. Y luego grito: —¡Quiero vivir! ¡No quiero esta muerte injusta!

Moctezuma viene a mi lado. Sus ojos están encendidos. Da una orden y el sacerdote levanta el brazo, la mano que sujeta el cuchillo de obsidiana. La mano le tiembla. En cualquier momento caerá sobre mi pecho y me sacará el corazón.

—¡Vivir! —grito.

---

[72] me... *they tie me up*

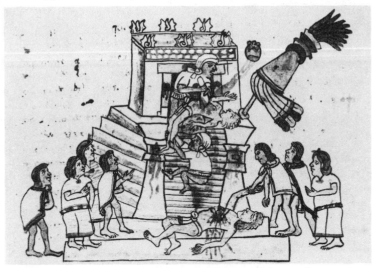

El sacrificio a Tonatiuh, dios del sol. «Sé que debo pedir el honor de esta muerte.... Debo decir que me alegro de vivir y morir en esta...era gloriosa...del Quinto Sol. Pero no puedo... »

Siento un dolor intenso en todo el cuerpo, como una pequeña serpiente que viaja por mi sangre y me muerde por dentro. *Vivir.* Luego un sueño intenso. *Vivir.* Me hundo.[73] Me hundo hasta el corazón y el centro de una enorme montaña... taña...

---

[73] Me... *I sink*

Parte III

Los volcanes Popocatépetl e Iztaccíhuatl.

Daniel escucha una voz de mujer que viene de lejos, que pronuncia su nombre. Trata de despertar. Siente frío. Se cubre con la cobija y de inmediato siente un calor confortante. La voz se hace más fuerte... «Daniel». Abre por fin los ojos y ve a Luvina, su madre, a su lado.

—¡Mamá!

—¿Quieres un cafecito, mijo?

—Sí, sí...

—¿Dormiste bien?

—Sí... Bueno... Tuve un sueño increíble, mamá.

—Soñaste con Chalchi, ¿verdad?

—Sí. ¿Cómo lo sabes?

—Murmuraste varias veces su nombre.

—Qué alegría estar aquí contigo, con ustedes, ¡en mi casa!

—¿Vas a contarme tu sueño?

—Sí, más tarde, cuando esté... más despierto.

Daniel se levanta. Recorre con alivio y con gusto la casita de sus padres. Nada ha cambiado: allí está el nogal, el establo, las dos vacas, el maíz. Y allí está su madre, su madre que le prepara ya una taza de café fuerte y dulce.

Ahora, aliviado por la calma de la mañana y feliz de estar vivo, Daniel repasa en su mente los detalles de aquel extraño «viaje». Y recuerda, por fin, la leyenda del guerrero Tozani, una de las más populares de Ayapango. ¿Por qué no podía recordarla en su sueño? Según la leyenda, el desobediente Tozani fue sacrificado junto a su esposa, porque ella pidió morir con él. Pero al momento de su muerte, los amantes recibieron un gran premio. La diosa del amor, Xochiquétzal, los convirtió en volcanes.

Daniel se acerca a la ventana y ve en la distancia sus dos viejos amigos, Iztaccíhuatl y Popocatépetl. El guerrero y su amada están allí, no muy lejos de Ayapango, eternamente juntos...

En su maravilloso sueño, Daniel era Tozani y estaba casado con Chalchiunenetl. En el espacio de su fantasía, él había salvado a su esposa. Sí, Chalchi le prometió que iba a vivir, que no le entregaría el corazón a Quetzalcóatl... *Porque mi corazón te pertenece sólo a ti, Tozani...*

Daniel se dirige al recipiente de barro donde está el agua fresca. Siente que necesita mucha agua en la cara para despertar. Ahora sí: despertar y ver la luz de los ojos de Chalchi. Casarse con ella. Vivir...

Epílogo

La figura del guerrero Tozani Águila de Guerra es legendaria, mítica. No hay ningún dato histórico que corrobore su existencia. Y sin embargo, para muchos habitantes de Ayapango. Tozani es el más real de todos los personajes del Descubrimiento.[1]

Según los relatos orales de Ayapango, por el pueblo pasó Hernán Cortés en su ruta hacia Tenochtitlán. Un mensajero viajó a la capital y le contó al emperador de aquellos seres monstruosos, mitad hombre y mitad animal, con armas que vomitaban fuego.

La orden del emperador fue no hacer resistencia. Pensó que se trataba del regreso de Quetzalcóatl. Mandó una comisión a encontrar a los blancos, y al frente puso a un joven guerrero llamado Tozani.

Tozani nunca creyó que aquellos hombres barbudos eran dioses. Desobedeció las órdenes del emperador y trató, inútilmente, de matar a Hernán Cortés. Luego regresó a Tenochtitlán y habló con Moctezuma. Le dijo que aquellos invasores eran seres humanos; le contó del mal olor[2] de sus cuerpos, de su obsesión por el oro. Aquellos «dioses» no reaccionaban al nombre de Quetzalcóatl, o de Tenochtitlán,

---

[1] *Discovery (Conquest of the Americas)*   [2] mal... *foul smell*

y se comunicaban en una lengua extraña muy diferente al náhuatl.

El valiente guerrero le advirtió al Reverendo Padre que debía prepararse para combatir a los invasores, porque venían a destruir a los aztecas. Pero Moctezuma se enfureció, no sólo porque Tozani le había desobedecido, sino también porque ahora el dios Quetzalcóatl estaría ofendido y dejaría caer sobre Tenochtitlán su furia.

Para contentar a Quetzalcóatl, Moctezuma mandó otra comisión cargada de regalos: semillas de cacao, piedras preciosas, plumas y, especialmente, oro. Y para limpiar la ofensa cometida por Tozani, sacrificó a éste en la Gran Pirámide.

Tozani estaba casado. Su esposa se llamaba Chalchiunenetl y, a petición de ella, fue sacrificada junto a su esposo. Sus corazones fueron guardados, y luego presentados a Hernán Cortés cuando éste llegó por fin a la capital azteca.

Muchas personas de Ayapango piensan que el espíritu de Chalchi vive aún en el volcán Iztaccíhuatl, y que el de Tozani habita en el centro y corazón del Popocatépetl.

Actividades para los estudiantes

Mi querida cuñada

A. INTRODUCCIÓN

Mire el mapa de Puerto Rico que se encuentra en la página 4 de este libro. ¿En qué mar está situada esta isla? ¿Cómo se llaman las islas vecinas? ¿Qué sabe usted de la historia de Puerto Rico?

La historia de la isla es rica en anécdotas de esclavos, piratas y tesoros perdidos en el mar. Muchos llaman a Puerto Rico «la isla del encanto». ¿Cuáles son los elementos de «encanto» en «Mi querida cuñada»? ¿Cree que el encanto de la isla está relacionado con el misterio en este cuento?

B. LA HISTORIA, MARIE Y VICENTE

Puerto Rico fue una colonia de España desde que llegó Colón, en 1493, hasta 1898, año en que España perdió sus últimos territorios en América y los Estados Unidos tomaron posesión de la isla. Hoy día Puerto Rico es un Estado Libre Asociado (*Commonwealth*) a los Estados Unidos. Esto significa que la isla tiene su propio gobierno, pero está bajo la protección norteamericana.

Como resultado de estos acontecimientos, en Puerto Rico se han formado dos facciones políticas: los «independentistas», que quieren la independencia total de la isla, y los «estadistas», que son los partidarios de la unión total de Puerto Rico a los Estados Unidos. Considerando esta información histórica, ¿cuál facción política posiblemente representa Marie y por qué? ¿Cuál facción podría representar Vicente? ¿Cómo son las relaciones entre los dos personajes?

C. LA CIUDAD/EL CAMPO

Vicente y Marie hablan de varias cosas en el coche; una de ellas es la vida en la ciudad. Es evidente que Marie prefiere la ciudad y Vicente el campo. ¿Qué dice cada uno del lugar de su preferencia? Según usted, ¿cuáles son las ventajas y desventajas de vivir en la ciudad? ¿las de vivir en el campo? ¿Dónde preferiría vivir usted? ¿Por qué?

D. LA PLURALIDAD DE CULTURAS

Una persona que ha recibido la influencia de más de una cultura (ha vivido en otro u otros países, sus padres son inmigrantes, etcétera) se puede considerar «bicultural» o «multicultural». ¿Conoce usted a alguien que pueda considerarse multicultural? ¿Qué culturas contribuyeron a formar el carácter de esta persona? ¿Cuáles son los aspectos más interesantes de su personalidad? Considerando los problemas que causa la discriminación en nuestra sociedad, ¿por qué es importante tener una conciencia multicultural?

Considere el personaje de Marie: Nació en Quebradillas pero vivió por mucho tiempo en Nueva York, Estados Unidos, hasta que murió su esposo estadounidense. También le fascina lo francés. ¿Podemos decir que Marie es multicultural? ¿Qué detalles en la personalidad de Marie revelan la influencia de la cultura norteamericana? ¿Y cuáles reflejan la cultura puertorriqueña? ¿Cómo puede interpretarse su admiración por lo francés? ¿Representa Marie una imagen positiva o negativa del multiculturalismo? ¿Por qué?

E. EL REGRESO A CASA

Vicente tiene muchas ganas de volver a su casa en el pueblo de Quebradillas. Está cansado, no tiene dinero y dice que la comida de su madre es la mejor.

1. ¿Qué es lo que tiene la casa en Quebradillas que es tan importante para Vicente? De cierta forma, Marie también regresa a casa: Después de morir su esposo decide quedarse a vivir en San Juan.
2. ¿Qué significa el regreso al hogar para estos personajes?
3. ¿Qué otros cuentos, novelas o películas ha leído o visto usted que tienen como tema el deseo de «regresar a casa»?
4. ¿Qué implica el regreso para sus protagonistas?

F. LA CONFUSIÓN DE VICENTE

Vicente está confundido porque su madre le dice que el camionero, don Manuel, lo llevó a casa. Él está seguro de que fue Marie quien lo dejó en Quebradillas. ¿Qué pasó de verdad cuando Vicente pensó que viajaba con Marie? Comente las siguientes hipótesis con un compañero (una compañera). Escojan la explicación que ustedes consideran más razonable y prepárense para compartirla en detalle con la clase.

1. A causa del calor y el cansancio, Vicente tuvo alucinaciones; vio a un monstruo y después a una mujer en un Cadillac.
2. Vicente tenía mucha hambre y se desmayó. Luego, soñó que hacía el viaje a Quebradillas en el Cadillac con Marie.
3. Vicente se desmayó después de ver en la guantera la foto de las hijas del camionero. Soñó con una de las hijas y por eso le era familiar la cara de Marie.
4. Vicente tiene una visión del futuro y toda la situación con Marie es una profecía de lo que va a pasar.

G. ¿DOS CAFETINES O SOLAMENTE UNO?

Marie invita a Vicente a comer en el cafetín ya que él no tiene dinero. La mesera dice que no tiene menús y empieza a recitar de memoria la lista de los pocos platillos que se sirven en el restaurante. ¿Cómo es la mesera? ¿Cómo trata a Vicente y a Marie? ¿Hay mucha gente en el cafetín? ¿Es el ambiente relajado o tenso?

Compare esta primera escena del restaurante con la escena en que Vicente regresa solo para investigar el misterio de Marie. ¿Cómo ha cambiado el menú? ¿Es el ambiente igual? ¿Cómo trata la dueña a Vicente? ¿Cómo trata Vicente a la dueña? ¿Por qué es tan diferente la escena esta vez?

H. CONVERSACIONES IMAGINARIAS

Con un compañero (una compañera) de clase, escoja una de las siguientes situaciones. Imaginen una conversación entre los personajes y luego compártanla con la clase.

1. Cuando llegaron a Quebradillas, Marie invitó a Vicente a visitarla en casa de su hermana. Vicente decide un día ir a

visitar a Marie. ¿Cómo sería esta reunión? ¿De qué hablarían los personajes?

2. Marie va a la casa de su hermana, Laura, después de dejar a Vicente cerca de su casa en Quebradillas. Marie le cuenta a Laura del su encuentro con Vicente y Laura opina que ella no le debe dar pon a los desconocidos. ¿Por qué? ¿Qué opina Marie?

3. Los padres están preocupados por la desorientación de Vicente, su hijo, y conversan sobre el caso. ¿Qué pueden hacer para ayudarlo?

4. Vicente se encuentra con el camionero que le dio pon. Quiere hacerle muchas preguntas que lo torturan. ¿Cuáles son esas preguntas? ¿Qué responde el camionero?

5. Vicente y Laura están casados. Marie los visita de vez en cuando. Un día Vicente decide hablarle a Marie de su experiencia en aquel viaje y de lo que ella le dijo que piensa de él. ¿Cómo cree usted que va a reaccionar Marie?

I. VICENTE, EL DETECTIVE

Usted es Vicente y se ha convertido en detective de su propio caso. Además de visitar el cafetín para hablar con la dueña, y de hablar del asunto con sus padres, ¿qué otras pistas (*clues*) buscaría para resolver el misterio? ¿Con quién(es) más hablaría? ¿Qué esperaría encontrar? Apunte los datos en su cuaderno de detective.

J. LOS ESTEREOTIPOS

1. Compare las semejanzas y diferencias entre el personaje de Marie y el de la madre de Vicente. ¿Cómo es la madre tradicional? ¿Cómo representa Marie la imagen de la mujer moderna? ¿Son éstos estereotipos de la mujer? ¿Hay aspectos de la mujer tradicional en Marie y elementos de la mujer moderna en la madre?

2. Cuando Vicente vuelve de vacaciones, su madre le dice: «¡La capital corrompe a los jóvenes!». ¿Está usted de acuerdo con ella? ¿Cuál es la reputación que tienen los jóvenes de las ciudades grandes en comparación con la de los jóvenes de las provincias? ¿Son éstos puramente estereotipos de los jóvenes? ¿Es la corrupción producto del ambiente de la ciudad o hay algo innato en el individuo que lo inclina al vicio?

K. LA RESEÑA

Usted escribe para la revista *Ficción de hoy* y tiene que escribir una reseña (*book review*) de «Mi querida cuñada». Usando las preguntas básicas, **¿quién?**, **¿qué?**, **¿cuándo?**, **¿dónde?**, **¿cómo?** y **¿por qué?**, haga un breve resumen escrito de la trama. Luego, dé su opinión sobre la obra. Use estas preguntas como guía.

1. ¿Quién es el protagonista?
2. ¿Cuándo y dónde tiene lugar el cuento?
3. ¿Qué le pasa al protagonista?
4. ¿Cuál es su conflicto? ¿Qué busca?
5. ¿Cómo termina el cuento? ¿Le parece un final interesante? Explique.
6. ¿Cuál es su opinión de la obra?

L. REFLEXIONES PERSONALES

¿Con cuál personaje de «Mi querida cuñada» se identifica usted, con Vicente, Marie, la madre, o el padre de Vicente, el camionero o posiblemente con Laura? (Aunque no conocemos a Laura en detalle, sabemos algo de ella por los otros personajes). ¿Por qué? ¿Tiene usted espíritu aventurero o es usted una persona prudente? ¿Se puede encontrar aventuras en la vida cotidiana (*daily life*)?

El último sol

A. EL VIAJE DE LOS AZTECAS

Los antiguos mexicanos salieron de Aztlán, tierra árida y fría, para buscar una zona más fértil. Pensaban que al sur había un mejor lugar para vivir.

1. Piense en los éxodos del mundo moderno. ¿Por qué emigra la gente hoy día? Mencione por lo menos tres razones.
2. ¿Ha tenido usted que emigrar? ¿Tiene antepasados o parientes inmigrantes? ¿Cuándo llegaron a este país? Cuente algunas de sus experiencias.
3. Una de las características de la sociedad moderna en los Estados Unidos es que la gente se muda con frecuencia. ¿Se ha mudado usted recientemente? ¿Por qué?

4. ¿Cuáles son las ventajas y desventajas de mudarse, especialmente de una ciudad a otra, o de un país a otro?

5. ¿Tiene usted una visión de un lugar ideal, es decir, de una utopía? Imagínese este sitio y descríbalo en detalle. ¿Cuáles son los símbolos que representan este lugar ideal, tal como el águila sobre el nopal representaba el lugar ideal para los aztecas?

B. EL EXPANSIONISMO Y LA HISTORIA

Los aztecas no sólo querían buscar un lugar más fértil; también buscaban la expansión de su imperio. Por eso en las Guerras Floridas conquistaban otros territorios y a otras tribus. El sacrificio humano tuvo un papel importante en su política de expansionismo.

1. ¿En qué se parecen la invasión española de México y las Guerras Floridas de los aztecas? ¿Tienen estas dos invasiones elementos en común? ¿Cuáles son?

2. ¿Existen ejemplos de expansionismo hoy día? ¿Dónde?

3. ¿Por qué quieren los países conseguir más territorio? Mencione por lo menos tres motivos. ¿Qué se sacrifica en el expansionismo moderno?

4. ¿En qué se parecen el sistema de sacrificio de los aztecas y los sacrificios del mundo de hoy?

C. UN LUGAR ESPECIAL

En el poema que lee Daniel en la antología *Los Metzli*, el poeta expresa el amor que siente por su ciudad, Tenochtitlán. Piense en un lugar que usted aprecia mucho. ¿Cómo lo describiría? Use el poema que aparece en «El último sol» como guía y... ¡escriba un poema para su lugar especial!

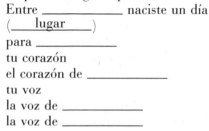

Entre _____ naciste un día
(___lugar___)
para _____
tu corazón
el corazón de _____
tu voz
la voz de _____
la voz de _____

D. EL CALENDARIO AZTECA Y LA DESTRUCCIÓN DE ERAS

En el calendario azteca, el tiempo estaba marcado por eras (soles) que se cerraron con catástrofes y destrucción. El primer sol fue destruido por tigres, el segundo por vientos, el tercero por lluvia ardiente, el cuarto por agua y el último por la invasión de los españoles.

1. En la concepción moderna del tiempo, ¿es necesaria una catástrofe o algún tipo de destrucción para marcar el fin de una era?
2. Piense en la historia del siglo XX. ¿Cuántas eras distintas se encuentran en este siglo, en su opinión?
3. ¿Cuáles serían los nombres de estas eras? ¿Qué evento marca el fin de cada una? ¿En qué era estamos ahora?
4. ¿Qué demuestran estas eras de nuestra civilización?

E. LOS SÍMBOLOS Y LA CULTURA

El calendario azteca era el símbolo de su civilización entera. El águila sobre el nopal también era símbolo para los aztecas; representaba el lugar ideal o soñado.

1. ¿Cuál es la importancia de los símbolos para una cultura?
2. ¿Cuánto tiempo duran estos símbolos?

Cada país del mundo tiene una bandera que contiene símbolos. En la bandera de los Estados Unidos, por ejemplo, cada estrella simboliza un estado. Mire la foto de la bandera de México.

3. ¿Cuál es el símbolo predominante de esta bandera?
4. ¿Qué significa este símbolo?
5. ¿Cómo figura el pasado en la selección de los símbolos del presente?
6. ¿Cuál es la función de estos símbolos nacionales?

F. PLANES PRÁCTICOS Y LA PASIÓN DE LA VIDA

Daniel va a estudiar ingeniería en la capital para poder ayudar a sus padres con la finca cuando termine sus estudios. Sin embargo, su verdadera pasión es la historia. No sigue esta carrera porque no la considera práctica.

1. ¿Qué hace Daniel para satisfacer su pasión por la historia?
2. ¿Adónde lo lleva su pasión?
3. ¿Puede la pasión llevarnos a otros mundos? ¿Cómo?
4. ¿Cuál es la carrera que ha seleccionado usted? ¿La escogió por razones prácticas o porque lo/la apasiona?
5. ¿Cuál es la pasión de usted? ¿Qué hace para seguirla?

G. EL AMOR Y LAS LEYENDAS

A Daniel le gusta mucho contemplar la vista de los dos volcanes, Iztaccíhuatl y Popocatépetl. Según la leyenda, estos volcanes contienen los espíritus de Tozani, el guerrero rebelde, y su esposa Chalchi. La diosa del amor los convirtió en volcanes en el momento de su muerte; así podían estar juntos por la eternidad.

1. ¿Cómo representan estos volcanes también a Daniel y a su novia Chalchi?
2. Imagínese que usted es un personaje en una leyenda y está muy enamorado/a. Quiere vivir con su amante eternamente, después de morir. ¿En qué quiere que los dioses los conviertan? Sigan el modelo.

Quiero que los dioses nos conviertan en _____ porque _____.

volcanes
flores
mariposas
árboles
plumas
¿   ?

H. LA SUPERSTICIÓN: EL NÚMERO 13

Cuando Daniel/Tozani visita a Moctezuma en su palacio, el emperador le encarga la misión de llevar regalos a Cortés y de averiguar la razón de su llegada. Moctezuma le da trece soldados porque dice que el número trece le va a traer buena suerte. Daniel/Tozani recuerda entonces que el quinto sol nació en la fecha de 13-caña. Para los aztecas el número trece significaba buena fortuna. También, ellos dividían su calendario anual en trece meses.

1. ¿Qué significa el número trece en nuestra cultura moderna? ¿Qué ejemplos hay en nuestra sociedad del miedo al número trece?
2. ¿Por qué tiene nuestro calendario anual doce meses en vez de trece, como el de los aztecas?
3. ¿Es usted una persona supersticiosa? ¿Qué supersticiones tiene? ¿En qué se basan sus supersticiones? ¿en experiencias negativas que ha tenido? ¿Son parte de una tradición cultural? ¿Son creencias de su familia?

I. OBEDECER SIN PENSAR

Tozani no obedeció las órdenes de Moctezuma y peleó con Cortés. Él tenía buenas intenciones—quería evitar la conquista de México—, pero recibió la pena de muerte porque desobedeció las órdenes de su emperador.

1. ¿Cree usted que Tozani simplemente debía haber obedecido, sin pensar en las consecuencias?
2. ¿Qué habría hecho usted en su lugar? ¿Habría matado a Cortés?
3. En general, ¿obedece usted a sus superiores (su jefe, sus padres, el gobierno) sin pensar, o rompe a veces las reglas cuando tiene mejores ideas o cuando cree que tiene razón?

J. LOS SUEÑOS Y EL VIAJE EN EL TIEMPO

En su sueño, Daniel viajó por el tiempo y vivió en otro momento histórico.

1. Si usted tuviera una máquina del tiempo, ¿adónde iría? ¿En quién se convertiría? ¿Cómo viviría? ¿Por qué?

El tema del viaje en el tiempo es muy popular hoy día en la televisión y en el cine.

2. ¿Ha mirado usted algún programa o ha visto una película con este tema? Describa el episodio o la trama de la película. ¿Le gustó? Explique.

3. ¿Por qué tienen tanto interés los seres humanos en la idea de viajar en el tiempo? ¿Cuál es la posible base de esta fascinación?

K. CONVERSACIONES IMAGINARIAS

Con un compañero (una compañera) de clase, escoja una de las siguientes situaciones. Imaginen una conversación entre los personajes y luego compártanla con la clase.

1. Justo antes de tener su sueño, Daniel le propone matrimonio a Chalchi. Al dormirse, piensa en Chalchi y luego sueña con la Piedra del Sol, los volcanes y Tonatiuh. Imagínese que Daniel y Chalchi, además del matrimonio, hablaron también de la historia y la cultura de los aztecas. ¿Qué dijeron?

2. Según la leyenda, el guerrero Tozani fue sacrificado en el Templo de Huitzilopochtli por ser desobediente. Su esposa Chalchi fue sacrificada con él. Ellos intercambiaron sus últimas palabras en el templo justo antes de morir. ¿De qué hablaron?

3. Cuando Daniel/Tozani se encuentra con Hernán Cortés, quiere matarlo pero no puede; admite que no es un asesino. Toma a Malinche, amante e intérprete de Cortés, como rehén (*hostage*) para poder escaparse. Luego la abandona en el campo. Imagine una conversación entre ellos en ese momento. ¿Qué mensaje le dio Daniel/Tozani a Malinche para Cortés? ¿Qué le dijo del futuro? ¿del papel que ella va a tener en la historia de México?

4. La noche en que Daniel tuvo su sueño del viaje en el tiempo, dio gritos mientras dormía. Al escuchar los gritos, sus padres fueron a su cuarto para ver qué le pasaba. Encontraron a Daniel dormido, y decidieron no despertarlo. ¿De qué hablaron sus padres?

L. LA REESCRITURA DE LA HISTORIA

Daniel/Tozani quiere reescribir la historia de México.

1. ¿Cómo sería México hoy día si Cortés hubiera muerto antes de

la conquista y los españoles nunca hubieran ocupado Tenochtitlán?

2. Si usted pudiera cambiar el curso de la historia, ¿qué evento en toda la historia del mundo cambiaría? ¿Cómo lo cambiaría? ¿Por qué?

M. LA MALINCHE

Además de ser la intérprete de Cortés, Malinche tuvo un hijo con él. Por eso muchos dicen que fue la madre de una nueva raza: una mezcla de lo español y lo indígena. Ocupa un lugar especial en la historia de la conquista. Para otras personas, Malinche es una traidora. Ya que ella era la traductora, tenía el poder de la palabra. Podría haber engañado a Cortés para ayudar a los aztecas, pero no lo hizo. ¿Qué opina usted? ¿Fue ella una traidora, aliada de Cortés en la conquista, o fue simplemente víctima de las circunstancias?

N. REFLEXIONES PERSONALES

El tema del sacrificio es importante en «El último sol» pues aparecen un sacrificio ritualista y uno personal.

1. ¿Cuáles son las creencias o ideas en que se basan los sacrificios ritualistas, es decir, los sacrificios de seres humanos y de animales?

2. En la leyenda, Chalchi se sacrifica por su esposo Tozani porque lo quiere con toda su alma y no desea vivir sin él. ¿Se sacrificaría usted por alguien o por algo? Explique.

O. LA RESEÑA

Usted escribe para la revista *Historia y ficción* y tiene que escribir una reseña (*book review*) de «El último sol». Usando las preguntas básicas, **¿quién?, ¿qué?, ¿cuándo?, ¿dónde?, ¿cómo?** y **¿por qué?**, haga un breve resumen escrito de la trama. Luego, dé su opinión sobre la obra. Use estas preguntas como guía.

1. ¿Quién es el protagonista?
2. ¿Cuándo y dónde tiene lugar la historia?
3. ¿Qué le pasa al protagonista?
4. ¿Cuál es su conflicto? ¿Qué busca?
5. ¿Cómo termina el cuento y por qué? ¿Le parece un final interesante? Explique.
6. ¿Cuál es su opinión de la obra?

P. LOS DOS CUENTOS

Ahora que usted ha leído los dos cuentos, es hora de pensar en los elementos que tienen en común.

1. En las dos obras aparecen los temas del amor y la familia. ¿Qué otros temas tienen en común los cuentos?
2. En «Mi querida cuñada» y «El último sol», el protagonista es un joven que tiene una experiencia extraordinaria, un «viaje fantástico». ¿En qué se parecen los dos viajes?
3. ¿En qué manera son diferentes los dos viajes? ¿Son grandes las diferencias entre los dos?
4. Ambos jóvenes regresan de la capital al hogar de su familia y adquieren cierto conocimiento de sí mismos. ¿Qué aprenden? ¿Qué aspectos de su personalidad o qué sentimientos descubren?
5. Para los protagonistas, ¿valió la pena hacer el viaje? ¿Por qué? Explique.
6. Piense en la cultura puertorriqueña en que se basa «Mi querida cuñada» y en la historia de México que sirve de base para «El último sol». ¿Qué aprendió usted sobre la cultura puertorriqueña y la historia mexicana al leer *Viajes fantásticos*?
7. ¿Hay un mensaje en este libro? ¿Cuál es? ¿A quién(es) va dirigido? ¿Le parece un mensaje importante? ¿Valió la pena leer este libro para descubrirlo? Explique.

Sugerencias para el profesor/la profesora

Note: The following suggestions are coordinated activity by activity with those in the preceding section, **Actividades para los estudiantes.**

It is not necessary to have students complete all of the suggested activities. Most activities are best done after students have read the stories in their entirety, but you may find suggestions that you can implement to guide class discussion as students are working their way through the novellas.

Mi querida cuñada

A. INTRODUCCIÓN
The first part of this activity is appropriately done before students begin to read the novel. If you find that the class as a whole does not know much about the history of Puerto Rico, ask for a volunteer (or volunteers) to research it and make a brief class presentation in outline form.

B. LA HISTORIA, MARIE Y VICENTE
Before starting this activity, discuss Marie and Vicente as characters, helping students organize what they know about them. You may want to do this on the board by listing short phrases under the name of each character as students make suggestions.

Marie: le gusta lo francés, prefiere la ciudad, tiene coche...
Vicente: prefiere el campo y la casa...

Then discuss the two political factions.

C. LA CIUDAD/EL CAMPO
As a whole-class activity, discuss the advantages and disadvantages of city and country life. You may want to list ideas on the board as students mention them.

A stimulating mini-debate could follow the discussion of this topic. In preparation for the debate students should think about where they live now, the location of their university, where their families live, other places they have lived in their lives, and so on. Debate topic: **¿Es mejor vivir en la ciudad o en el campo?**

D. LA PLURALIDAD DE CULTURAS
Share this information with students before or during class discussion resulting from this activity: Puerto Ricans are U.S. citizens and many have relocated and now make their homes on the mainland. The largest community is in New York. "New-yorican" is one term used to describe this crosscultural community.

E. EL REGRESO A CASA
Before discussing these questions, you may want to have students answer the questions in writing. Have them divide a sheet of paper into four squares, one for each question. The squares should be numbered horizontally from left to right.

1   2
3   4

Ask students to write their answer to each question in the box with the corresponding number. Here is an example of possible student answers for squares 3 and 4.

3 *Gone with the Wind*	4 «Regresar a casa» para Scarlett es buscar la seguridad, escaparse de su situación con Rhett, olvidar la guerra.
E.T.	Para E.T., regresar a casa es volver a su lugar de origen, a lo conocido, a su gente.

Have students compare charts, focusing primarily on the information in squares 3 and 4.

As a whole-class follow-up, see how many different ways **regresar a casa** can be expressed figuratively.

As an individual follow-up, ask students to answer the following question (perhaps on the back of their charts, prior to handing it in): **¿Qué significa «regresar a casa» para usted?**

F. LA CONFUSIÓN DE VICENTE

A whole-class debate is recommended following the discussion generated by this activity. Debate topic: **¿Cuál de las explicaciones de la experiencia misteriosa de Vicente es la más lógica? ¿la más interesante?**

G. ¿DOS CAFETINES O SOLAMENTE UNO?

Working in groups of four, have students compare the two scenes by discussing and jotting down similarities and differences between them on a sheet of paper divided vertically into two sections. Label one section **RM (restaurante con Marie)** and **RS (restaurante solo)**. Then have students list a variety of reasons which could account for the differences in the scenes (in answer to the last question) and vote on the two most interesting explanations. Finally, each group shares the winning explanations with the whole class. You may wish to have the whole class vote on the best idea.

Example explanation:

Economic conditions change over time. Perhaps the economy was in recession when Vicente visited the restaurant with Marie and was more vigorous at the time he went there alone.

H. CONVERSACIONES IMAGINARIAS

Have pairs of students present their situation to the class.

Note: This activity is more interesting if the situations are discussed by a relatively equal number of pairs of students. At the least, try to ensure that each situation is discussed by one pair of students.

I. VICENTE, EL DETECTIVE

Have students answer the questions as homework. Then have them discuss their ideas in groups of four. Suggestion: Ask each group to develop a two or three-step program for Vicente to follow while investigating the mystery. Then have one person from each group list the steps his or her group came up with on the board. The class can then vote on which steps are the most important for Vicente to follow in order to solve the mystery.

J. LOS ESTEREOTIPOS

Have students form discussion groups of four and choose one of the groups of questions (1 or 2). Be sure that at least one group in the class works on each group of questions. Students may find it helpful to answer some of the questions by preparing charts, for example, contrasting Marie and Vincente's mother or young people in the city versus the country. Then have them answer the final two questions in each section with a few sentences or a paragraph that the group as a whole composes.

If you wish to conduct a whole-class discussion of either or both topics, it is a good idea to make the charts and answers prepared by each group available to all students. You can do this by dittoing or photocopying them; alternatively, if you have students work on butcher paper or poster board, you can hang the charts around the classroom and have students circulate to read the comments of other groups.

K. LA RESEÑA

After students have completed their reviews, discuss the six questions as a whole-class activity. For the last question, which asks for students' opinions about the story, take a survey by asking who liked the story, who didn't, and who was ambivalent about it. Then create groups that are as equally balanced as possible between students with different opinions. Have students discuss their opinions, creating lists of positive or negative reactions.

After students have worked in groups, follow up by having each group write its positive and negative points on the board. See how much overlap there is between groups. What is the overwhelming opinion of the class?

L. REFLEXIONES PERSONALES

You may wish to assign these questions as a composition (for homework). As a follow-up, have pairs of students who have written on the same character exchange compositions and write a comparison of the reactions expressed in their own composition with those of their partner.

El último sol

A. EL VIAJE DE LOS AZTECAS

You may find that class conversation drifts a bit when you use these questions, which is fine. Allow the discussion to go where the class wants to take it. Some of the questions (the advantages and disadvantages of moving, for example) lend themselves to being handled as lists on the board.

Not all students will be interested in question 5. You may wish to ask those who have "gotten into" this idea to present their concepts to the class and to create a visual representation of the symbol of their utopia.

B. EL EXPANSIONISMO Y LA HISTORIA

It is useful to have a world map in Spanish available for consultation when discussing these questions. Have students point out places currently or recently in the news where expansionism is a factor: Bosnia and Herzegovina, Georgia, Moldora, and so on. You may wish to supply other 20th-century examples if students cannot come up with them: Germany (Hitler, Nazism), for example. It is also appropriate to discuss expansionism throughout history; if you do, be sure to include the United States as an example.

Compare the Aztec system of sacrifice with modern day sacrifices. Do not be limited to examples of concrete sacrifice (such as the death of individuals and the destruction of property); be sure to include more abstract examples such as the sacrifice of human rights, of dignity, and so on. Are the concrete and the abstract really that different? What do these sacrifices imply about human nature?

C. UN LUGAR ESPECIAL

Assign this activity as homework. As a follow-up, have students share their poems with the whole class or in groups. Do not force any student to participate.

As an alternative, you may want to collect all of the poems and "publish" them in photocopied form for the class. Then have students vote on the three best poems. Ask the winners if they would like to read their poems to the class. (If you choose this alternative, it is a good idea to have students hand in their first drafts so you can correct obvious errors and make suggestions. Then "publish" the second draft.)

D. EL CALENDARIO AZTECA Y LA DESTRUCCIÓN DE ERAS

Before starting this activity, work with students to make a list of the major events of the 20th century: the world wars, major revolutions (Russia, Mexico, Cuba), the Cuban Missile Crisis, political assassinations, space exploration and the first man on the moon, the atomic bomb, major inventions (television, the computer.)

Have students work in groups to answer question 2. You may want to have them design a model of 20th-century eras. It might be round (like the Aztec calendar), linear, triangular, and so forth. Have groups share their models with the rest of the class prior to discussing questions 3 and 4 with the whole class. Remember, there is no one "right" answer.

E. LOS SÍMBOLOS Y LA CULTURA

Use questions 3 through 6 as the basis for a discussion of the U.S. flag. If your class is multicultural, ask students who are originally from another country (or those who know about the country of their immigrant ancestors) to bring in a picture of the flag of that country and explain its symbolism to the class.

F. PLANES PRÁCTICOS Y LA PASIÓN DE LA VIDA

Have students work in pairs or groups to answer the questions. Then, as a whole class, survey students to find the answers to questions 4 and 5. Is there any overlap? That is, what is a passion for one student, may be a career for another, and vice versa.

G. EL AMOR Y LAS LEYENDAS

As an optional creative-writing assignment, ask students to develop their own original legend, based on their answer to question 2. Alternative: Make the same assignment as a group project.

H. LA SUPERSTICIÓN: EL NÚMERO 13

Here are some social manifestations of the aversion to the number 13: Buildings do not usually have a 13th floor; airplanes do not have a row 13; beliefs about Friday the 13th; and so forth.

I. OBEDECER SIN PENSAR

A whole-class debate is recommended following the discussion generated by this activity. Debate topic: **Las ventajas y desventajas de una cultura que exige la obediencia ciega y una que permite que a veces se rompan las reglas.**

J. LOS SUEÑOS Y EL VIAJE EN EL TIEMPO

Here are some recent examples to get class discussion going:
Movies: *Back to the Future, Somewhere in Time*
Television: *Time Trax, Quantum Leap*
Note also that many episodes of *Star Trek* involve time travel.

K. CONVERSACIONES IMAGINARIAS

Have pairs of students present their situation to the class.

Note: This activity is more interesting if the situations are discussed by a relatively equal number of pairs of students. At the least, try to ensure that each situation is discussed by one pair of students.

L. LA REESCRITURA DE LA HISTORIA

Here are some 20th-century events to suggest in order to get discussion going: the decision to drop the atomic bomb, the assassination of Martin Luther King, Jr., or of President Kennedy.

M. LA MALINCHE

A whole-class debate is recommended following the discussion generated by this activity. Debate topic: **La Malinche, ¿cómplice de la conquista o víctima de las circunstancias?**

N. REFLEXIONES PERSONALES

You may wish to assign these questions as a composition (for homework). As a follow-up, have pairs of students who have written on the same topic exchange compositions and write a comparison of the reactions expressed in their own composition with those of their partner.

O. LA RESEÑA

After students have completed their reviews, discuss the six questions as a whole-class activity. For the last question, which asks for students' opinions about the story, take a survey by asking who liked it, who didn't, and who was ambivalent about it. Then create groups that are as equally balanced as possible between students with different opinions. Have students discuss their opinions, creating lists of positive or negative reactions.

After students have worked in groups, follow up by having each group write its positive and negative points on the board. See how much overlap there is between groups. What is the overwhelming opinion of the class?

P. LOS DOS CUENTOS

This activity could turn into a lively discussion and summary of the stories, as you compare and contrast the two. Assign it as homework, then conduct a whole-class discussion of the questions. Use the board to list the different elements the stories have in common (1-5). Or have students work in groups to come up with several **elementos** (1-5) and **mensajes** (7), then present them to the class. Students are likely to offer interesting ideas. You may want to offer the following **mensajes** for discussion if students don't mention them.

1. El tiempo no es lineal. Hay dimensiones y experiencias del tiempo que no podemos explicar con datos científicos.
2. Las experiencias que tenemos en los sueños son tan válidas y reveladoras como las experiencias cuando estamos despiertos.
3. Es importante tener una relación especial en la vida.
4. El amor triunfa sobre todos los obstáculos.
5. Vale la pena conocer bien la historia (el pasado) del país de uno. El conocimiento de la historia hace más interesante y rica la vida en el presente.

Vocabulario

The Spanish-English vocabulary contains all the words that appear in the text, with the following exceptions: 1) most close or identical cognates; 2) most conjugated verb forms; 3) diminutives in **-ito/a**; 4) absolute superlatives in **-ísimo/a**; 5) most adverbs in **-mente**; 6) personal pronouns; 7) cardinal numbers. Only the meanings that are used in the text are given.

The gender of nouns is indicated, except for masculine nouns ending in **-o** and feminine nouns ending in **-a**. Stem changes and spelling changes are indicated for verbs: **dormir** (**ue, u**); **llegar** (**gu**). Consult a grammar textbook for the proper conjugation of verbs.

Words beginning with **ch**, **ll**, and **ñ** are found under separate headings, following the letters **c**, **l**, and **n**, respectively. Similarly, **ch**, **ll**, and **ñ** within words follow **c**, **l**, and **n**, respectively. For example, **fachada** follows **facilitar**, **allá** follows **alucinación**, and **año** follows **anunciar**.

The following abbreviations are used:

adj.	adjective	*m.*	masculine
adv.	adverb	*Mex.*	Mexico
coll.	colloquial	*n.*	noun
conj.	conjunction	*p.p.*	past participle
f.	feminine	*pl.*	plural
fam.	familiar	*poss.*	possessive
form.	formal	*prep.*	preposition
inf.	infinitive	*pron.*	pronoun
interj.	interjection	*rel. pron.*	relative pronoun
inv.	invariable in form	*sing.*	singular
irreg.	irregular	*Sp.*	Spain
L.A.	Latin America	*v.*	verb

a to; at
abajo below, underneath
abierto/a *p.p.* open; opened
abrazar (**c**) to hug; **abrazarse** to hug each other
abrazo hug
abreviar to reduce, shorten
abrir to open
aburrido/a boring
aburrir to bore
acabar(se) to finish, end; **acabar con** to put an end to, kill; **acabar de** + *inf.* to have just (*done something*)
acampar to camp; (*coll.*) to halt and rest
acariciar to caress
acercarse (**qu**) (**a**) to approach, come near (to)
aclaración *f.* clarification, explanation
aclarar to clarify, explain
acolchonado/a padded
acomodarse to find or settle into a comfortable position
acompañar to accompany
aconsejar to advise
acordarse (**ue**) (**de**) to remember
acostarse (**ue**) to lie down
acostumbrado/a customary; **más de lo acostumbrado** more than usual
acostumbrarse a to become accustomed to
actualizar (**c**) to bring up to date
adelante ahead
además moreover, besides
adentro inside
adorno decoration
advertir (**ie, i**) to warn
afuera *adv.* outside
afueras *n. f.* outskirts, suburbs
agarrar to grab
agitado/a excited; disturbed

agradecer (**zc**) to be thankful for
agrónomo/a agricultural, farming
agua (*f. but* **el agua**) water
águila (*f. but* **el águila**) eagle
ahí there
ahora now
ahorrar to save
aire *m.* air; **al aire libre** outdoors
ajustarse (**a**) to fit (on)
alarmarse to become alarmed
alcance: a mi alcance within (my) reach
alegrarse (**de**) to be glad (about)
alegría happiness
alejarse to go far away
algo something
alguien someone, anyone
algún, alguno/a some, any
aliviarse to get relief
alivio relief
almacenado/a stored
almorzar (**ue**) (**c**) to have lunch
almuerzo lunch
alojamiento housing, lodging
alquilar to rent
alrededor de *prep.* around
alrededores *m.* outskirts, environs; **a mi alrededor** around me
alto/a tall; high; **¡alto!** halt!; **altos y bajos** ups and downs; **en voz alta** aloud
alucinación *f.* hallucination
allá there; **para allá** over there
allí there
amable kind
amado/a beloved
amante *m., f.* lover
amargo/a bitter

amarillo/a yellow
amasar to knead; to mix
amenazar (**c**) to threaten
amigo/a friend
amistoso/a friendly
amor *m.* love
amplio/a wide
ampliar to extend, enlarge
anda *interj.* come on
anillo de compromiso
  engagement ring
animarse a + *inf.* to
  encourage (*someone*) to +
  inf.
ánimo spirit, energy; **estar de
  ánimo para** + *inf.* to be in
  the mood to (*do something*)
anoche last night
ansiedad *f.* anxiety
ansioso/a anxious
ante before, in front of
anterior previous
antes de *prep.* before; **antes
  (de) que** *conj.* before
antiguo/a former; ancient
antología anthology
antorcha torch
antropología anthropology
anunciar to announce
año year; **hace** (**dos**) **años**
  (two) years ago; **tener...
  años** to be . . . years old
aparato appliance
aparecer (**zc**) to appear
apasionar to excite, fill with
  enthusiasm
apenas barely
apestar (**a**) to stink, smell (of)
apoyar to support
apreciar to appreciate
aprender to learn;
  aprenderse de memoria to
  memorize
aprensión *f.* apprehension
aprovechar to take advantage
  of

apuntar to point, aim
aquel, aquella *adj.* that (*over
  there*)
aquél, aquélla *pron.* those
  (*over there*)
aquí here; **aquí mismo** right
  here
árbol *m.* tree
arco bow
ardiente burning
ardilla squirrel
arepa (*L.A.*) cornmeal
  griddlecake
arma (*f. but* **el arma**) firearm,
  weapon
armadura frame, framework
armario chest of drawers
armonía harmony
arrastrar to drag
arriba up
arroz *m.* rice
arruga wrinkle
artesano/a craftsperson
asesino/a murderer
asfixiar to smother
así *adv.* so, thus; like this; **así
  que** *conj.* so
asiento seat
asistir (**a**) to attend
aspecto appearance
asumir to assume
asustado/a frightened
ataque *m.* attack
atar to tie, tie up
atender (**ie**) to wait on, serve
atolli (*Mex.*) *m.* creamy, corn-
  based drink
atractivo attraction
atrás *adv.* behind
atreverse a + *inf.* to dare to
  (*do something*)
aun *adv.* even
aún *adv.* still, yet
aunque although
ausencia absence
autónomo/a autonomous

avenida avenue
avergonzado/a ashamed, embarrassed
ayuda help
ayudar to help
azotea flat roof; attic
azteca *m.*, *f.* Aztec
azul blue
azulejo tile

baile *m.* dance
bajarse to go down, descend
bajo *prep.* under
bajo/a *adj.* low; short (*in height*); altos y bajos ups and downs
banco bank
bandera flag
bañarse to bathe; to swim
bañera bathtub
baño bath; bathroom
barato/a cheap
barba beard
barbudo/a thickly-bearded
barco boat
barro mud; clay
bastante quite a bit
batalla battle
bello/a beautiful
bendito: ¡ay, bendito! (*Puerto Rico*) *interj.* dear Lord! (*expressing pain, surprise, or pity*)
besar to kiss
beso kiss
bienvenida *n.* welcome; dar la bienvenida to welcome
bienvenido/a *adj.* welcome
billete *m.* bill (*currency*); ticket
blanco/a white
boca mouth
boda wedding
bonito/a pretty
bordado/a embroidered
borrar to erase

botones *m. pl.* bellhop
bravo/a fierce; brave
brazo arm
brillar to shine
broma joke
brotar to spring, gush (*water*)
buen, bueno/a *adj.* good; buenas noches good evening/night
bueno *adv.* well; O.K.
buscar (qu) to look for
búsqueda search

caballero gentleman
caballo horse
cabello hair; head of hair
cabeza head
cabo: al cabo de at the end of
cabrito kid (*young goat*)
cacao cocoa
cada *inv.* each, every
caer (*irreg.*) to fall
café *m.* coffee; café
cafetín *m.* small coffee shop
cajero/a cashier
caliente hot
caliza: piedra caliza limestone
calor *m.* heat; hace color it's hot (*weather*)
callar to be quiet
calle *f.* street
cama bed
cambiar to change
caminar to walk
caminata long walk; dar una caminata to go for a long walk
camino road, path
camión *m.* truck
camionero truck driver
camisa shirt
campamento camp, campsite
campesino/a *n.* peasant; *adj.* country
campo field

canoa canoe
cansado/a tired
cansancio tiredness, weariness
caña reed; year on the Aztec
  calendar
cañón *m.* cannon
cara face
carga cargo, freight
cargar (**gu**) to carry; **cargar**
  de to load with
Caribe *m.* Caribbean
caricia caress
carnal carnal, of the flesh
carne *f.* meat
carrera career
carretera highway
carro car
cartera wallet
casa house
casarse (**con**) to get married
  (**to**)
casco helmet
casi almost
caso: hacer caso to pay
  attention
castaño/a chestnut-colored
casualidad *f.* coincidence
caza: de caza hunting
cazuela cooking-pot
celda cell
cena dinner, supper
centro center; downtown
cerca *adv.* near, nearby; **cerca**
  de *prep.* near
cerrar (**ie**) to close
cerveza beer
cicatriz *f.* (*pl.* **cicatrices**) scar
cielo sky; heaven
cierto/a certain, true
cima summit
cincho girdle, belt
cintura waist
ciudad *f.* city
claridad *f.* clarity
claro (**que sí**) *interj.* of course
clima *m.* climate

cobija (*L.A.*) blanket
cocina kitchen
cocinar to cook
cocinero/a cook, chef
cola tail
colgar (**ue**) (**gu**) to hang
colina hill
colocar (**qu**) to place, put
colonizador(**a**) colonizer
combatir to fight
comer to eat; **comerse** to eat
  up
comenzar (**ie**) (**c**) to begin
comerciante *m., f.*
  businessperson
cometer to commit
comida food; meal
comienzo beginning
comisión *f.* committee
comodidad *f.* comfort
cómodo/a comfortable
compañero/a companion
compartir to share
cómplice *m., f.* accomplice
comportarse to behave
comprar to buy
comprender to understand
compresa compress, cold pack
comprometerse (**con**) to
  become engaged (**to**)
compromiso: anillo de
  compromiso engagement
  ring
comunicarse (**qu**) to
  communicate (*with one*
  another)
con with
concentrarse to become
  concentrated
concluir (**y**) to conclude
condenar to condemn
conducir (**zc**) (**j**) to drive
conductor(**a**) driver
confesar (**ie**) to confess
confianza confidence
confiar to trust

confortante comforting
confundido/a confused
conmigo with me
conocer (**zc**) to know; to meet
conquistador *m.* conqueror
conseguir (**i, i**) (**g**) to obtain, get
consejero/a adviser
consejo advice
construir (**y**) to build
contaminado/a polluted
contar (**ue**) to tell (*a story*)
contemplar to contemplate
contentar to please
contento/a happy
contestar to answer
contigo with you
contra against; **en contra de** against
convencer (**z**) to convince
convertirse (**ie, i**) **en** to become, turn into
corazón *m.* heart
correr to run
corroborar to corroborate
corromper to corrupt
corte *m.* cut; *f.* court (*royal*)
corto/a short (*in length*)
cosa thing
costa coast
creador(**a**) creator
crecer (**zc**) to grow
creer (**y**) to believe, think; **no creo** I don't think so
crianza raising, breeding
criar to raise
criticar (**qu**) to criticize
cuadro painting
cual *rel. pron.* which; who
cualquier any
cuánto/a how much
cuántos/as how many
cuarto room
cuarto/a fourth
cuate, cuata (*Mex.*) buddy, pal
cubierto/a *p.p.* covered

cubrir to cover
cuchillo knife
cuello neck
cuenta: darse cuenta (**de**) to realize
cuento short story
cuerda rope
cuerpo body
cueva cave
culpar to blame
cultivo cultivation
cuñado/a brother-/sister-in-law
curso course

chango (*Mex.*) monkey
Chapultepec: Parque (*m.*) **de Chapultepec** park in Mexico City
chévere (*Cuba, Puerto Rico, coll.*) great, terrific
chimenea chimney
choque *m.* shock
chuparse los dedos to lick one's fingers

dar (*irreg.*) to give; **dar fin a** to destroy, finish off; **dar la bienvenida** to welcome; **dar las gracias** to thank; **dar miedo** to scare; **dar una caminata** to go for a long walk; **dar unos pasos** to take some steps; **darse cuenta** (**de**) to realize
dato fact
debajo de underneath
deber *m.* duty
deber to owe; **deber** + *inf.* should, ought to, must
decimosegundo/a twelfth
decir (*irreg.*) to say, tell; **querer decir** to mean
dedicarse (**qu**) to dedicate oneself (to)

dedos: chuparse los dedos to lick one's fingers

defenderse (**ie**) to defend oneself

dejar to leave; to let, allow; **dejar de** + *inf.* to stop (*doing something*)

delante *adv.* in front; **delante de** *prep.* in front of

delgado/a thin

demás: los/las demás the others

demasiado *adv.* too much

demasiado/a *adj.* too much

dentro: (**por**) **dentro** inside

derecho/a *adj.* right

desaparecer (**zc**) to disappear

desayuno breakfast

descansar to rest

descanso rest

descifrar to decipher

desconocido/a stranger

describir (*p.p.* **descrito/a**) to describe

descubrimiento discovery

descubrir (*p.p.* **descubierto/a**) to discover

desde *prep.* from, since; **desde que** *conj.* since

desear to desire, wish

desenfocado/a out of focus

deseo desire, wish

desesperadamente desperately

deshabitado/a uninhabited

deshonroso/a dishonorable

desilusionado/a disillusioned

desmayarse to faint

desmayo fainting spell

desnudar to undress, strip

desnudo/a nude

desobedecer (**zc**) to disobey

desolado/a desolate

despedirse (**i, i**) (**de**) to say good-bye (to)

despertar(se) (**ie**) to wake up

despierto/a awake

después *adv.* afterward; **después de** after

destruir (**y**) to destroy

detalle *m.* detail

detenerse (*like* **tener**) to stop

detenidamente at great length

detrás de behind

devolver (**ue**) (*p.p.* **devuelto/a**) to return (*something*)

devorar to devour

día *m.* day

diablo devil; **para qué diablos** why the devil

diario/a daily

dicho/a *p.p.* said

difícil difficult

difunto/a deceased

diminuto/a diminutive

dinero money

dios(a) god/goddess; **por Dios** for heaven's sake

dirigirse (**j**) **a** to head toward

diseñar to design, draw

diseño design

disfrutar de to enjoy

disparar to shoot

dispuesto/a ready, willing

distinguir (**g**) to distinguish

distinto/a different

divertirse (**ie, i**) to have a good time

doler (**ue**) to hurt

dolor *m.* ache, pain

domingo Sunday

dominio dominion

don title of respect used with a man's first name

dorado/a golden

dormido/a asleep

dormir (**ue, u**) to sleep; **dormirse** to fall asleep

duda doubt; **sin duda** doubtless

dueño/a owner

dulce sweet

durante during

durar to last
duro/a hard

e and (*used instead of* **y** *before words beginning with* **i** *or* **hi**)
echarse to throw oneself
edad *f.* age
edificio building
ejemplo: por ejemplo for example
ejército army
electricidad *f.* electricity
embargo: sin embargo however, nevertheless
emborracharse to get drunk
emperador *m.* emperor
empezar (**ie**) (**c**) to begin; **empezar a** + *inf.* to begin to (*do something*)
empleo job
empujar to push
enamorarse (**de**) to fall in love (with)
encabezar (**c**) to head, lead
encender (**ie**) to light
encerrar (**ie**) to enclose
encima de on top of
encomendar (**ie**) to entrust
encontrar (**ue**) to find
encuentro meeting
enemigo/a enemy
energía energy
enfermo/a sick
enfurecerse (**zc**) to become furious
enorme enormous
ensalada salad
enseñar to teach; to show
entender (**ie**) to understand
entonces then, next
entrada entrance
entrar (**en**) to enter, go in
entre between, among
entregar (**gu**) to turn over, hand over
entusiasmado/a enthusiastic

enviar to send
envolver (**ue**) to wrap, wrap up
época epoch, age
equivocado/a mistaken
era era, age
escalofrío shiver
escaso/a scarce
esclavo/a slave
escoger (**j**) to choose
escribir to write
escrito/a *p.p.* written
escritor(**a**) writer
escuchar to listen (to)
escudo shield
escultura sculpture
ese, esa *adj.* that
ése, ésa *pron.* that (one)
esfuerzo effort
eso *pron.* that, that thing; **por eso** that's why
esos/as *adj.* those
ésos/as *pron.* those (ones)
espacio space
español *n. m.* Spanish (*language*)
español(**a**) *n.* Spaniard; *adj.* Spanish
especialidad *f.* specialty
espejo retrovisor rearview mirror
espera waiting
esperar to wait (for); to hope; to expect
espíritu *m.* spirit
espontáneo/a spontaneous
esposo/a spouse; husband/wife
estar (*irreg.*) to be; **estar a punto de** + *inf.* to be about to (*do something*)
establo stable
estación *f.* station; **estación de tren** train station
estampa illustration, engraving
estatua statue
estatura height

este, esta *adj.* this
éste, ésta *pron.* this (one)
estimular to stimulate
esto *pron.* this, this thing
estómago stomach
estos/as *adj.* these
éstos/éstas *pron.* these (ones)
estudiante *m., f.* student
estudiar to study
estudio study
estufa stove
estupendo/a stupendous
eterno/a eternal
evitar to avoid
exagerar to exaggerate
exasperado/a exasperated
exclamar to exclaim
excluir (y) to exclude
exhausto/a exhausted
experimentar to experience
explanada esplanade (*level,
   open space of ground*)
explicación *f.* explanation
explicar (qu) to explain
explorador(a) explorer
extinto/a extinct
extrañar to miss, long for
extraño/a *n.* foreigner, alien;
   adj. strange

facción *f.* gang, band; faction
fácil easy
facilitar to facilitate
fachada facade
faenas chores
falda skirt
falo phallus, penis
faltar to be lacking
fascinado/a fascinated
favor: por favor please
fecha date
felicidad *f.* happiness
feliz (*pl.* felices) happy
fertilidad *f.* fertility
fiel faithful
fiesta party

figurilla small figure
fijar to fix, set (*date*)
fijo/a fixed, unmoving
Filosofía y Letras Humanities
filtrado/a filtered
fin *m.* end; dar fin a to destroy,
   finish off; en fin in short, in
   brief; por fin finally
finca farm
flecha arrow
flor *f.* flower
floreado/a floral
florido/a florid, flowery;
   guerra florida Aztec war
   (hunt for sacrifical victims)
flotante floating
flotar to float
fogón *m.* (de leña) (wood)
   cooking stove
foto *f.* photo
flamboyán *m.* (*Puerto Rico*)
   type of tree
francés *n. m.* French
   (*language*)
francés, francesa French
frecuencia: con frecuencia
   frequently
frente *f.* forehead; *m.* front; al
   frente in front
frente a *prep.* in front of
fresco type of painting
fresco/a fresh; cool
frío/a cold
frito/a fried
frontera border
frustrado/a frustrated
fuego fire
¡fuera de aquí! *interj.* get out
   of here!
fuerte strong
fuerza force
fundar to found, establish

ganar to win
ganas: tener ganas de + *inf.*
   to feel like (*doing something*)

gandules *m.* pigeon peas
garganta throat
gastado/a worn-out, shabby
general: por lo general in general
generoso/a generous
gente *f. sing.* people
gesto gesture
gigantesco/a gigantic
gobernante governing
golpe *m.* strike, blow
golpear to hit, strike
gordo/a fat
grabado/a engraved; recorded
gracias thank you; **dar las gracias** to thank; **gracias a** thanks to
gracioso/a charming
gran, grande great; big
grasa fat; grease
grave serious
gritar to shout, yell
grito shout; scream
grueso/a thick; stout
guante *m.* glove
guantera glove compartment
guarache *m.* (*Mex.*) leather sandal
guardar to keep; to hold
guardia *m.* guard, guardsman
guerra war; **guerra florida** Aztec war (hunt for sacrificial victims)
guerrero soldier
guía *m., f.* guide; *f.* guidance
guiar to guide
gustar to like; to be pleasing to
gusto: a gusto at ease; **con gusto** gladly; **de mal gusto** in bad taste

haber (*irreg.*) to have (*auxiliary*); **había** there was/were; **hay** there is/are
habitación *f.* bedroom
habitante *m., f.* inhabitant

habitar to inhabit
hablar to speak, talk
hacer (*irreg.*) to do; to make; **hace calor** it's hot (*weather*); **hace** (**dos días**) (two days) ago; **hace** + *period of time* + **que** + *present tense* (I) have been (*doing something*) for (*period of time*); **hacer caso** to pay attention; **hacer la maleta** to pack (*suitcase*); **hacer un viaje** to take a trip; **hacer una pausa** to pause; **hacerse** to become; **se hace tarde** it's getting late
hacia towards
halagado/a flattered
hambre (*f. but* **el hambre**) hunger; **tener hambre** to be hungry
hambriento/a hungry, starving
hasta *prep.* until; up to; **hasta que** *conj.* until
hecho/a made; done
hermano/a brother/sister
hermoso/a beautiful
hierba grass
hijo/a son/daughter
historia history; story
hogar *m.* home
hoguera bonfire
hombre *m.* man
hora hour; time
hoy today; **hoy en día** nowadays
humilde humble
humo smoke
hundirse to sink

idioma *m.* language
iglesia church
igual que the same as
imagen *f.* image
imaginar to imagine
impedir (**i, i**) to impede, hinder; to prevent

imperio empire
imponente imposing
importar to be important; to matter
impregnar to impregnate
impresionante impressive
improvisado/a improvised
incesante unceasing, continual
incómodo/a uncomfortable
inconsciente unconscious
incorporarse to sit up
incrédulo/a incredulous
increíble unbelievable
indeciso/a indecisive
indefenso/a defenseless
indígena indigenous, native
indio/a Indian
inesperado/a unexpected
infancia childhood
infierno hell
infinidad *f.* infinity
ingeniero/a engineer
iniciado/a initiated
injusto/a unjust, unfair
inmediato: de inmediato immediately
inodoro toilet
inquieto/a restless, uneasy
insaciable insatiable
insignia badge, emblem
insoportable unbearable
inspeccionar to inspect
inspirar to stimulate; inspire
intercambiar to exchange
interés *m.* interest
interesante interesting
interesar to interest
intérprete *m., f.* interpreter
interrumpir to interrupt
intervenir (*like* **venir**) to intervene
introducir (**zc**) (**j**) to put (into), insert; **introducirse** (**en**) to get in, break in
inundado/a inundated

inútil useless
ir (*irreg.*) to go; **ir a** + *inf.* to be going to (*do something*); **irse** to leave, go away
ira ire, anger
isla island
izquierdo/a *adj.* left

jalar to pull
jardín *m.* garden
jefe, jefa boss
joven *n. m., f.* young person; *adj.* young
junio June
junto/a together; **junto a** along with
jurar to swear

laberinto labyrinth
lado side; **de un lado** on one side
lago lake
lágrima tear
lanza lance
largo/a long; **a lo largo de** along
lástima pity; **¡qué lástima!** what a pity!
lectura reading
leche *f.* milk
lechuga lettuce
leer (**y**) to read
legumbre *m.* vegetable
lejano/a distant
lejos *adv.* far, far away; **a lo lejos** in the distance; **lejos de** *prep.* far from
lengua language
lento/a slow; **a paso lento** slowly
Letras: Filosofía y Letras Humanities
levantar to lift, raise up; **levantarse** to get up
leve light, slight
leyenda legend

libre: al aire libre outdoors
libro book
ligero/a light (*not heavy*)
limón *m.* lemon
limpiar to clean
limpio/a clean
loco/a crazy
locura craziness
lucha fight
luego then; soon
lugar *m.* place
luna moon
luz *f.* (*pl.* **luces**) light

llamar to call; **llamarse** to be named
llegada arrival
llegar (**gu**) to arrive; **llegar a** + *inf.* to manage to (*do something*); **llegar a ser** to become
llenar to fill
lleno/a full
llevar to wear; to carry; to bring; **llevar puesto/a** to have on (*clothing*), be wearing
llorar to cry
lluvia rain

madera wood
madre *f.* mother
maíz *m.* corn
mal *adv.* badly
mal, malo/a *adj.* bad; **de mal gusto** in bad taste
maleta suitcase; **hacer la maleta** to pack (*suitcase*)
mandar to send
mandato command
manejar to drive
manera manner, way
mano *f.* hand
manta blanket
mantener (*like* **tener**) to maintain, support

manto mantle, cloak
manzana apple
mañana tomorrow; morning
maquahuime wooden club studded with obsidian knives
maquillado/a made up, with makeup applied
maquillaje *m.* makeup
mar *m., f.* sea
maravilloso/a marvelous
marcado/a marked, pronounced
marcharse to leave, go away
mareo dizziness
mármol *m.* marble
más more; most; **más o menos** more or less; **más que nada** more than anything
matar to kill
matrimonio matrimony, marriage
máximo maximum
mayor great; greater; older
mediano: de mediana estatura of medium height
medio *n.* middle; means; *adv.* half; **en medio de** in the middle of; **por medio de** by means of
mejor better
mejorar to improve
menor younger; slightest, least
memoria memory; **aprenderse de memoria** to memorize
menos: más o menos more or less
mensajero/a messenger
mente *f.* mind
mentir (**ie, i**) to lie
mercado market
mes *m.* month
mesa table
mesero/a waiter/waitress
metro metro, subway

mexica *inv.* Aztec
mexicano/a Mexican
mi *poss. adj.* my
mí *obj. of prep.* me
miedo fear; **dar miedo** to scare; **tener miedo** (**de**) to be afraid (of)
miel *f.* honey
mientras while
mijo/a (*shortened form of* **mi hijo/a**) my son/daughter
milla mile
mío/a *poss. adj.* my, (of) mine
mirada look
mirar to look (at); **con sólo mirar** just by looking
mismo/a same; **aquí mismo** right here; **sí mismo/a** oneself
misterio mystery
misterioso/a mysterious
mitad *f.* half
mítico/a mythical
mito myth
mitología mythology
mochila backpack
mole *m.* (*Mex.*) dish prepared with chocolate, chili sauce, and spices
molestar to bother, annoy
monótono/a monotonous
monstruo monster
montaña mountain
morder (**ue**) to bite
morir (**ue, u**) to die
mostrar (**ue**) to show
mover(se) (**ue**) to move
movimiento movement
muchacho/a boy/girl
mucho/a a lot
muchos/as many
muebles *m. pl.* furniture
muerte *f.* death
muerto/a *n.* dead person; *adj.* dead; *p.p.* died
mujer *f.* woman; wife

mundo world
muñeca doll
murmurar to murmur
muro wall
musculoso/a muscular
museo museum

nacer (**zc**) to be born
nada nothing, (not) anything; **más que nada** more than anything
nadie nobody, (not) anybody
natal *adj.* native
naturaleza nature
necesidad *f.* necessity
necesitar to need
negro/a black
nervioso/a nervous
ni nor; **ni siquiera** not even
nido nest
nieve *f.* snow
ningún, ninguno/a none, (not) any
niño/a boy/girl; child
noche *f.* night; **buenas noches** good evening/night; **esta noche** tonight
nocturno/a nocturnal
nogal *m.* walnut tree
nombre *m.* name
nopal *m.* prickly pear cactus
nordeste *m.* northeast
norte *m.* north
norteamericano/a North American
notar to notice
noticia (piece of) news; *pl.* news
noviazgo courtship
novio/a boy/girlfriend; fiancé(e); bride/groom
nuez *f.* (*pl.* **nueces**) walnut; nut
nuestro/a *poss. adj.* our
nuevo/a new
número number
numeroso/a numerous
nunca never, (not) ever

o or
obedecer (zc) to obey
objetivo objective
objeto object
obra work; work of art
obsesionar to obsess
obsidiana obsidian
obviamente obviously
octli pulque (*beverage made of fermented sap of maguey plant*)
ocupado/a occupied; busy
ocupar to occupy
ocurrir to occur
oeste *m.* west
ofendido/a offended
oferta offer
ofrecer (zc) to offer
ofrecimiento offering
ofrenda offering
oído (inner) ear
oír (*irreg.*) to hear
ojo eye
olor *m.* odor
olvidar to forget; olvidarse de to forget
olvido forgetfulness
opaco/a dark
opinar to think, have an opinion
orden *f.* order, command
ordenar to order
orgullo pride
orgulloso/a proud
oro gold
oscuridad *f.* darkness
oscuro/a dark
otro/a other, another; el uno al otro to each other
oxidado/a rusted

paciencia patience
padre *m.* father; father (*form of addressing a priest*); padres parents
pagar (gu) to pay (for)

país *m.* country
paisaje *m.* countryside
palabra word
palacio palace
pálido/a pale
palmera palm tree
pan *m.* bread
pantalón, (*pl.* pantalones) *m.* pants
pañuelo handkerchief
papá *m.* dad
papel *m.* paper
para *prep.* for; in order to; para allá over there; para que *conj.* so that; para qué diablos why the devil
parada stop
parar to stop; parar a + *inf.* to stop to (*do something*)
paralizado/a paralyzed
parecer (zc) to seem, appear; parecerse a to resemble
pared *f.* wall
párpado eyelid
parque *m.* park
parte *f.* part
partir to leave
pasado *n.* past
pasar to pass, pass by; to happen; to come in; to spend (time); ¿te pasa algo? is something the matter?
pasaje *m.* passage
pasillo hallway
paso step; a paso lento slowly
pata foot, leg (*of animal*)
pausa: hacer una pausa to pause
paz *f.* (*pl.* paces) peace
pecho chest; breast
pedazo piece, bit
pedir (i, i) to ask for, request; pedir prestado/a to borrow
pegado/a stuck, glued
pelea fight
pelear to fight

pelo hair
peluca wig
penetrar to penetrate
pensamiento thought
pensar (**ie**) to think
pensativo/a pensive
pequeño/a small; little
perder (**ie**) to lose; **perderse**
to get lost
perdonar to pardon, excuse
perro/a dog
personaje *m.* character (*in a
story*)
pertenecer (**zc**) to belong
pesadilla nightmare
pesar to be heavy
pesar: a pesar de in spite of
petate *m.* (*Mex.*) sleeping mat
pico beak
picosito/a spicy
pie *m.* foot; **a pie** on foot;
quedarse de pie to remain
standing
piedra rock; **piedra caliza**
limestone; **piedra preciosa**
precious stone, gem
piel *f.* skin; fur; hide
pierna leg
pieza piece
pila heap, pile
pintado/a painted
pirámide *f.* pyramid
placer *m.* pleasure
plano/a flat
plátano banana
plato plate
playa beach
pluma feather
pobre poor; **pobre de ti** poor
you, you poor thing
poco *adv.* little; **poco a poco**
little by little
poco/a *adj.* little
pocos/as few
poder *m.* power
poder (*irreg.*) to be able

poderoso/a powerful
poesía poetry
poeta *m., f.* poet
policía police (force)
pollo chicken
pomada ointment; salve
pon *m.* (*Puerto Rico*) ride
poner (*irreg.*) to put, place;
ponerse to put on (*clothing*);
ponerse a + *inf.* to begin,
set about (*doing something*);
ponerse de acuerdo to agree
por for; by; through; because
of; **por aquí/allí** around
here/there; **por dentro**
inside; **por Dios** for heaven's
sake; **por ejemplo** for
example; **por eso** that's why;
por favor please; **por fin**
finally; **por la mañana/
tarde/noche** in the
morning/afternoon/evening,
night; **por lo general** in
general; **por medio de** by
means of; **¿por qué?** why?;
por suerte luckily; **por
supuesto** of course; **por
último** finally
portarse to behave
posibilidad *f.* possibility
posponer (*like* **poner**) to
postpone
práctico/a practical
prado meadow
preciosa: piedra preciosa
precious stone, gem
preferir (**ie, i**) to prefer
pregunta question
preguntar to ask (a question);
preguntarse to wonder
premio prize
preocupado/a worried
presenciar to be present at
prestado/a: pedir prestado/a
to borrow
primer, primero/a first

principio: al principio in the beginning
prisa: de prisa hurriedly
prisionero/a prisoner
probar (**ue**) to try, taste; to prove
prometer to promise
pronto soon; **de pronto** suddenly
pronunciar to pronounce
propio/a own
proponer (*like* **poner**) to propose; **proponerse** to plan, intend
propósito purpose; intention
provinciano/a provincial
prueba proof, evidence
pueblo town
puerta door
puesto/a *p.p.*: **llevar puesto/a** to have on (*clothing*), be wearing
punto: estar a punto de + *inf.* to be about to (*do something*)
puñal *m.* dagger

quedar to remain, be left; **quedarse** to remain, stay; to be; **quedarse de pie** to remain standing
quehacer *m.* chore
quejarse to complain
quemadura burn
quemarse to burn oneself
querer (*irreg.*) to want; to love; **querer decir** to mean
querido/a dear
quien(es) *pron.* who, whom
¿quién(es)? who?, whom?
quinto/a fifth
quitar to take away; **quitarse** to take off (*clothing*)
quizás perhaps

raro/a strange
rascacielos *m. sing.* skyscraper

rato while, short time
razón *f.* reason; **tener razón** to be right
reaccionar to react
real real; royal
realidad *f.* reality
realizar (**c**) to carry out, fulfill
rebozo shawl
recibimiento reception
recibir to receive
recipiente *m.* container
recoger (**j**) to pick up
reconocer (**zc**) to recognize
recordar (**ue**) to remember
recorrer to travel; to go through
recuerdo memory
recuperar to recuperate; to regain
redondo/a round
reescrito/a rewritten
reflejado/a reflected
refrescar (**qu**) to refresh
regalar to give as a gift
regalo gift
regla rule
regresar to return
regreso return; **de regreso** *adj.* return
reinar to reign
reino kingdom
relacionado/a related
relato story, narrative
reliquia relic
repasar to review
repetido: repetidas veces repeatedly
repetir (**i, i**) to repeat
repleto/a full
representado/a represented
reprochar to reproach
rescatar to rescue
residir to reside
respirar to breathe
responder to answer
respuesta answer
resultar to turn out to be

retrovisor: espejo retrovisor
rearview mirror
reunión *f.* meeting
revivir to revive
rey *m.* king
rico/a rich
ridículo/a ridiculous
riesgo risk
rincón *m.* corner
riqueza wealth
rito rite, ritual
roca rock
rodear to surround
rojo/a red
ropa clothing
rostro face
rubio/a blond(e)
ruido noise
rumbo a bound for
ruta route

saber (*irreg.*) to know; **saber
a** to taste like
sabor *m.* flavor
saborear to savor
sabroso/a tasty
sacar (**qu**) to take out, get out
sacerdote *m.* priest
saciar to satiate, satisfy
sacrificar (**qu**) to sacrifice
sagrado/a sacred
sala room
salir (*irreg.*) to go out, leave
salón *m.* drawing room,
reception room
salsa sauce
saludable healthy
saludar to greet
salvar to save
san, santo/a saint
sandalia sandal
sangre *f.* blood
sartén *f.* frying pan
satisfecho/a satisfied
seco/a dry
sed *f.* thirst

seguir (**i, i**) (**g**) to continue; to
follow
según according to
segundo second (*measure of
time*)
segundo/a second
semana week
semilla seed
sencillo/a simple
sensación *f.* sensation
sentarse (**ie**) to sit down
sentencia sentence, judgment
sentido: tener sentido to
make sense
sentir(se) (**ie, i**) to feel
seña sign, signal
señalar to point out, point at
señor *m.* Mr.; sir
señora Mrs.; ma'am
separado/a separated
ser *m.* being
ser (*irreg.*) to be; **llegar a ser**
to become; **o sea** that is
serio/a serious
serpiente *f.* serpent
significado meaning
signo sign, symbol
siguiente following
silencioso/a quiet
silla chair
símbolo symbol
simplicidad *f.* simplicity
sin without; **sin duda**
doubtless; **sin embargo**
however, nevertheless
siquiera: ni siquiera not even
sirviente, sirvienta servant
sitio place
sobre on, on top of; about;
sobre todo especially
sobrino/a nephew/niece
sol *m.* sun
soldado soldier
soledad *f.* solitude
sólo only; **con sólo mirar** just
by looking

solo/a alone; single
soltero/a single, unmarried
sombra shadow
someter to subdue
sonido sound
sonreír (**i, i**) to smile
sonrisa smile
soñar (**ue**) (**con**) to dream (about)
sopa soup
soportar to endure, put up with
sorprender to surprise
sorpresa surprise
sospechar to suspect
sostener (*like* **tener**) to hold up, support
su *poss. adj.* his, her, its, your (*form. sing., pl.*)
suave smooth, soft
subir to go up; to get into (*vehicle*)
subyugar (**gu**) to subjugate
sucio/a dirty
sucumbir to succumb
sudor *m.* sweat
suelo floor
sueño sleep; dream; **tener sueño** to be sleepy
suerte *f.* luck; **por suerte** luckily; **tener suerte** to be lucky
sufrimiento suffering
sufrir to suffer
sujetar to hold, grasp
superficie *f.* surface
supermercado supermarket
suponer (*like* **poner**) to suppose
supuesto: por supuesto of course
sur *m.* south

tal such, that; **ésa tal** that woman
tampoco neither, (not) either

tan so
tanto *adv.* so much; **mientras tanto** meanwhile; **un tanto** somewhat, a bit
tanto/a *adj.* so, so much
tantos/as so many
taparrabo loincloth
tardanza tardiness
tardar to take a long time; **tardar... en** + *inf.* to be or take (*period of time*) to (*do something*)
tarde *adv.* late; **más tarde** later; **se hace tarde** it's getting late; **tarde o temprano** sooner or later
tarde *f.* afternoon; **por la tarde** in the afternoon
taza cup
teatro theater
techo roof
teja roof tile
tela cloth
temblar (**ie**) to tremble
temblor *m.* tremor
temer to fear
temor *m.* fear
temprano early; **tarde o temprano** sooner or later
tender (**ie**) to spread out
tener (*irreg.*) to have; **tener... años** to be . . . years old; **tener frío** to be cold; **tener hambre** to be hungry; **tener miedo** to be afraid; **tener que** + *inf.* to have to (*do something*); **tener razón** to be right; **tener sueño** to be sleepy
tercer, tercero/a third
terminar to finish
ternura tenderness
terreno terrain, land
testigo witness
ti *obj. of prep.* you; **pobre de ti** poor you, you poor thing

tibio/a warm
tiempo time
tienda store
tierno/a tender
tierra land; ground
tiesto flowerpot
tigre *m.* tiger
típico/a typical
tipo kind, type
tirar to throw
título title
tobillo ankle
tocar(se) (qu) to touch
todavía still; **todavía no** not
  yet
todo/a all
tolerar to tolerate
tomar(se) to take; to drink; to
  eat; **tomar una decisión** to
  make a decision
tomate *m.* tomato
tonto/a silly, foolish
tortilla (*Mex., Central America*)
  tortilla (*round, flat bread
  made of corn or wheat flour*)
torturado/a tortured
tostón *m.* deep-fried plantain
  slices
trabajar to work
trabajo work
traducir (zc) to translate
traer (*irreg.*) to bring
traición *f.* : **a traición**
  treacherously
traje *m.* suit; costume
tranquilidad *f.* tranquility,
  peace
tranquilo/a calm, peaceful
transportar to transport
trastornar to upset, disturb; to
  make dizzy
tratar de + *inf.* to try to (*do
  something*)
través: a través de through
trayecto journey
tremendo/a tremendous

tren *m.* train
trenza braid; tress
tristeza sadness
triunfo triumph
trono throne
tu *poss. adj.* your (*fam. sing.*)
tubo pipe
tuyo/a *poss. adj.* your (*fam.
  sing.*), (of) yours (*fam. sing.*)

últimamente lately
último/a last; **por último**
  finally
único/a only; unique
uniformado/a in uniform
universidad *f.* university
untar to smear; to apply
  (*ointment*)

vaca cow
vacaciones *f. pl.* vacation
vacío void, emptiness
vacío/a empty
vagabundo/a vagrant, tramp
valer (*irreg.*) to be worth
valiente brave
valle *m.* valley
vano: en vano in vain
variado/a varied
variedad *f.* variety
varios/as various; several
vecino/a neighboring
vejez *f.* old age
vela candle
vena vein
vencer (z) to win, be
  victorious
venda bandage
vendedor(a) salesperson
vender to sell
venir (*irreg.*) to come
ventana window
ventanilla train window
ver (*irreg.*) to see; **a ver** let's
  see; **verse** to be seen; to look,
  appear

verano summer
verdad *f.* truth; **de verdad**
truly, really
verdadero/a true
verde green
vestido dress
vestirse (**i, i**) to get dressed
vez *f.* (*pl.* **veces**) time; **a veces**
sometimes; **de vez en
cuando** once in a while; **otra
vez** again; **repetidas veces**
repeatedly
viajar to travel
viaje *m.* trip
vibrar to vibrate; to quiver
víctima *f.* victim
vida life
viejo/a *n.* old person; *adj.* old
viento wind
vigilar to watch, keep guard
villa town
vino wine

Virgen *f.* Virgin Mary
visitar to visit
vista view
visto/a seen
viviente living
vivir to live
vivo/a *p.p.* alive; living; lively,
bright
volar (**ue**) to fly
volcán *m.* volcano
volver (**ue**) to return
voz *f.* (*pl.* **voces**) voice; **en
voz alta** aloud
vuelta turn
vuelto/a *p.p.* returned
vuestro/a *poss. adj.* your
(*fam. pl., Sp.*), (of) yours
(*fam. pl., Sp.*)

y and
ya already; **ya no** no longer

—Pregúntales quiénes son —le ordena a la mujer.

Ella nos habla en náhuatl. Ahora comprendo quién es. Se trata de Malinche,[46] la intérprete y amante de Cortés.

Le pido a Ollín que conteste.

—Somos nobles de la corte del emperador Moctezuma —les explica Ollín—. Venimos mandados por él para hacerles llegar estas ofrendas en su nombre. Y también, si así lo desean, para guiarlos hasta nuestra capital, Tenochtitlán.

Malinche traduce al español lo que acaba de decir Ollín. Alvarado sonríe, satisfecho.

—Entonces, ¿queréis ver al capitán Cortés? —nos pregunta.

Decimos que sí con un gesto.

Hernán Cortés está acostado sobre una cama improvisada. Se levanta cuando nos ve llegar. Es un hombre de mediana estatura; tiene pelo negro, barba. Nos saluda amablemente. Nosotros le mostramos los regalos.

—¡Qué bienvenida! —exclama. Luego nos habla por medio de su intérprete Malinche—. Acepto vuestra invitación. Estamos aquí precisamente porque queremos llegar a esa gran ciudad de la que todos hablan.

Cortés sonríe. Está tan cerca, tan a mi alcance.[47] Con un leve corte[48] de mi cuchillo, puedo acabar con él y cambiar el curso de la historia. Sería tan fácil. Pero no. Yo no

recuerdo aparece Tozani. ¿Quién es? ¿Por qué estoy ocupando su cuerpo y viviendo su vida?

Me dejo caer sobre la cama. Es muy suave. La muchacha regresa y me trae la cena: los platos más sabrosos y variados que he comido en mi vida.

Después de comer vuelvo a la cama y duermo tranquilo, sin sueños.

---

[46] Malinche (−ca. 1530), indígena que interpretó para Cortés y con quien el capitán tuvo un hijo   [47] a... *within my reach*   [48] *cut*

For the suns that rise on the horizons we've yet to see,
for my brothers and sisters, my sons and daughters.

For my father, Bee Yang,
who sings his lonely songs so that we may hear
the trembling of the still, fluttering heart.

Kwv txhiaj is, in the words of Ralph Ellison on
   American blues,

"an impulse to keep the painful details and
episodes of a brutal experience alive in one's aching
consciousness, to finger its jagged grain, and to
transcend it, not by the consolation of philosophy
but by squeezing from it a near-tragic, near-cosmic
lyricism. As a form, the blues is an autobiographical
chronicle of personal catastrophe expressed
lyrically."

✧

Kwv txhiaj songs can be duets: the voices of fathers
   and daughters coming together, different verses
   within the same song, stanzas in the same poem.

Contents

The
Song
Poet

Album Notes

My father would never describe himself as a poet. In Laos, he was a fatherless boy. In Thailand, he was a refugee waiting in the dust. In America, he is a machinist. Through it all, he has been a poor person yearning for a father and living to be one.

My father is Chue Moua's husband and the father of seven children, five girls and two boys. My father says that on his gravestone he wants it known that his wife and his children are his life's work. He would love it if we could add: "All of Bee Yang's children became good people."

I am the only person I know who describes my father's work as poetry. I am not referring to the pieces of hard metal he polishes, the rough edges he makes smooth, the coarseness he evens into shine. I am talking about the songs he composes, day and night, in Hmong, our language, his *kwv txhiaj*.

My father is not a writer. He does not write down his compositions. He is a singer. He sings them.

It has taken me a long time to gain the courage to call my father's work poetry. For much of my life I have described my father to the world as a machinist, not as the poet I know him to be. I didn't have a way of conveying how being my father's daughter has taught me not how machines work but how the human heart operates.

I grew up hearing my father digging into words for images that will stretch the limits of life for my siblings and me. In my father's mouth, bitter, rigid words become sweet and elastic like taffy. His poetry shields us from the poverty of our lives.

On the colorful woven plastic mat in the middle of our living room floor, we sit around my father. We look at the walls with him. The mold growing wild becomes the backdrop of the beautiful paintings we see on television, the peak of this mountain, the descent of that river, the sliver of tree that clings to life on the edges of the rocks, open and exposed. We point at the things we did not see before our father's words gave them shape, alternatives, possibilities. My brother Xue sees a crane at the river's edge. Sib Hlub points to the sky with its cloud families, gray and rumbling, and whispers of bad weather approaching. For a moment, we are living in a priceless, ageless piece of art.

In the deep of winter, after months of unceasing cold, my father points outside our front window at the ice-covered mounds of snow shining in the bright sun, under a cloudless sky of blue, and says, "Look at the garden of winter, the snow flowers are blooming today." My siblings and I leave our places by the big heater with its opening's single blue flame, and we look out into a picture of winter we thought we had grown sick of. We blink against the shine. Beneath our lashes, in the sliver of open eyes, stars twinkle in the colors of the winter rainbow. The children marvel while my older sister Dawb and I take deep breaths and breathe foggy air onto the glass pane. We draw the flowers of early spring on the cold, wet glass with our fingers: buds of tulips and daffodils, the bursts of dandelions and fragrant lilac blooms. The sweet, clean scent of magnolia blossoms and the images of the flowering trees—stocked with soft white, pink, pinkish-red, and purplish-white petals—remind us that warm weather and abundant flowers are coming our way. The world of winter becomes bearable in the promise of spring.

In perfect <u>pentatonic</u> pitch my father sings his songs, grows them into long, stretching stanzas of four or five, structures them in couplets, repeats patterns of words, and changes the last word of each verse so that it rhymes with the end of the next. He is a master at parallelism; the language is protracted, and the notes are drawn deep and long. The only way I know how to describe it as a form in English is to say: my father raps, jazzes, and sings the blues when he dwells in the landscape of <u>traditional Hmong song poetry</u>. Different shapes come forth from the dirty places, different possibilities are born in the shadows of our lives, and windows emerge in the places my brothers and sisters and I have only ever seen walls.

I grew up surrounded by my father's words. They are familiar to me as the wind outside the thin walls of our old house across the different seasons.

In the cool of autumn, the wind carries the dry, crackling leaves along the sides of York Avenue. Empty cans roll along the broken cement walk and abandoned plastic bags fly with their ghostly goods. An occasional voice is carried in the wind, a brother looking for a sister as night falls, a baby crying for its mother, the bark of a hungry dog.

In the cold of winter, the wind blows the snow off the ground and waves of white come sweeping across our tiny stretch of lawn and hit the house in sprinklings of icy snow. Invisible streams of air seep through the cracks of the old windows and the smell of our rice-scented home swims in the currents of cold. Outside, the sound of police sirens resonates in the rippling, urgent winter winds.

In the warmth of spring, the wind transforms the empty parking lot by the corner Laundromat into a field of fallen petals as crab apple trees release their blooms and the hard pavement feels the soft brush of tender, ephemeral beauty. Wet rain falls into shattered concrete and the pools of black water lie still for the pink and white and red petals to swim in. The wind carries the voices of laughing children into our house as we watch the petals sway to and fro in the dark puddles across our street.

In the heat of hot summer, the green grass grows while the yellow dandelions die, and in the wake of their demise the wind carries their spirits and their seeds across open lots, rotting houses, small yards, littered avenues, and everywhere there are little parachutes of pollen floating away. Late into the night, we listen to the voices of friends and neighbors talking outside on their porches, hear the clinking of cans, turn our heads toward their laughter and their tears, and the wind loses its appeal for a season because the pull of people grows strong across the fertile green.

My father was a young man who carried on his broad shoulders hundred-pound sacks of rice while I ran fast as I could to open the front door lest he beat me there. Then came the season when there was no danger that my father would get there before me, when I stood with the door wide open, my fingers soft against the hard wood; I watched my father age with each sack of rice we bought and ate. My wait at the front door of our house grew long as my father's steps grew heavier on the ground and his shoulders shook beneath the burden of feeding us.

Once in a while, there was something undeniably lonely that

seeped into me when I caught and understood pieces of my father's songs, heard the tears leaking through, creating ripples of husk in the smoothness of his voice. As a child peeking through crowds, my hand secured in my mother's, I watched groups of people cry around my father's songs, and I saw how sorrow could be shared.

My first absolute memory of my father as a poet happened at the Hmong American New Year in November of 1989. Someone had put my father's name down as a performer at the annual celebration. We were in the old Civic Center, now renovated and renamed. The younger kids hadn't been born yet. They were still high up in the clouds, in their race across the sky. It was only the five of us: my mother, my father, Dawb, me, and Xue, our baby brother. My mother pushed Xue in the old stroller we'd gotten from a garage sale during the summer. Dawb was ten years old. I was in the last months of my eighth year. It was the first year I was growing out my hair from its Thai schoolgirl bob, and I had borrowed my mother's hair spray and done a tiny pouf on the bangs that were getting long over my eyes. My father had not been excited about my decision to let my hair grow out—he thought I was too young—but my mother had agreed that it was time I learned how to take care of long hair, so my father had relented. I was learning how to be critical of my father that year, our second year in America.

My father owned two suits, the brown one that Grandma had paid for in Thailand and then a black one that my mother had chosen for him at Men's Wearhouse. He wore the black suit to the Hmong New Year that year. His straight shoulders lifted high in the suit. My father looked like a man who worked in an office building. My mother wore a black sweater with shiny beads, purple pants with seams down the front that she created carefully with the iron, knee-high stockings that made the skin of her feet dark and smooth, and a pair of heels that clicked gently on the floor with each step. When my mother and father walked together, I thought they both looked good enough to be secretaries; the only challenges to the image were the sleeping baby boy in the stroller, Dawb and me, and the backdrop of Hmong people in their finery.

The New Year celebration was a day dedicated to dreams, dreams of prosperity for the Hmong people and the Hmong family. Since our arrival in America in 1987, my family had gone regularly to the celebrations. We all looked forward to the two days of seeing and greeting family, friends, and strangers. Our mother and father would stop to chat with the adults they knew while Dawb stood solemnly by and I bit my bottom lip and tried not to look too shy. Occasionally, I sneaked behind the stroller to feel the stiff tiny pouf of hair on my forehead with my fingers. In the bright fluorescent light of the Civic Center, the yellow in everybody's skin changed into a pale shade of whitish gray. The women with lots of makeup looked like clowns. The thin old men with their hollowed eyes brought to mind the plastic skeletons at the stores during Halloween. Despite these scary possibilities, there was movement and color all around, and more comfort than fear to be found in the big building. I imagined that we were all performers in a great circus.

That year had begun like the previous years: My family and I spent the first hour or two walking around the large arena admiring the glitter and noise that surrounded us, the clinking coins and swishing silver bracelets, women in heels that clicked on the hard floor along with the gentler clicking of camera shutters. We stopped to look at the young men and women who stood in lines and threw handmade cloth balls sewn with silver and gold thread, or the familiar fluorescent green of tennis balls, at each other. It was an old courtship tradition. We made room for the old men and women who helped each other through the crowds, stopping every few feet to admire the beauty of the young. All around us there were little babies like Xue in their strollers with the sunshade drawn forward despite the fact that there was no sunshine to protect them from. Some of the babies looked intently at the world around them while others fell into exhausted slumber, heads sagging to rest against the sides of their strollers. A few of the sleeping babies were drooling. I checked Xue regularly to make sure that his mouth was clean. Our family moved slowly through the standing, shifting bodies.

When we heard "Bee Yang, Bee Yang, if you hear this please come to the stage. Your name is being called for a traditional *kwv txhiaj* performance. Bee Yang, Bee Yang, please report to the stage," it did not register that they were calling the Bee Yang we knew. It was not until the familiar faces of family, aunts and uncles, second and third cousins, emerged from the crowd and each of them pointed my father toward the stage that we knew our father was being called.

My father shook his head. He was like me. He was shy. He did not want to go on the stage. He shook his head slowly again, this time smiling. The faces did not disappear into the crowd. They came closer. When old friends and acquaintances started pulling him toward the stage, my father looked at my mother and shrugged his shoulders, both his hands raised, palms up. He allowed himself to be led toward the sound of the amplified voice calling his name. Near the empty outskirts of the stage, where the people had cleared room so that the raised platform seemed a small island in the sea of smooth concrete, my father straightened his spine and walked slowly to the woman and the man waiting for him with a microphone extended. My father's name was announced as a contributor to the New Year's festivities. The people around me applauded. I stood by my mother, my older sister, and my baby brother in the crowd, and we watched my father take the extended microphone from the male host, shake his hand, nod to the female host, and then climb the stairs to the stage. I was nervous for my father. I was also scared that I would be embarrassed by him. I had heard stories of how he had been requested to sing at the Hmong New Year's celebrations in Ban Vinai Refugee Camp, but it was not something I could remember. I imagined the dust rising in the yellow dirt field, the young men and women standing opposite each other, my father standing on a makeshift stage, his voice muffled by the debris of our lives in Thailand, struggling to be heard. I knew that my father's singing was valued by the adults. I looked at the faces of the men and women standing still, eyes on my father, and I realized that they did not know that I was his daughter. I was just another kid in the crowd of Hmong people celebrating the New Year. The fluorescent bulbs continued to cast their unfriendly light upon us. If I grew embarrassed, I figured I could always pretend I didn't exist.

When my father began to sing, I watched him as a stranger would. I saw a man standing still, his left hand holding a microphone, his right smoothing the side of his suit jacket. There was firmness to the set of his jaw, an appearance of reckoning in his straight stance. The steadiness of my father's voice reached out

to me. His "*Niajyah* . . . ," the preamble to the form, called out
across the crowd. He looked at the people, from one side of
the arena to the other. He trained his gaze high over us, at the
people sitting up in the stands. As he sang, it seemed he saw
through the steel beams and cement walls that surrounded us
and out into the world we had ventured from. It was a song of
grieving. The song was a cry for a New Year that once was a
time for rest after the bountiful harvest, for the old to call upon
the young, for all to walk together toward the future of a sun
on the rise. There was a moment of transition, and then my
father sang, "The flash of light that turned the world dark, the
sounds of exploding suns across the sky, the cries that rang forth
in the place of laughter." A new quiet entered into the arena;
his voice softened, his tones lengthened. "Lost are the ones who
run through jungles without shoes, the young screaming for
their elders to run faster, a giant moon on the other side of a
river, the glittering water a mirror for what will come." People
started weeping. Men and women reached into pockets and
purses and came forth with folded pieces of wrinkled napkins;
they tore up the napkins to share; those with nothing in hand
began wiping away their tears on their sleeves.

I saw my father bend his head, searching within for the
words that would send away the sorrow he had unleashed. He
walked a few steps forward, to the edge of the stage, and raised
his right hand to the audience, opened his palm, closed it again,
slowly dropped his hand, and allowed the fingers to round into
a fist. My father sang, "A brother and a sister search the world
for each other, one caught on the side of the trees, the other has
traveled far across the wide seas." His rhythm and his rhyme were
one. His words grew louder, his voice stronger. He sang: "Like

the eggs hatched upon the same nest, they huddle to themselves and call out for the same feathery bed. The future takes us to the same place, our hearts hover close to the same space . . . where once our mothers and our fathers held us close, and made us safe."

My fear of embarrassment vanished. In its place there was no pride, just an understanding of the man I had always seen exclusively as mine, now standing before his people, with his heart open, bleeding hardship and harrowing hope. The words had nothing and everything to do with my being in the big arena. There was no room for refusal, for thoughts or ideas, it was all just a moment felt, emotions bubbling forth from losses the Hmong had endured. In his song, I was no longer young. I was one with a people who had lived for a long time, traveled across many lands, a people clinging to each other for a reminder, a promise, of home, that place deep inside and far beyond where the Hmong people had hidden our hearts so that we could heal. There was nothing to be embarrassed about.

After my father's song ended, there was a stretch of silence, noses being blown, breath exhaled, and then the echoing ring of applause. Men and women rushed toward him at the stage's edge and they clapped their hands on his back as he walked back down to the floor. Some wept on his shoulders. My mother stood aside, just a woman with her children, and we waited patiently for him to make his way toward us. I slipped my hand from my mother's and moved away from my family so that I could see the moment when they met, my mother and father. I watched how my father approached my mother, my big sister, and my baby brother sleeping in his stroller. My father placed both his hands on Dawb's smooth hair. He leaned close to my mother and whispered something in her ear. She turned to him and smiled and nodded, and then I watched the smile fade from her face as she started looking for me.

In the car home, we were silent. There were words that I wanted to say but did not know how or why they felt necessary. I didn't tell my father that I'd finally listened and found meaning in his songs. No longer were the phrases just bits and pieces of a long story floating from the past into my present. I did not say that I was not embarrassed or that I thought he had done a good job. All I did was stare out the car window and hear the work of the wind in the dark, cold night. I squinted hard at the lights in the distance. I urged my world to dissolve into a blur of light circles. Dawb sat quietly beside me, lost in her own thoughts. Her new shoes were a small heap on the floor of the car beneath her dangling feet. Xue, our baby brother, slept in his car seat between us. Our brown Subaru made its hiccupping noise at every stoplight, and I watched puffs of smoke balloon behind us when the lights turned from red to green. I could smell the exhaust from our car. I hoped other people weren't able to smell it as I did. I listened to the wind blow hard against the car. I felt the car shake. I did not want to tell my father that his song had shaken my heart, taken me to a place that I did not want to visit for fear I would never return. Now that I had heard, I could not forget the suffering and sorrow of the Hmong story.

After my father's Hmong American New Year's performance we received many calls from friends and family, from strangers who had heard him, and from people from other states who had heard of him, asking my father to please make a tape of his songs and send it to them. The people said that they would be happy to pay my father for a recording of his songs. The winter passed and the phone calls did not stop. My cousin Pakou was married to a man in a band who played and recorded music from his basement. The cousin-in-law had the equipment we needed to make a cassette album, including the ability to duplicate taped recordings. After a particularly busy day of the phone ringing with strangers' requests, my mother approached my father and said, "You love your poetry. Let the people love it with you."

My cousin Pakou and her husband lived in a town house in the Roosevelt Housing Project. My father and I drove into the busy parking lot on a gray day. It was early spring. The afternoon air was cool against the bare skin of my arms. The uniform yards, small designated squares of grass, were beginning to green. My hair blew against my neck and I felt the maturity of my years scratching at my shoulders; it was the first time I was going to have long hair. My father offered his hand out to me and I considered it for a brief second before I extended my hand into his. We held hands as we walked to my cousin and her husband's tan wooden door with the small peephole that was distinguishable from the other doors only by its number.

My cousin opened the door with her usual huge smile, and the familiar aroma of sweet coconut milk wafted into the cool day. We greeted her children and then she ushered us down the staircase into their basement. At the bottom of the stairs, in the darkened room, I saw her husband behind a dashboard of controls, red and green bars rising and falling before him on black screens. The corners of the large cement-block room were full of cardboard boxes stacked in pyramid-shaped heaps. In the center of the basement, there was a microphone and a chair on wheels with a handle underneath to adjust the height. There were sound boxes and amplifiers connected with black wires that tangled on the floor. I got to sit with my cousin's husband on a stool behind the dashboard during the session. My cousin came down the stairs quietly with a cup of cool, slippery tapioca dessert for me.

I sat quietly spooning the long strands of tapioca into my mouth, careful not to slurp the sweet creaminess going down my throat. With my tongue, I pushed the round tapioca pearls against my front teeth, trying to squeeze them through the small spaces. It baffled me how my father could just recite his songs from memory. They were long, winding tales of rhymed poetry. Each was about ten minutes long. I thought that eventually my father would have to close his eyes, search for the words in his head. For someone who had so little schooling, for someone who forgot clinic and dentist appointments and our birth dates, my father had an astounding memory for his songs. He kept his eyes open the whole time; he looked at my cousin's husband and me alertly, lost to no one. Between sips of water and the occasional clearing of his throat, my father made an album of song poetry in a single day. Once my amazement over his memory dimmed, I lost track of his words and focused on savoring the sweetness in my mouth. The tapioca cup was long empty before I heard the final beep and my cousin-in-law say to my father, "The final track has been recorded." The door closed gently behind us with Pakou and her husband's words of "Farewell" and "Come again."

The day was done. The sky was a blanket of black. The stars glimmered down in their scattered fashion. The cool breeze had turned cold and little bumps rose on my arms. I moved close to my father. He placed his arm around my shoulders. In the dark, the night felt more autumn than spring. On our way to the brown Subaru in the crowded lot, I couldn't stop my shivers. It was easier to see the stars in the sky than to see into my father's face in the night.

My father coughed all the way home in the car. He told me that his voice was no longer what it had once been. He laughed and said that he had gained too much weight; there was a heaviness in his throat now when he sang that had not been there before. I wondered if you could put your throat on a special diet. I had seen old men and women whose throats were weighed down by folds of skin, even if they weren't fat. I had heard the age in their talk. I assured my father that he didn't sound like them yet, but the thought of him one day sounding like the old Hmong men at family gatherings made me sad. I just shrugged my shoulders. Maybe he saw. Maybe he didn't. My father didn't talk much after his comment. His voice had grown tired in the studio. The headlights of our car took us to our own busy parking lot in the McDonough Housing Project.

Bis Yaj: Kwv Txhiaj Hmoob was released in 1992. Like my father, the title of his album was very concrete, Bee Yang: Hmong Song Poetry. It was a Hmong song poetry hit in the early 1990s. The album consisted of six songs. They were songs of love, of yearning, of losing home and country. We sold the album at the 1993 July 4 soccer tournament in St. Paul. Dawb and I tried to make the family's booth more modern and American by attempting to sell boiled hot dogs. We thought the American fare would bring in young people. It didn't. In fact, we lost money because our shriveled, pale hot dogs were unappetizing next to the coolers of steaming sticky rice and the smell of barbecued ribs, flattened game hens, Hmong sausages, and the sizzling pork skin that crackled and popped on the hot grills. The scent of good food came wafting in from neighbors on either side of us while we stood looking at our boiled hot dogs, some with slimy relish on them, others with just ketchup, and a few with bright yellow mustard. Young people passed before our booth with plates full of papaya salad, leaving the taste of hot chili peppers, the sour of lime, and the sweetness of tamarind in our mouths. Only a few kind men and women looked in on our hot dogs after they had stopped by and purchased our father's cassette. The sale of my father's tapes made a profit and allowed us the loss of our hot dogs.

After the tournament, we received more phone calls from people asking that we put the cassettes in local Hmong grocery stores so that they would be more accessible to the community. My mother, my father, Dawb, Xue, Sib Hlub, our new baby girl, and I traveled throughout Minneapolis and St. Paul in our Subaru, dropping off tapes at stores. For the next few years, my mother and I would collect whatever money there was (once the grocery stores had deducted their percentage) and restock supply as necessary. My father, Dawb, and the babies never came into the stores with us: they said they were shy. My mother said that selling your art is nothing to be ashamed of, although once we were in the stores it was always hard for her to ask about the money. We would stand for long minutes between aisles of dusty cans of Chinese bamboo shoots, coconut milk from Thailand, and rice flour from Vietnam. The scent of star anise powder surrounded us, a little like cinnamon but reminding me of the tree barks my grandma kept in her medicine bag. I examined the packaging of the food on the shelves as I held my mother's hand to give her silent support.

My father's album was a small venture, and in the end my parents made a profit of a little more than five thousand dollars.

Originally, my mother wanted to invest the money they had made in a second album and my father agreed, but we were going to school and needed new clothes and books and pencils, and each year Dawb and I wanted new backpacks. Then Xue and Sib Hlub started school, too, and then Shell and Taylor were born, and eventually all the money was gone, translated into food on the table and supplies in our bags. My mother and father never had the funds for a second album, although my father spent years composing songs. He would record one or two on our old tape recorder, label the cassette, and put it away. We saw him doing this but we did not ask any questions about his poetry. We did not ask him what the new songs were about, or offer to listen to them. We understood his *kwv txhiaj* in American terms, as little more than our father's hobby. There were mornings, afternoons, and evenings when our father would recite his songs to his brothers on the phone or to my mother when they found a moment together. All around us, we heard fragments of his words coming together in song and we took it for granted that this would always be so.

My brothers, sisters, and I never thanked our father for the money his first album made or regretted that a second one was not possible because we had used the money, and he never expected us to.

When Youa Lee, our father's mother, died in 2003, he forgot all his songs. He had never written them down. They were either recorded on old scratched tapes or memorized in his heart. His heart had broken. The songs had leaked out. The poetry was gone from our house.

I was thirty years old when I took out my father's cassette album and listened to it. By then, I had become a writer. By then, I had learned enough about poetry and literature, about art, to see my father as a literary force in my life. By then, I had grown to understand that my father was a fine poet in the Hmong tradition, and as poets across traditions and time have done, my father has suffered for his poetry. What I found in the old cassette tape, however, was not a work of suffering. The first time I listened through my father's album as an adult, it was striking to me that there was humor, irony, and astute cultural and political criticism. There was so much more than the hurt that I thought he had harnessed in his songs. There was the beauty of endless hope. Hearing his voice on the side of a tape scratched by time, then turned into a CD without tracks, a continuous stream of stories, I felt I could hear my father speaking to me, not as his daughter, but this time as a fellow artist.

My father is a poet. My father's art is his *kvw txhiaj*, his song poetry. His poetry complicates what he says to us, my brothers and sisters and me. We are not the walking and talking, quick-acting and hard-feeling products of his creativity; it is instead the songs that he composes, songs born deep inside, rising forth to find improvised life in the very breath that he breathes, that are his art and his contribution to our world. Because the second album never came out, because he turned his words into grains of rice and strings of meat to feed us, shirts and pants and underwear to clothe us, my father has allowed us and the people in our lives, for a long time, to believe that we are the output of his life's work. Because my grandmother died and she took with her the shelter of her love, our father's heart could not save the beauty he had stored inside from disappearing. I want my father to understand that aside and apart from my mother and his children, he has offered the world a gift all his own.

I want to tell Bee Yang that once upon a time, at a Hmong American New Year's celebration, his words sank deep into the heart of a little girl. I want to tell him that the seeds his words planted sprouted into life and that way down where the water of her tears wells up, they have grown green, stretching their limbs far to touch the world with their blooms. I want to show him that my siblings and I have grown rich and full from his songs, journeyed not only to the Hmong past but to our possibilities, and while I will never know *kwv txhiaj* the way he does, I want to pay my respect to his form and the many Hmong men and women who share it.

When my first book, *The Latehomecomer: A Hmong Family Memoir*, came out, my family was interviewed by a local public television station. I sat between my mother and father on our brown microfiber sofa in our living room in Andover, Minnesota, with its faded 1970s wallpaper. The camera was on us. We each had a microphone tucked into our shirts. The hot summer breeze entered through the old screened windows and ruffled our hair.

The young producer, breathing heavily with her belly round with child, asked my father, "How does it feel to be a writer? How does it feel to give birth to one?"

I couldn't look at my father as I interpreted her questions. I couldn't look at my father as I interpreted his words. I looked at my small, crooked fingers, clasped together in my lap. I watched the skin of my hands, plump with the moisture of summer and youth, grow tight around the bones of my fingers.

My father's words in response to her question: "I am not a writer. I can barely write my own name. My daughter has made possible in English the stories I cannot tell."

✧

This is and can never be your second album, Father. It is an answer to the songs that you've sung but have not recorded because of us. I take on your voice so that you may write the stories of your life through me in English for those fluttering hearts that are still coming.

Birth of a Song Poet

Bee Yang

Birth of a Song Poet

"I didn't have very many people around to say beautiful things to me."

"I used to go from the house of one neighbor to the next collecting the beautiful things people had to say to each other."

"By myself, I whispered the words to comfort my heart. One day, the words escaped on a sigh and a song was born."

No one looked at a calendar or wrote down the date of my birth. I only know what my mother remembered and what my brothers have told me.

My brothers say that I was born at the beginning of 1958, in the midst of the Laotian Civil War. In the bigger cities of Luang Prabang, Savannakhet, and Vientiane there were battles and debates between members of the Royal Lao Government and coalition groups of Communist revolutionaries. On the world stage, Laos had become a faraway place for the super-powers of the Cold War to test their might against each other. But on the high mountains of Phou Bia, in the province of Xieng Khuoang, in the village of Phou Khao where I was born, the Hmong continued the life we knew.

In 1958, according to my mother, the Hmong still believed that the young would outlive the old. Mothers and fathers continued to give birth to children. The living called out to the dead. Shoots of green rice were planted along the sides of steep hills and fertile valleys. Harvests were had. In 1958, according to my mother, my father was thinning but he continued his long shaman's treks across the mountaintops to different villages to do healing ceremonies for those who were sick, weary of soul, or those whose spirits were in need of a call to come home. In 1958, my father believed that there was still life in him.

My brothers and my mother tell me that I was a harvest baby, an early birth in the New Year. The grain sheds were full to the top with rice and unshelled corn. Dried buffalo jerky hung from the rafters of the houses. Big clay jars full of fermented pork and greens rested in the corners of houses. The temperature had dropped, and white frost covered the green of the mountain foliage in a thin layer each morning. The wind had grown cold, and it swept through the village, cooling the uneven mountain terrain so that children with bare feet complained unceasingly when they traveled the distance away from the house to pee or poop. At each house, a fire burned around the clock. Mothers sat in open doorways sewing French coins to Hmong embroidered shirts, pants, sashes, and skirts. Fathers checked on cows, pigs, and chickens to ensure that there would be enough meat for the ancestral feasts and streams of visitors. The young gathered around their elders and whispered wishes for new clothes to be made for the New Year's celebrations, new cloth balls to be fashioned so they could be tossed in the courtship rituals, new musical instruments to be crafted so that they could be played in the village circles, and new *kwv txhiaj plees*, love songs, to be taught so they could be sung at the festivities.

The whole village was deep in preparations for the beginning of a New Year—except my mother, who could barely walk with the strength of my struggles inside of her.

My mother's pregnancy had been difficult. Her daughters-in-law watched as she struggled to keep up with the younger women along the road to the garden and moved clumsily around the hard-packed floor of their communal home. By the time my mother had me, she had had nine children already. I would have been the tenth if the little girl with the pale skin and straight hair had not died. As it was, the adults knew that I would be her ninth and final child. My mother was in her late forties. She could not sit for long in the open doorway preparing clothes for her children for the New Year. Her back ached after just a few minutes. She could not bend down to stoke the fire close to the ground. She knelt by the fire, a short, stout woman, big belly before her, a bamboo fan in her hands, leaning awkwardly, fanning the flickering flames. Legs widespread, she went through the days, a hand on her back, heaving great, long sighs with each step she took.

My mother was weak and without energy during the long months it took for me to grow within her belly. There were nights when she woke up shivering because she had kicked the harsh woolen blanket off in the sweat of a moment, and then grown too weak and exhausted to pull it back up. For the last few months of her pregnancy, she woke up each morning in sweat as cold as a mountain stream. The chilly air traveled through the split bamboo walls. The hand of morning stretched its fingers through vivid dreams of dense jungle laden with the calls of wild creatures. In the gray, my mother made out the shallow breathing of my father beside her and saw how his body sank in with the exhalation of each breath. My father had been a slender man for most of his life, but in old age he was little more than thin muscle clinging to bones. He slept with their youngest child, a two-year-old boy, cuddled to his side. My mother struggled off the bed as quietly as she could. Her wide feet on the smooth, cold earth, she took in the cool mountain air, exhausted already by the thought of the journey to the bathroom.

When my mother first felt me drop low in her belly, she knew I had made the decision to venture from the clouds and into the world, and her exhaustion grew into a state of anxiousness. As a medicine woman, a healer, and a shaman, she had seen many old mothers who could not muster the energy to push their babies from their bodies. She had seen too many blue babies, colored like the monsoon sky, who never got to breathe the air of earth. My mother did not want this to happen to her youngest child. When she felt the familiar liquid rush down her legs and a pressure build low in her back, she told her daughters-in-law to stand aside. She crouched on her knees, legs widespread on a bamboo mat. She placed both hands on her thighs, looked straight ahead. My mother breathed the air of earth into her body and pushed as hard as she could so that I would know the air that waited for me at the gate of life. She did not stop until she could feel my wet, round head against her fingers. When my loud cries split the quiet of the early morning and called in the day with more gusto than the family rooster's crow, her daughters-in-law rushed in close to help my mother. I was passed between different hands. My brothers' wives crooned and they shushed me. They helped each other bathe me in the old plastic tub by the light of the family's fire ring. The women wrapped me up in a warm blanket and handed me to my mother. My mother held me in her arms, safe against her body as she had all her children, and would her grandchildren to come.

✧

I am almost two and I have learned how to walk slowly by myself. I am a sturdy balancing act on the dirt floor of our house. There is the dark outline of a man sitting in the late afternoon shadows. A fire burns in the center of the room, warming the cold air filtering through the open doorway. His body is turned toward the flames of the fire pit. There is a bamboo basket of dried bark by his side. His hands are busy, rolling out the long stretch of bark, twisting and turning it into rope. The doorway is an uneven rectangle of light. Outside, there are the sounds of children playing, laughing, and talking, peals of delight and joy rising in rhythmic, predictable intervals. I want to join them. I make my way carefully to the open door. I put both my hands on the door's slight frame, and I try and try to lift one leg high enough to cross the door's ledge to the other side. I try hard to raise the leg higher and higher but it grows too heavy, and it falls down in a swoosh. I look at the man by the fire for help. I don't understand that my father has grown weak with old age and the endless coughing that brings his shoulders high and shakes them. I do not know that it will be only months before my father will go to bed and not get up again. I look at the man and then point to the open doorway where I can see Hue, my big brother by two years, playing with a spinning top.

I will remember for the rest of my life the voice that carried his words to me, the only words I have directly from my father: "*Me tub me me los nws txiv mog. Kuv tus me tub los ntawm kuv. Los koj txiv ua txoj hluag rau koj khi qaib me me. Txiv tus tub tsis quaj nawb.*"

"My little boy, come to your father. My son, come to me.

Your father is making a rope for you to tie around the little chicken. My little son, don't cry."

✧

I was only two years and several months old when my father died.

My father had made it through the harvesting of the crops and the New Year's celebrations. He, a frail man, more bone than flesh, had leaned on the frame of our front door and sung into the night the traditional New Year chant to call all of our wandering spirits home from the depths of the jungle and the tops of the mountains. He had rested heavily on both elbows at our low dining table and called our ancestors' spirits to partake of the herb-boiled chickens, big bowls of pork belly fat and greens, little bowls of spicy red chili pepper sauce, and heaping plates of freshly harvested rice. He himself did not eat much from the meal but he sat by and smiled as he watched his children, their spouses, and his grandchildren feast upon the hard year's work in anticipation of the new.

The cold mountain air had lost its bite and the birds had begun to sing their mating songs. The mountain sun shone brightly in the early mornings and the sun's rays lingered long into the late afternoons. My mother had burned many sticks of incense and boats of folded gold and silver joss paper for the ancestral spirits to keep my father's body whole and his heart strong. Friends and relatives traveled from nearby villages to visit our house and pay their respects and speak their gratitude for my father's generous and tireless work as a shaman. The stream of visitors made my father happy. His voice, weakened, called out greetings and goodbyes to the people who passed through our door. His parting words were always "Come again. We will meet each other soon."

Now it was the beginning of the planting season. The visitors had stopped their coming. Each was busy in his or her field, softening the earth with gardening hoes the size of palms, creating fields large enough to feed whole families, working with their backs angled away from the hot sun, their dirty toes anchored tightly to the mountainous terrain the Hmong farmed on. All over the villages in the high mountains of Laos, families gathered to go to bed early each night, to rise before dawn, to prepare for the next day's toil. Each morning, before the crow of the roosters, the women in my family got up in the dark of night to make rice and prepare meat and greens for our day's work in the garden. By the time the gray light entered through our split-bamboo walls and the roosters sounded their morning cries, all the adults would be ready for the fields and the children awake. The littlest of the children were assigned to stay home with my mother and my father. I was among them.

My father's death, like much of his life, was simple.

My father, an early riser his life through, did not get up that morning. He had had trouble breathing through the night. His shallow breath had whistled upon the wind that crept into our room. My mother thought that she would let him sleep for a while longer. The household was busy in its morning routine. My brothers were looking over the farming equipment in the morning shadows. One of them sharpened the dull garden hoes by the light of the fire on a smooth mountain stone, adding drizzles of water from a nearby pail. Those with young children greeted them with hair tousling and hugs as the little ones sleepily chased the household dogs around the table. My older brothers talked of which sections of the garden to weed, which animals needed additional attention, and what repairs needed to be made to the thatched roof or a section of the house wall.

Their wives had joined forces and prepared the morning meal. Hot food was on the table. We could hear the noise from nearby houses as neighbors went about their rituals for the day. My mother went into their little bedroom to wake up my father for breakfast. He was asleep. She saw the rise and fall of his chest. She called his name, "Nao Lor, Nao Lor, time to get up." His eyes did not open but he shook his head at her lightly. He raised his right hand a little, a gesture to slow down the morning, she thought. She left him in his bed.

Breakfast was had. The adults and older children made their way to the gardens with their woven bamboo baskets on their backs and gardening hoes in hand. My mother stood by the doorway with her youngest children and grandchildren around her and watched as the long line of family trailed into the rising sun. The morning fog, close to the ground, shrouded the disappearing figures in the mist.

My big brothers and sisters ran from their gardens when they heard the news that our father was calling for them with his last breath. It was midafternoon. The sun was high in a clear sky when they reached the house and saw my father in his bed. What had been a quiet day grew loud with the wailing of my mother, sisters, and sisters-in-law as my father's head fell back into the arms of my big brother Palee. The tousled gray hair fell across his forehead. His mouth was open.

My father's last words to his older sons were: "I have lived this life like a young man, even when age came to me. I have two baby boys that I am leaving behind. They are mine but I cannot take them with me. They cannot care for themselves. I have nothing left to leave them except for the two small colts in the pen. Please raise my youngest sons for me. One day, if they become intelligent men, then maybe they will love you in return. If they do not, then raise them simply because I have raised you."

Streams of salty water flowed down my mother's cheeks. She now sat on the dirt, in front of the doorway to our house. Inside, friends and family crowded around my father's still, stiff form, mourning him in a chorus of cries. My mother did not mourn with them. Instead, she sat on the dirt, a guard against the leaving of his spirit. Her strong hands balled into fists and she pounded on the brown earth. Her voice grew stormy as she cited the many reasons why my father could not leave. People tried to calm her. They tried to stop her hands from beating the earth, to help her up off the ground, to comfort her when they couldn't do either, but my mother would not be comforted. She raged against my father's departure until her hands bled and her voice grew hoarse.

I was too young to remember my father's death or much of his life. I know only the stories that people tell me of him. I carry only foggy memories of the man in the shadows sitting by the fire, making ropes of tree bark for me to tie around little chickens, calling me to come close, telling me not to cry. Sometimes I come across the smell of dry lemongrass and the powerful scent of mint and I feel a pull toward that distant, thin shadow of a man who once loved me.

The only good thing about my father's death is that he did not see the Land of the Million Elephants fall to the roar of the iron birds that dropped balls of fire from the sky. My father died in 1960, before our village of Phou Khao was turned into a military-prisoner site by the Americans. My father did not live to see his son yearn for a father, or struggle to become one.

A Fatherless Boyhood

My mother started coughing shortly after my father died. Her coughs were so jarring, they woke me from deep sleep. Between fits of coughing she tried to speak and tell Hue and me that she was all right. In the dark, all we heard was her struggle for a voice. Her breath was heavy and constricted. The bouts of coughing left her exhausted. On the small bamboo bed we shared we could feel the heat evaporate off her sweat-dampened body in the cool of the night. When the coughing grew harsh, I would put my hands on my mother's arm to try to steady her. I could feel the slippery sweat of her skin as it shook in the wake of her coughs. My little hands could not slow down the movement of muscle and flesh. The scent of menthol oil and herbs emanated from my mother's body. She shifted from my hold and gasped out, "Go to sleep, go to sleep. I will be okay."

During the day, my mother spent long hours searching for herbal remedies in the wilds surrounding our village. The shadow of her round back walking away was a fixture of our day. Hue and I used to ask to go with her. She would shake her head, place her hands on both our heads, and say, "When you get bigger, you can go with me and help me. Now you two are still too young. I will not be able to hold both your hands through the jungle brush and gather my herbs and medicines to carry home."

My mother came back each evening with her bamboo basket full to the top with jagged roots and bundles of wild greens. Each night, she sat by the fire sorting through the finds of the day and stirring pots of brown broth made from tree limbs and fallen leaves, sacred roots, and hard, round nuts. Hue and I sat on our haunches beside her on low wooden stools as our mother made her medicine. We watched as she carefully emptied the steaming brown broth into the old tin cans we used as cups. She blew on the steam and its rich scent, like the wet earth after a heavy rain or the garden in the morning dew, reached us. We didn't ask to try and she didn't offer us any. Each time she took a sip of the bitter brews she concocted, our mother would say she hoped the cough would go away.

The cough did not go away.

In fact, my mother's coughing fits in the night grew so loud that they woke my older brothers and sisters in their different sleeping rooms. My older siblings grew worried. One of the ailments that had killed my father was a chronic cough. They were concerned that the cough could be infectious. My mother's decision to move Hue and me away from her bosom and her bed was driven by a desire to preserve our health.

My older brothers built a bamboo bed for Hue and me to sleep on in the same room we had shared with our parents. Our mother moved our blankets to the new bed. Hue and I went along with the plan without objection, but that first night of being away from our mother was hard. We couldn't sleep. The fresh bamboo felt too hard against our thin backs. We had grown used to the suppleness of our mother and father's old bed. The wind whistled through the small holes in our wall. The village dogs barked and we wondered what ghostly spirits had awakened them. The dark night expanded around us and the few feet between our mother and us grew vast. When our mother coughed on her bed, we saw the dark outline of her body turn away from us to face the wall. We went through a long season of falling asleep looking upon the dark of our mother's heaving back.

When the wet of the monsoons eased and the mountain breezes grew calm, our mother's coughing fits grew slower and lighter, but by then she had gotten used to sleeping in her own bed, on her side, facing the wall. She had grown accustomed to the empty bed around her, sleeping without our father and us. Our mother did not invite us to return to the way things had been.

I grew up sleeping with my brother Hue. In the beginning, when the nights were cold, he held me close to his side. He wrapped his skinny arms around me and patted my bony shoulder. On the nights when I awoke suddenly from a nightmare and struggled to fall back asleep, when I battled the urge to cry for our mother, it was Hue's voice that shushed me to rest. When we grew bigger and more comfortable in our aloneness, we kept warm by tucking our hands beneath our armpits. Hue's quiet, even breathing took me to sleep each night. Its absence in the early morning was my call to start the day.

Each morning we woke up to a house busy with the sounds of people talking and work being done. My six older brothers, two older sisters, my sisters-in-law, and their children all continued to live with our mother and us in the family's long bamboo house. My older brothers tended different fields but stored their harvests in the same sheds and ate from the same table. Two of my older brothers had daughters who were months younger than me. Each day, Hue and I played with the girls and took care of them as best we knew how while the adults went with woven bamboo baskets and garden hoes and large Hmong knives to tend to the fields. The work was endless. Each day the adults had to chop up mounds of green to feed the ever-hungry pigs, drive the large gray water buffaloes with their curved horns to the river, and work as the American and Hmong soldiers who frequented our village demanded.

Every few months, groups of soldiers entered our village and called for the eldest son of a family to join them to fulfill village obligations to the war. I was too young to know or ask questions about the particulars of the war being fought. All I remember is that one month the soldiers came to our house and demanded that not only my eldest brother, Nhia, but Sai, the third one, follow them. The soldiers wanted my brothers to serve as mules to carry their heavy packs across the mountain passes away from our village. My mother pleaded with the soldiers. She told them that her sons had huge fields to tend and many mouths to feed. The soldiers brushed her off as an old grandma who did not and could not understand the ways of men and war. Their loud voices rang throughout the surroundings when they told my mother that her sons would be sent back once they had served successfully as mules on the crossing through the mountains. They told my mother that her crying would not help their cause.

I watched as the soldiers with their guns and urgent voices shuffled my brothers away from the small clearing around our house. I gathered with the village children to watch as my brothers walked away from our village with heavy packs on their bent backs. They had their eyes on their feet lest they fall into the ruts of the road and ruin the goods they carried. Everybody in the village knew that the soldiers dared call upon two sons from one home only because we didn't have a father to protect us and the might of a mere woman in a war was not enough to stop the work of guns. No one said anything to console my weeping mother, whose hands were clenched in fists by her side as she looked upon the line of young men disappearing around the bend of the dirt road.

Nhia and Sai would tell us years later that being mules for the burdens of war was the most humiliating experience of their lives. My mother prodded and asked for details, but neither of my brothers said anything more upon their return about what happened to them. Instead, they worried that the fighting would consume all of us. They were concerned that we would not be able to harvest our fields in time and store up enough food to carry us through to a New Year. They collected their children into their arms and fixed their gaze on the flames of our family's fire. Hue and I stood in the corner and we watched our big brothers hold their little ones close.

By the time I was five, we could no longer tend to the fields around our village. It was not safe to do so. The war effort at Long Cheng, an American settlement that housed more than forty thousand people, had grown intense. There were North Vietnamese and Pathet Lao soldiers sneaking up into the high mountains, and the adults whispered of farmers with familiar names dying in their fields. Big planes flew across the sky and we could hear the falling bombs at all hours of the day and night. We watched as the rice fields of our neighbors and friends became craters of burning earth. There was no guarantee of a harvest if we kept to our old fields. My family made the decision to go farm in the lowlands.

I remember the stretch of even land beneath my feet. Used to clinging to rocks and climbing up jagged mountain paths, my feet and my leg muscles had grown accustomed to the continual task of holding to nature. On the flat earth, I felt like I was asleep in my bed, standing there in the middle of the wide expanse of brown earth. The sky looked farther away. The air felt sticky. I thought we had walked into the bottom of the earth's vast bowl.

The adults did not complain about the far distance we had to travel to get to the new fields. They did not argue about how best to till even ground. On the rises that we were used to, a person could farm the earth that rose from their feet and still stand up. In the expanse of the wide plain, backs had to bend low. The sun was merciless. Sweat trickled down necks and dampened shirts. Dry throats called out weakly for something to drink.

Hue and I delivered water to the adults in hollow tubes of dried bamboo. In the moments when there were no calls to quench thirsts, we tried to help with the planting, but the mosquitoes were so bad I could not manage. I found myself in the middle of the fields, waving the endless swarms of mosquitoes away from my face and body. Clouds of black-winged mosquitoes and large biting flies buzzed and buzzed around my head. I flung my arms and I jumped up and down in the soggy earth, but the mosquitoes found bare skin, and when they didn't, they landed on top of my clothing and sank in for blood. I could not keep count of how many mosquitoes bit me. All I know is that one day, in the hot afternoon, my vision grew blurry and I fell. The last thing I saw was Hue running toward me, his tired eyes round and shiny.

I did not wake up for many days and nights. I could hear

my mother cry endlessly in my stormy sleep. It was dark. I was lost. I couldn't find my way. I felt a desperate need to concentrate but my mother kept calling my name, crying for me. She reached me from far away, telling me I couldn't leave her, shouting for my father to return me to the world of the living, demanding that the ancestors, the spirits of the land and rivers, bring me back to her. I kept waiting for my mother's voice to fade, for her cries to stop; they never did. I couldn't figure out a direction to travel or a place to stop and rest. I was overcome with exhaustion and restlessness at once. From the shadows, I thought I saw a figure like my father. I tried to reach for him, but my fingers touched upon nothing. Except for my mother's voice, I knew I was alone, and the loneliness grew inside until I could no longer contain it. I began imagining a place full of sunlight, sweet-smelling flowers, and the sound of a gurgling mountain stream. The clearer the world in my imagination grew, the dimmer my mother's voice became.

At some point, I heard my mother's voice rise in anger. She started threatening my spirit if I left. She said she was going to find me, in whatever incarnation, and teach me the wrath of a mother denied her child. At another point, she started begging for my return, promising me a chicken and an egg, a spirit-calling ceremony. All I wanted to do was wrestle myself from the darkness and enter the bright world of imagination, lose the feeling that I was in a world all by myself. But that was impossible with my mother's voice in my head, crying and calling, again and again, for my return to her.

I believe I would have died if my mother hadn't scared my spirit from leaving. I woke up because I worried that she would grow sick herself with all the yelling. I opened my heavy eyes to bright, intrusive sunlight. My mother's and Hue's faces were peering at me. I realized slowly that I was on our bed, in our room, in our home.

There were no pills to take or shots to give.

My mother did everything she could to bring me back to health. She gave me her herbal remedies. She made me drink from endless medicinal and herbal concoctions. They were all hot and steaming. The green ones tasted of concentrated jungle leaves. The thick brown broths tasted like the soil where she had found them, heavy and wholesome. My mother handed me pieces of bark and the dry root of hard, bitter trees to chew on. I grew sick of her medicinal brews and herbs, but my body grew strong because of them. The sad thing is that while my body came back, a part of my mind did not. After malaria, I couldn't remember well the things that I had learned or needed to learn. My memory became a fleeting thing with wings that perched on the different limbs outside the school room, hovering near but beyond my grasp.

My mother never blamed me for the loss of my memory. I became a cheerleader in Hue's incredible journey through school. Each year, I watched him excel in the highest ranks of his peers. I saw myself standing and clapping with all the village boys and girls as my brother stood before us with the teacher's hand on his back. I never gave up on school, but I lost interest in being the best one. I spent more time outside, observing nature, visiting people's houses, watching people's stories coming together, and listening to the zoom of planes overhead, trying to gauge from a distance the destruction of the bombs falling down. I fell in love with birds and chickens and all feathered things.

I once captured a beautiful songbird. I was so proud of it. I had been looking for days through the different seasons. In Laos, it usually took a father to capture a songbird. They were so rare. I was only a boy. My brothers were busy in the fields. My mother was busy searching the mountainside for her healing herbs. I had a lot of time to myself. I could go anywhere and do anything I wanted so long as I didn't hurt anyone or come across the path of soldiers. There were no thieves to steal a child in a village the size of ours. We all knew each other.

One lucky day, I was walking the path from the garden back to the village. I was stopping every few steps to listen to the sounds around me. If I hadn't been so careful, I would never have heard the nesting birds. Theirs was a thin cry. At first, I thought it was the chirp of a cricket, but then I heard the twists and the turns in the high melody and recognized the sound as a birdsong. I started looking all around me at the low branches of the trees and the bushes on either side of the skinny dirt path. Close to my head, on the left side of the path, I found a bird's nest made of twigs and feathers. I was careful not to move too close. I saw a pair of green-tinted songbirds and their babies. The babies were wrinkled and pink. My discovery made me so happy. I didn't tell anyone. Every single day, I spied on the nest. In a week, I heard the mother bird's song grow more urgent and loud because the babies had all begun chirping their hunger songs. I knew I didn't have much time left. I came up with an idea. I asked my mother for a piece of thread.

The next day, I stood quietly by and waited until the mother and father birds went searching for food. I sneaked up on the babies, wings still only developing, and I chose the one that was closest to me. I tied one of its feet to the tiny twigs of the nest.

I tied the knot loosely. I was careful to be gentle so that the little bird would not get hurt. Each day, I went to look at the birds. Their mother and father fed them. Feathers grew on their bodies. Wings sprouted like the stalks of rice fields as the fluffy feathers fell off. One day, the mother and father birds flew away and didn't come back. The next day, all the baby birds, except the one with its feet tied to the twig, walked to the edge of the small nest. One by one they flew away. The little bird with its foot tied to the nest could not fly away. I knew it could not survive without its mother and father. I came out of the leaves and I approached softly. I offered my hand gently to the young bird in the nest. It hopped right into my palms. I cupped the bird carefully with both hands, held the little body close to my chest, and then snipped the thread that tied it to the nest with my teeth. I felt the bird's warm, light weight, the softness of its feathers, the beating of its small heart, and I heard its song.

I was walking into the village when this big boy saw me with my little bird. He was a bully. He was mean to everyone. He had a father who loved him very much. I did not have a father. I was scared of the boy. He walked right in front of me. He held out his hand for the singing bird. I knew he would kill it. I shook my head. He yelled a few angry words, and then his punch flew at me. The bird dropped from my hands to the ground. It made a noise and then scurried away. In that moment, I started to fight for myself. There was no one waiting to help, it was me and what I loved falling from my hands; there was a punch in the air coming at me, and I had no place to run. I pushed him as hard as I could. He fell. I fell on top of him. I punched hard. He punched back. The pain took my breath away.

That was my first fight with anyone other than the normal pushes and pulls with Hue, but it was not my only fight.

When I was eight years old I got into another fight with a boy who was three years older. We went to the same school. We were in the same grade because the older boy had failed his exams. We were on the dirt path that led from our school back to the village. The sky was a heavy gray, thunder sounded from nearby, and then rain started to pour. We were laughing and pushing each other along the dirt path.

We were with two girls who were about my age, too. They had grown up in the same village with us. They attended the same school. One of the girls was a Yang like me. We were distant relatives. The other girl was her best friend, a girl from a different clan.

The dirt path home took about two hours, and we were told by the adults to walk together. Most days, the girls followed after the two of us, holding hands, stopping here and there to pick at wild blooms on either side of the path. All four of us were friends. Sometimes we played tag, chasing each other all the way home. Occasionally it was hide-and-go-seek, which always made us a bit squeamish because of the thrill of hiding and then the real danger of wild animals lurking close by. All of us had grown up hearing the same stories, stories of little boys and girls getting lost in the jungle foliage, of the bodies turning first green like the high leaves and then brown like the fallen trunks of old trees.

The rainstorm was exciting for us. The rain from the gray sky was warm on our brown skin. We boys took off our flip-flops and held them in our hands so we could feel our feet meet the thick mud. We watched as the imprints of small toes penetrated the once hard earth, felt the sagging give of smooth mud.

We twisted our ankles first right then left to carefully pull our feet from the clinging kiss of the soaking soil. We marveled as the imprints of our feet filled with rainwater and puddles formed inside our steps. The girls laughed in the near distance, walking slower because their wet sarongs clung to their skinny legs, which made walking tricky. In the rainstorm, we all knew it would take us longer to get home.

I didn't notice when my friend slowed down and lagged behind. I just thought he would catch up with me soon or perhaps that he was talking to the girls, telling them some made-up scary story. The walk in the rain was too wet, too clingy, too slippery, too much fun to ponder the whereabouts of friends. My black hair was soaked through and the normally spiky needles fell heavy and flat on my forehead. My clothes, black wide-legged Hmong trousers and a black shirt secured in front with a shiny safety pin, were growing brown with streaks and streams of mountain mud. I worried a little about what my mother would say when I got home, or what my sister Ka, the one who did the laundry, would do. Her short temper, her irate, irritated voice washed over me in a moment of sobriety before the spirit of the wind and the rain took over again, forces I could not control, so much bigger, older, and wiser than I could ever be.

When the girls started screaming, I thought it was because they were all having fun, so I ignored them and kept on walking. I checked behind me only when the screams got louder. I turned all the way around on the little path and looked through the rain. I could hear they were coming closer. I was not prepared for the expressions on the little girls' faces. Through the dark, soaking foliage, beneath the heavy, wet clouds, I saw the little girls grabbing at their sarongs, hair fallen in wet strands across their faces, running and screaming in terror. Before

I could form a reaction, either take flight as they were doing or start screaming with them, the girls were behind me, their hands painfully clinging to my arms. I was going to ask questions. What happened? Did they come upon a wild animal? Was my friend hurt? But there was no time. My friend, the one who had been sliding down the path with me earlier, walked around the bend and approached the group slowly. He took measured steps toward us. His hair, flat against his head, was not long enough to cover his eyes. He was looking at the girls, first one and then the other. It was as if he didn't see me standing there. When he was a few feet away from us, he stopped walking.

In a low, quiet voice, he said, "When the girls walk in the rain, I can see everything. Bee, let them go first so we can both watch. Let them go first and we can touch."

The girls screamed.

"Help us. Don't let him hurt us. He tried to touch us!"

I was eight years old. I did not understand fully what my friend was saying but I knew the girls were scared of him and I, too, grew scared. The girls sank their nails into my arms. The pain jerked me into action.

"You stay away from us," I said as I backed away, the girls slipping and struggling for balance behind me. "We have to go home. The adults are waiting."

The boy advanced. He was unafraid. I was younger.

"You go home. Leave the girls with me. Run now or you will regret it," he said.

The girls squealed like little piglets about to be slaughtered. Their hold on my arms tightened and I could feel their nails pinching harder into my flesh. There was a thrumming in my heart. All I could see was the wash of rain protecting us. A stirring began inside of me, vibrating from my heart to my extremities. I moved away from the hold of the girls. They cried in unison and tried to grab me.

I did not look at the girls as I spoke to them.

I said, "Run home. Go tell the adults. Tell them what happened."

I could hear the girls through the pouring rain. In my mind's eye, I saw them take a few slow, hesitant steps backward and then watched them turn and scramble away from us.

Thunder roared on the mountainside. Lightning flashed across the gray. It felt as if we were in the eye of the storm, me and this boy who had been my friend, a stranger now. I watched him but it seemed he saw through me. The boy charged after the girls. I lunged at him as he passed.

We fell into the slippery path. At first, I was on top because of the surprise impact and because of my height, but then experience and age shifted the odds and the older boy took the lead. Pain blossomed on my face, in my arms, in my belly, right up against my heart. Hard, throbbing blows from his clenched fist crashed into me. I felt my arms being jerked. My scalp burned from the boy's pull on my hair. Heat erupted inside of me. I knew I was being slammed, again and again, into the path. I could hear the hot breath from our bodies, loud as the thunder had been. I opened my eyes in the falling rain. I saw the lights of heaven flash and then the awful face of the boy above me, blood and snot running down his face. My vision wavered. In a last surge of desperate strength I pushed, I kicked, I clawed, and the boy went tumbling down the sloping path. I stumbled to my feet, blinked against the pounding hurt in my body, looked to where the boy was rising, spitting out blood, yelling, "You will pay for this, Bee. You pathetic little orphan. You will pay for what you've done to me."

The warmth of the rain was now flowing off me, a mountain stream running down my body. I started shaking. The boy got to his feet and started to run away. I didn't know how far the girls had gotten. I had tried to buy them time.

I chased after the boy, my friend whom I had chased countless times before. I focused on the mud-soaked back of his shirt, tried to close the growing distance between us. My flip-flops were no longer in my hands. I had no idea where they were. I ran through the rain, falling every few steps because the world had turned into clay; it was soft all over; each step was a mess, a guess at stability. I could feel the mud pulling me down. The eleven-year-old boy was sturdier and faster in the squishy, slippery mud. I kept falling, and each time I had to crawl my way up, but he did not fall once. Still, I chased and chased and even as I felt the burning in my chest, I did not stop running. The world grew darker, the sounds of steps disappeared, and then I lost sight of the boy.

I saw the dark jungle foliage pass. I found myself in the grass field surrounding our small village. My heart was beating so fast, my chest rose so high I could not see my own feet on the ground. I stood still and battled for breath. The smoke from my house beckoned. I heard the pigs in the pen. I knew the silent huddle of the ducks and the chickens in their feathery coops. I knew the girls had made it home because I had seen no sign of them on the path. I had looked for tattered skirts, torn shirts, for blood. There had been no sign of the boy, either.

My feet were heavy, weighed down with wet mud. My muscles gave way as I reached for the bamboo latch at our front door, felt it come undone, and toppled into the thatch-roofed hut, startling the family.

There was a clamor of questions.

I recounted the incident by our fire when the shaking calmed and I found the words. I waited to hear what would happen. My brothers listened to the story, asked some questions, and then they talked among themselves about what might happen the next day. My mother walked to the doorway, held the door wide open to the storm, and called into the angry night: "My son, come home. Do not wander in the dark and the wet of the falling rain. Come home." My mother wanted my spirit to come home to my body and my family. Then she took no chances. She prepared a clear poultice from thick green leaves and applied it to the parts of my skin that had broken open—my arms with the mark of the girls' nails, my bleeding knees and elbows, one corner of my lip, parts of my back, and the side of my head. She made an herbal drink for me so I wouldn't get the chills in the night. Once my mother was sure that I had drunk my share of warm vegetable broth and eaten a helping of rice, she told me to go to bed. My sister Ka did not complain about the dirt on my clothes or my missing flip-flops. She just gathered the wet, muddy clothes in her arms and said she would wash them in the morning light. Hue waited for me to slip into bed before he whispered his questions. I talked until my words slurred with sleep.

As the house grew quiet and my eyes grew heavy, the sounds of the storm lost their power and the familiar smell of smoke on my blanket comforted me. The image of the boy in the storm disappeared. I fell asleep to Hue's quiet, even breathing.

In the dawn, the sun came through the slits in the woven bamboo walls. I woke up to the voices of adults speaking.

I could smell the steam of the rice cooking. I knew the parents of the girls were visiting. Beside me, Hue nestled deeper into his blanket. My mother's bed was empty.

I could hear the fathers' voices saying, "Thank you. Thank you so much."

The girls' mothers kept repeating, "The girls were so scared."

When I entered the communal area, no one looked at me. My sisters-in-law were busy with the work of preparing the morning meal. My brothers and my mother sat with the guests on low stools close to the main fire ring. My bare toes curled on the earthen floor, felt in its damp coolness the storm that had passed. The adults kept on talking. I found an empty stool by the open doorway. The leaves on the nearby bushes were wet with dew. The chickens were in the yard pecking at the worms that had surfaced in the storm. The air felt clean and crisp and wet. My body ached. I swallowed the air as if it were water. I heard the small bustle of the adults getting up from their seats and the goodbyes and more words of gratitude from the girls' parents.

In response, my eldest brother, Nhia, said, "It was Bee's place to make sure the girls were safe. No more needs to be said. Everybody made it home. This is what matters in family."

When the guests came close to the door on their way out, the father of the Yang girl stopped by my side and said, "Bee, the boy's parents came early to apologize this morning. They brought chickens to call in the spirits of the girls. They were very sorry. They say that they have spoken to their son and he is sorry, too, but I think you should be careful. You hear?"

I looked at the man's rough, leathery feet. His toenails were thick and yellowed by years of hard work in the fields and exposure to the elements. I was quiet. I listened with my head down and nodded at the closure of his words. I had been careful all my life. The admonishment was a familiar one. My mother had taught Hue and me that to take care was the way fatherless sons protected their way to manhood. I felt exhausted by the man's words. I watched as his cracked heels headed out our door. I wondered if my father, too, walked the earth as an old man with broken feet.

$\diamond$

Instead of talking to the world, I took to listening to it. I heard how the night wind whistled through the bamboo walls and accompanied the gentle snores of those sleeping around me. I heard the whisper of morning light in the throats of the roosters. I heard how the children of the village laughed and cried and talked among each other and to their mothers and fathers about their pains and their fears. I heard how the mothers and fathers talked to their children about gardening, hunting, games, and fun. I noticed the difference between their conversations and the warnings and precautions my mother and my brothers gave Hue and me. Did the adults in our lives talk to us? Not unless something was wrong, and many times when they did talk to us, it was about how things could go wrong.

I understood my mother: with a garden hoe the size of a man's palm, she took to the mountain slopes to feed a house of hungry children. My mother did not fail me. She was the reason I survived despite all that life has delivered. For my mother, life was not to be taken lightly. Each moment was a confrontation of essentials.

I understood my big brothers and sisters: they were young men and women trying their best to grow up and grow families of their own. Time was scarce and life was hard. Hue and I were both more work for them to do, more people for them to take care of, more reminders of a life without a father.

But it was not until I was a grown man with children of my own that I could speak of my endless yearning for a father. Day by day, I stored my loneliness and the constant missing deep inside of me. To appease the hungry heart inside, I started gathering the beauty of flowers that blossomed from people's lips in the presence of those they loved and adored. I used to run away to repeat the words to myself whenever the yearning grew unbearable.

The late afternoon sun glazed the mountainside in its oily glow. The whole world was both too silent and too loud. The birds were chirping and chattering on the trees. Every few minutes, one or two of them cut a path through the cool air. Like butterflies, they chased each other, fluttering by. They landed first on one spot and then the next. The winged bugs were nowhere to be seen, taking a late-afternoon break before their nighttime duties commenced. Before I could conjure the words I wanted to hear, I reckoned with the ones I had heard. The sound of human voices played loud in my ears, like records, continuous tracks in my head.

A sister-in-law was concerned that the rice rations were dangerously low. A big brother had tried to control the frustration in his voice but it had leaked out.

"I am doing everything I can."

"It is not enough."

"Are you saying we have too many mouths to feed?"

"You want your children to eat corn mush!"

"You will be lucky if there is even a harvest!"

"When are the soldiers going to come?"

"How long do you think before you have to fight?"

Tense silence.

My head throbbed.

A married brother had taken a trip to Long Cheng, the provincial headquarters of the war effort, and returned with candy for his children. When the family had gathered by the fire after the evening meal and his children had proffered their hands, he had given them each a bag of candy. Of course, Hue and I had not held out our hands. Instead, we had stood silently by and swallowed our spit as the girls chewed. The little girls were too young to think to share candy that was so hard to come by, particularly with uncles who would not ask. Hue had whispered for me to pretend I hadn't seen the candy. He had told me to stare and to wash the wanting from my face.

Hue tried to set an example for me to follow. My skinny brother lifted his head and turned his gaze toward the far corner of the house. I don't know what he saw in the heavy shadows but they drew his full attention. I could not do the same. Instead, I looked at the girls eating their candy and my older brothers who did not see how much I yearned, and I tried to trample on the wanting in my heart. Later that night, in our room, my mother turned toward the wall, I listened to Hue, my quiet brother, whisper and whisper. He wouldn't let me sleep. He talked of the games he had played with the village children: first it was jumping the rubber rope, and then it was tossing and catching little pebbles on the backs of palms, and then it was throwing spinning tops into target objects. Hue waited until our mother was asleep, her breathing regular, before he approached the real topic keeping him up. His voice was hoarse when he told me how embarrassing the situation with the candy was for all involved. I told Hue that I was sorry I could not follow the example he worked hard to set. My mother cleared her throat in her sleep. We grew quiet, closed our eyes, kicked a little against each other's legs in search of comfort, grew still, and tried to visit her and our father in our dreams.

I ran away from home many times. Each time I left, I did not think about the coming of the night. My only plan was always to find the tallest tree I could away from the village and climb it. I thought I could stay there forever, somewhere between the earth and the sky. I would sit on the tree's high limbs and scan the jagged rise of the mountains that surrounded my village, look at the gentle curve of the valleys, and search for the place where my father was buried. All I knew was what my older brothers had told me, "Father is on a mountain that is in the shape of an uneven rectangle rising out of the treetops."

Up on the tree, I repeated the words I had gathered from friends and relatives, words I had heard my brothers say to their children, words of appeal, of love, of courage—words that traveled everywhere to come to the same place: "Do not be afraid. Everything will be all right. I will not let anything hurt you."

As the sun descended, the jungle foliage grew thicker and closer. I made out moving shapes. What had been clouds in the sky, puffs of white that had shielded the tops of the highest mountain peaks, now floated down and hovered over the ground in fog. I curled my legs up on the tree limb and felt the cool dampness of the mountain air settle into the smooth bark, felt the cold travel through the thin cotton of my pants. My shirt was little armor against the evening wind. I recalled the stories the village elders told of torched souls wandering the night, in lines of fire, seeking reparations from the living. From the safety of the storyteller's mat, it had been fun pretending that the fireflies hovering in the nearby brush were the tortured souls alight with anger. In the dark of my tree limb, I could not trust that the blinks of light I saw belonged to fireflies. My courage wavered and I started thinking about how perhaps I had acted childishly: running away was not the answer; it was no one's fault that I wanted a father I could not locate in the world.

Each time I ran away, I walked back home along the same path I had taken away from it. I went over the long list of things my mother did for all of us each day. I started thinking about all my older brothers and sisters. Nhia tended a huge field so that he could share his harvest with his mother and his little brothers. Chue had become a teacher so that he could share his government salary with everyone in the family. Xai got up before dawn each day and crawled into bed at first dusk each night so he could rise early again in the morning and be the first to attend to the communal work of the village. Palee worked hard at raising healthy chickens, ducks, pigs, and cows so that the family could have meat at each New Year feast. Eng carried books in his hands all the time and wrote notes of politics and humor so that he could be an example of education for Hue and me to follow. Ya cooked and cleaned without complaint. Ka did our laundry and helped with the house, and while she had long lists of complaints, they never stopped her busy hands and feet from working. They all did so much and what did I do?

Bee was too sensitive. Bee told himself that the concern over having enough rice was not about him but the war. Bee told himself that the brother who had bought candy for his children was simply being a good father. It was not his intention to make anyone sad. All his brothers were acting as best they knew how. The sadness was because he didn't have a father, nothing less and nothing more. Bee told himself that he needed to expand his heart and thicken his skin and become more of what the family needed him to be, more like Hue—although without his school smarts or big, round eyes.

I ran away so many times because I could not carry the weight of words, the ones inside of me and the ones around me. I could not use my mind to escape from the actions, conscious and unconscious, of those who loved me. There were words I yearned to hear and there was no one to say them. Each time I left, I found myself stumbling back home, embarrassed by my childishness and lack of competence.

My mother never asked why I ran away or where I had been. Upon my return, I said and she agreed: I had gone to play by myself because I was a loner and I had strayed too far and it had taken me much longer to get home than was good for me; my little feet could not beat the descent of a great sun; of course, I was young and I forgot, even after the other times she had admonished me and told me to remember. My mother accepted this, always only too happy that I had found my way home again. She moved close to me, surrounded me with the scent of menthol oil and dry herbs. A woman of strong, steady public words, my mother did not offer many private endearments, but when I returned home I made out the beating of her frantic heart.

The only person who knew that my late return was not an innocent mistake was Hue. I saw it in his eyes, a blend of hopelessness, disappointment, regret, and love.

Hue would lie very straight in the bamboo platform bed he shared with me. He pulled the rough blanket up to our necks. Hue folded his arms to pillow his head. He stared up at the thatch-roofed ceiling. His head did not turn. His eyes did not close. He took deep breaths. His bony chest rose high. Slowly, as sleep was coming to me, one of his hands unfolded from the other, and he reached out quietly to hold my smaller, meatier hand in his own. He gave a tiny squeeze. In the force of those thin fingers, I felt I was not alone. I understood that we inhabited the sadness together. I realized that if I had not returned, Hue would truly be alone. That's when I cried—for my own thoughtlessness and our endless yearning. I didn't dare make a noise. My body jerked in small hiccupping motions, and the hot liquid of my tears slipped out of my eyes and down either side of my face. The tears that I had held back by the firelight, on the trek away from the village, up high in the tree, became a small, salty stream of hurt unfurling.

Through the tears, I could see my mother's back, turned to the wall. In the dark, it seemed her body jerked in little motions similar to my own.

✧

I was twelve years old when I began singing Hmong song poetry. My body was changing. More and more girls were noticing me in the village. My mind was changing, too. I understood that school was not my arena but that I could find other pathways into manhood. The world we lived in was changing. Each day, I grew more certain that my future would rest at the point of a gun, not a pen. The drums of the dead battled with the cries of widows and orphans in our village. The only way I could meet their pain was to take it inside of me, melt it into my flesh, and feel the pull of the Hmong blood pulse through my veins, fill my heart, and overflow.

When I began singing song poetry I discovered I could share our stories of hurt and sorrow, of missing and despair, of anger and betrayal, conscious and unconscious, intentional and not—my silent sensitivities—with those around me.

In my songs, my brothers and sisters, family and friends, felt the fall of their own hot tears come down their cheeks. My songs allowed me and those around me to feel our longing for those words that were impossible to live up to but unforgettable to hear, the promise of eternal care: "Do not be afraid. Everything will be all right. I will not let anything hurt you."

Brothers and Sisters

I am sorry, dear heart, that I have more sorrows than joy.
I am sorry I made you scale mountains, heedless of your
    soft skin.
I am sorry I made you jump into rushing water, heedless
    of your inability to swim.
I am sorry, dear heart, that you must bear the scars.
Dear heart, that you remember . . .
The day my older brother told me to run.
In my flight away from our home, I heard the shotguns
    blast.
In my dreams, people found my brother, and they took
    him to the hospital in Sam Neua.
In my dreams, the wild dogs entered our house, and
    feasted on my brother's fallen body.
I am sorry, dear heart, that I wish to begin again,
My tender, my wounded heart,
Begin again before the mountains and the water, before
    the sorrows, when I knew joy at my brother's side.

I have six brothers and two sisters, and we all have one big
brother, Shong Moua Yang. Big brother Shong is not our birth
sibling. He is the son of our father's youngest brother; he is our
first cousin. I cannot sing the song of my life without singing a

song of gratitude to Shong, my big brother, my first teacher, my dearest friend.

Shong's father died when Shong was six years old. There was suspicion that his father's death was the result of foul play. Shong's father had been in the midst of defending a cousin in a clan-versus-clan dispute, and all the indications were that he and the Yang clan would win. The night before the final hearing in the provincial town where the case was being heard by a local magistrate, Shong's father died suddenly and unexpectedly. He was a young man of twenty-five and in excellent health. The other clan boasted that while Shong's father was good in the court of the living, he would be useless in the court of the dead. There was no proof that he was murdered, but a few hours before Shong's father's death, leading figures from the other clan had paid for the services of a black magician. The night after his burial, several members of the Yang clan had dreams where he visited them in a state of distress. His message to all of them was simple and direct: "I have been wrongfully killed. I leave behind my son. I will not let this death go unavenged. In the world of the dead, as in the world of the living, it is the long road that leads to justice. I will walk that road until my death is avenged. Do not let my son be orphaned by my death."

Shong and his younger sister lived with their mother for a short time after his father's death, but the young widow soon found the pressures of being alone too much to bear. In addition to the cooking and cleaning, the endless mending of the split bamboo walls and the thatched roof, she found herself chopping firewood and feeding the animals—jobs that her husband had always done. There was no privacy to be had in their little thatch-roofed home, no space to mourn and cry for her husband, or to complain before the wary eyes of her children about the heaviness of the workload. The little boy and girl carried pinched faces full of sorrow and concern. For the first several months after their father's death, the two followed their mother everywhere, as if their presence would ensure hers. It was only by the smoke of the fire ring that tears could fall freely from her eyes. She swatted at the dark rise of smoke from the burning logs as her tears fell from her face, hoping her children believed that it was the sting of the smoke that made their mother cry, not the life she was living with them. In these moments, the boy would lead the girl to the entrance so they could hold open the swinging bamboo door and let the wind enter their house, watch as the smoke dissipated. As the months passed and the children stopped following their mother everywhere, she asked the boy to watch over the girl. She told them she could get more work done in the house and the fields if they scattered with the village children with the rise of the sun.

The whole village watched the little family and it was obvious to everyone, including my parents, that my aunt was too young to live life alone.

One day while she was grinding kernels of corn in an open shed by the edge of the village, an older man approached Shong's mother and offered to help her. It had been six months since her husband's death. It was customary now for any man interested to introduce himself. She was not a stupid woman and understood that she should be cautious. She dared not speak to him, but she nodded and moved away from her basket of corn. She stood to the side as the squat, balding man, perhaps in his forties, approached the heavy, round stones at the shed's center. The village men had sculpted the contraption from two hard, flat rocks; they had used bamboo poles and donkeys to place the rocks atop each other, carved a hole in the top one for the kernels of corn to be fed into the grinder. She watched the rise of muscles under the thin fabric of the man's traditional black shirt. Sweat poured down his forehead, but he did not look up at her or stop to wipe away the wet rivulets seeping into his clothing. After the basket of corn had been turned into a rough powder, the man used both of his hands to cup the cornmeal into her woven bamboo basket. Only once he was done did he look up at her and gesture for her to come closer. She approached him slowly. He did not speak as he pointed for her to turn. She turned her back to him. He lifted the basket high and allowed her time to put her arms through the straps before settling the weight gently. His nod was polite when her hold was secured and she turned around. When he walked away from the shed, he did so silently. No words of goodbye. She watched his broad back, saw him lift his hands—perhaps to wipe away the sweat upon his brow, perhaps to run a hand over his mouth. His silence had triggered hers. She did not thank him for his help.

The next day as Shong's mother faltered beneath the weight of the water pail on her back, it was the same squat man whose hands reached from behind to steady the weight. He balanced the weight of the water for her the entire way from the stream to her house, matching his steps to her own. As she neared the empty yard, her eyes scanned the open area for her children, but they were not in sight. She moved farther away from him, spilling some of the water with her self-conscious movement.

Her reaction caused the man to clear his throat. When he spoke, his voice was gentle.

The man said, "The work of carrying a home is too hard on a woman alone. You need my help. Far away from here, I have a house full of children who need a mother. I would be happy to serve as a father to your children. Will you consider an offer of marriage from a humble man?"

Shong's father had been a song poet. They had followed a traditional courtship ritual. The two had met at the New Year's festivities in her home village, a few days' walk from his. It was his impressive height, resolute chin, and steady eyes that had attracted her, but it was his words when he sang his songs during their courtship ball toss that had sealed her decision to marry him. Unlike those of most of the young men on the courting field, his song was not a love song. Instead, the young man had told a tale of woe. He had sung a song about an orphan boy, the loneliness of a lifetime, and how throughout it all, it was the thought of a family that had sustained him, a wife's heart and her arms wrapped around their children, the embrace of a little boy or girl. His song had moved her like none she had ever heard. She yearned to put her arms around him, to give him that little boy and girl, to seal what she saw as a hole in his heart.

Shortly after their meeting, in a whispered conversation lit only by the moon, she on one side of a thin wall, lying on a bamboo platform with her younger siblings asleep beside her, he on the other side of the wall, crouching low beside a village dog, he asked if she would marry him. Her heart hammered in her chest. Instead of the response her mother had taught her was appropriate and modest for a young girl encountering a proposal of marriage—"Oh, someone handsome as you would not tie themselves to someone like me"—she said a firm "Yes."

Theirs had been a good marriage. He was well respected by many people for his wit and his intelligence, his artistry and his allegiance to family. While he had not been present as much as she had wished because of his work with the Yang clan, and though the night shadows grew scary in his absence, he was attentive when he was home. He doted on her. He made her laugh and held her close. He entertained his children with stories of ghosts and ghouls. He reminded her each day of the poetry inherent in life. He would cock his ear toward the cricket's song, slowly stamp his feet, snap his hands, break off a nearby leaf, and respond with a song of his own. She marveled at how a man could make music with a cricket. She knew each day they had together that there would be no other man like him in her lifetime.

Shong's mother missed my uncle very much. She longed for the company of a man. She was only twenty years old. In the days after the stranger's proposal, she spent sleepless nights thinking about her late husband's first song and how it had made her ache with loneliness. If she wasn't careful, his song would become her life.

Shong's mother's decision to remarry was driven as much by the hardships of a life on the mountains as it was by the loneliness that ate at her each time she saw men and women with their children going in and out of their homes, happy in their daily rituals and routines.

As she looked at the older man with his hands at his sides, waiting silently, a picture of patience and calm, the words came easily to her. "Yes. I will take my little daughter with me to your home. My son I will leave behind. It is what his father would have wanted. He will stay here in this village and live with his uncle to become the man his father wanted him to be, a member of the Yang clan."

Shong's mother left him with his one surviving uncle, my father. On her marriage day, she knelt before her young son, her head lowered. Her words were soft, soaked with unshed tears.

She said, "My little boy will not hate me because of the decision I've made. He will live with his uncle. He will grow up to be a man like his father. He will know that his mother has made the only decision she knows how to keep him united with his clan and his family."

So far as I know, Shong did not respond to his mother that day, and has never spoken of her since.

At the time, my father was an old childless widower who had just married my mother, a much younger woman of modest looks but strong constitution. My mother had also been orphaned at an early age and had grown up in her uncle's house. She had raised herself and her four younger siblings. There was no indication that my parents would have children of their own as my father had none with his previous wife, and estimates were that he was close to sixty years of age by the time he welcomed my mother into his home and his bed. My mother and father adopted Shong eagerly into their home as their son.

Two years into their marriage, to everyone's happy surprise, my mother found out that she was pregnant. She had wanted children badly; she had administered herbal drinks and medicinal brews, visited local shamans and medicine women. While my father had been resigned, my mother had grown despondent waiting for a child to enter their lives. My father had hoped that having Shong in their lives would be enough for my mother. He was a good boy with rare, insightful intelligence. Still, my mother yearned and everyone knew how much she wanted more children in their lives. When news of her pregnancy spread throughout the village, many people came to the house with their blessings. Shong was the most exuberant, excited about the prospect of having brothers and sisters. Although he loved his aunt and uncle, he was lonely for his sister and seeing the other village children with their many siblings made him sad. Life with my parents had been quiet. There was work to do and gentle words delivered, but no one to play with.

Each day, the three of them got up early and walked the path to the garden together. They tended to the fields in a line of three. On special mornings when my father's services as a shaman were needed in nearby villages to call in the spirits of the soul weary and attend to the health of the sick, Shong accompanied him with a red cloth bag across his shoulders. In the bag, he carried the assortment of shaman's tools that my father needed for his ceremonies: the dark steel gong, the ring of copper coins, the bull's horns, and other trinkets of the trade. In the stretch of gray dawn, when the fog lay low over the dirt paths, the two of them walked, my father talking quietly of the man Shong's father had been and of the man Shong would become. The young Shong listened earnestly. His own memories of his father grew dim with the passing of the seasons. My parents had learned early on of Shong's fortitude, his intelligence, and his fierce loyalty, but it was his uncanny ability to articulate truth that startled them and told them Shong would one day lead the Yang clan as his father had. As my mother's belly grew big and round, Shong and she had more and more conversations about the future.

He used to say to her, "You are having the baby for me, aren't you, Mother? A little brother or sister who will never leave me, who will become a part of me, a little boy or girl I could work hard for."

My mother nodded at his words, knowing they were true: that with each child, Shong would have to work harder.

As the years passed and the flicker of respect grew between my parents and the flames of love began to burn, their house grew warm with the bodies and the breaths of many children. My mother kept busy tending to the hungry mouths, the feisty tongues, the endless cries, and the bursts of unstoppable energy. With each baby, my father ate less and grew older. He became frail. He walked with a cane that he rested on heavily. His once wiry frame, muscled and strong, grew soft. The skin fell from his bones. His cheeks were sunken and the wrinkles formed deep ravines across the leathery plane of his face. Still, my father continued the long treks to surrounding villages attending to the sick, his breath coming harder with each trip. My parents were so busy taking care of the new babies and each other that much of the burden of attending to the fields and harvests fell on Shong.

My mother told stories of how Shong began harvesting whole fields of rice long before he was tall enough to stand beside a small Hmong donkey and saddle it with rice sacks. He used to have to pull the donkey next to a large fallen tree or beside a rising boulder just so he could hoist the heavy bags of rice onto the animal's back. For all the work that my mother saw Shong do, he never complained once. Instead, he used to say to her, "Mother, in this lifetime, I will never be able to return the love you and Father have given me. When you die, it is my wish to die shortly after so that I can help you make your way into the next life."

Shong lived to fulfill these words, but long before that he did so much more for my brothers and me.

Each of my brothers can speak for hours of Shong's love and the gentle strength of his guiding hands. At family dinners, when my brothers are together, inevitably there is mention of Shong. We talk about his meager height, his little frame, his spry movements and slow, even speech. We all have stories of Shong that make us laugh, give us pause for reflection, bring a shine into our aging eyes and a familiar constriction to our throats. Through the stories we tell of him, we want our children to know his goodness, to learn from his example and carry his stories into their futures, the distant futures that he enabled but could not share. If not for Shong, so many of us, my brothers and sisters and I, would be less than we are today. He is the example that many of us have followed our lives learning from.

◇

Shong taught me how to be kind to children.

I was just a boy and Shong was a young man then. He was not yet married. The French were still in Laos, but we felt the heaviness of their influence only once or twice a year when they sent uniformed men to collect taxes from the Hmong villages of Phou Bia mountain. My father had died a few years before. In the wake of his death, my mother spent the bulk of her days walking up and down mountain slopes collecting healing herbs and remedies. Her work as medicine woman helped her take care of us younger children. My mother had no spare moments.

I was five years old and Hue was seven. We used to spend entire days playing by ourselves or with village children our age. One day we decided to climb the small rise around the back of our village. We had never been there before. We wanted to go the farthest we had ever gone. Hue led us on the adventure. We imagined we were a pair of hungry tiger brothers. The village was a lone elephant. It would be our dinner. Hue scrunched his shoulders and held his head low. I did the same. Each of us had a thin stick in our hands because humans didn't have claws and sharp teeth and we needed to make an adjustment. It was a sunny day. The wind was light and crisp. A lone bird cried in predictable intervals. Groups of bugs flew together, forming small clouds along patches of the small dirt path that circled away from our village. We walked along the tree line. The grass was up to our knees. It seemed to grow more golden as we climbed closer to the top of the hill. Rocks the size of children's heads were scattered across the rise. We pretended they were children's heads. Earlier meals. We growled and pointed our sticks at each rock we encountered. We did this all the way up to the top. Neither of us spoke. We were tigers. We growled at each other.

When we made it to the top we could see the layout of our village. We could see the pig pens and rice bins behind the individual houses. The neighbor closest to the village's edge on our side had the cleanest yard. It was fenced in. There were no wooden stools lying around. The firewood shed was full of carefully stacked wood. We admired it for a moment before shifting our gaze to our own house. While we did not have a fenced yard, our mother had a fenced garden where the walls were green and lush with bitter melon vines. We knew the green spread on the ground consisted of herbs: green onion, cilantro, basil, mint, lemongrass, chili plants, and a variety of mustard greens. Our house looked small and long from where we were positioned. We saw neighboring girls taking turns jumping over a string of rubber bands in the empty circle of smooth ground that served as a gathering space for the village children. The mountains facing our village rose tall before our young eyes. They looked like a wall of green trees climbing higher and higher, narrowing until it reached a single peak. We lived at the base of a great triangle of trees. We tried growling once or twice in the direction of our home but the village was immune to our threats. The game had grown considerably less fun. It had taken us what seemed like hours to get to the top, but once there, after a perusal of the land, there wasn't much to do; our prey was too far away to feel our presence. The sun was hot and our mouths grew dry. I wanted a cool drink of water from the clay pot my mother kept full in the corner of our house, smooth water that she had boiled with medicinal herbs to ward off illness and disease. I spoke in my human voice.

"Let's go home. I want some water."

Hue nodded his agreement.

On the sloping mountainside that led down toward the village, we spied a large, circular rock we had never seen before. It looked like a broken column stuck in the ground. We approached and measured ourselves against it. The rock was taller than me but not quite as tall as Hue. I tried to wrap my arms around its thick middle but my hands wouldn't meet. The surface of the gray stone was warm against my touch. Its smooth, glittery surface against my skin felt nice. I rested against the rock. I closed my eyes. I opened my eyes. An idea had popped into my head. I turned around to look at Hue. An idea had also popped in his head. His eyes were round. The boredom I had seen earlier was gone.

Were we strong enough to move this rock?

We both nodded.

Of course we were. We were as strong as grown men.

At first each of us took a turn trying to push the rock. Our individual efforts yielded no movement. After a few tries, we decided to join forces. We positioned ourselves behind the tall rock, put our hands on its sun-warmed surface, counted to three, and pushed as hard as we could. We felt a small shifting, and then the rock ran away from our hands, slowly at first. We watched the rock tumble down and roll like a log. We saw the rock going faster and faster toward the village. It was too late. We could only watch in horror as the rock gained speed down the incline and crashed through the clean yard's neat bamboo fence, coming to a jarring stop at the neighbor's house. Half of the rock crashed into the wall. A small figure, the irate neighbor, ran out of his house, surveyed the damage, followed the trail of the fallen rock up the incline, and pointed at us. The man did not yell. If he had, we would have heard him. Instead, he stabbed at the air, once, twice, three times with his index finger high. Then he marched angrily the short distance from his house to our own.

Shong was not home. Our mother was somewhere on the mountainsides gathering her herbal remedies. We both knew that the neighbor would have to speak to one of our older brothers. Neither of us had much to say to the other. It was too late for words. We had caused a big problem: real damage. Neither Hue nor I wanted to return home but we knew that lingering outside would not help the situation. We held hands as we walked slowly down the incline. Our steps halted as we got closer to the site of the catastrophe. We kept a wide berth as we rounded the path to our home. The long split bamboo house with its thatched roof that had appeared small in the distance grew bigger and bigger in front of us. At the door, Hue cleared his throat to announce our presence. An angry voice from inside demanded that the culprits enter.

Our eldest brother Nhia's face was a rush of color. His words came out between heaves of air: the family were in the thick of the planting season; he had no time to go to neighboring houses to fix the mistakes of ill-behaved children; why didn't we think about our actions? He looked at the silent neighbor who stood in the darkened house, and he looked at us in the stream of light from the open door. Nhia shook his head. He spoke fast, his words hard and clipped. He told us to go and repair the fence. Nhia said for us not to return home until the broken fence was mended. The neighbor stood to one side, muttering low to himself, his hands crossed over his chest. We could only nod at our brother's words.

Hue and I dragged our feet to the neighbor's house. At the gate to the yard, we waited for a few minutes to see if someone would come and open it but no one did. We looked around for the neighbor but he had not followed us. Hue reluctantly opened the gate for us. We walked to the place where the rock had broken through the fence and followed its passage to the wall. We surveyed the damage. The hole in the wall of the house was big enough for children to crawl through. The torn edges of jagged bamboo bits were sharp as knives. Pieces of broken bamboo and broken twine fell about the ground. An entire side of the fence around the yard had fallen in the wake of the collision. We did not know where to start so we began picking up the bamboo pieces off the ground. Our arms cradled the bits of broken fence. The weight of the injured bamboo grew heavy. We began to cry quietly. Neither Hue nor I knew how to cut bamboo or split it, let alone to make a line of bamboo stand tall together. We had made a bad decision and caused serious damage to someone else's property and we did not know how to solve it. The more we thought about the stupidity of our actions, the more aware we became of the embarrassment we had brought to our family, and the harder it became to control the flow of our tears. Hue and I dared not lift our gazes because we feared meeting the neighbor's eyes or those of his wife and children.

We focused on our task, eyes to the ground. First, one piece of fallen bamboo and then the next. Hue spoke at one point to tell me to be careful when handling the edges. He had gotten poked by a particularly bad splinter. We made a small pile by the far wall when our arms were full. Not sure of where to proceed after picking up the broken pieces, we moved slowly through the work. Our motions slowed only when we heard a familiar voice at the neighbor's door. We looked up to find Shong standing by the side of the house. We would recognize his small figure anywhere, the softness of his voice speaking to the neighbor. We waited with the bamboo in our arms. When the conversation was through, Shong walked to us. We did not want to meet his gaze. He crouched down and pulled us into his arms, broken bamboo and all.

He wiped off our tears and snot with his shirt and said, "My little brothers, stop crying. Your big brother is here. I know you two are too young to know the speed and strength of a boulder rolling. Hush now. Little boys cannot do the work of grown men. There is no reason to cry. I will mend the fence."

When my brothers and I have lost patience with each other, when the older ones have forgotten the trembling heart of a boy, and when the younger ones have forgotten the sacrifices of their older siblings, Shong remembered for us. He was the balance that we needed in order to hold on, the necessary weight on either side on the scale of siblings.

Shong never spoke to my brothers and me about the sadness or loneliness of growing up in our home. He made us feel cherished and loved. To Shong, we were not burdens to bear, but gifts given to him so that he would not be alone in the world. Under Shong's watch and protection, my brothers and sisters and I grew up with a margin for error in a dangerous world full of death and destruction, a world rifled by war.

✧

Beneath the falling bombs, we grew into young men and women who could run fast on unsteady ground. The French had left the country. The Americans had come to take their place. Our village of Phou Khao was chosen as a prisoner-of-war site by the Americans. In the caves around Phou Bia mountain, the tall men in uniforms set up military jail cells for captured North Vietnamese and Pathet Lao soldiers. They brought the skinny men in rags, with hands tied behind their backs, in planes and trucks from other parts of the country. Many of the villagers were fearful, including my mother, who stood at our door and watched the iron eagles fly overhead, her hands to her heart. Our small village expanded its boundaries as more and more men in uniforms entered our lives, rows of bullets strung across their chests and guns strapped to their sides.

General Vang Pao, the respected Hmong military leader, recruited many of the Hmong men and boys in our village to fight for him on behalf of the Americans. My mother refused to let any of her sons become soldiers. Instead, we did the work of building coffins and attending to the rituals of the funerals of our childhood friends and neighbors. The number of widowed women in our village grew. More and more orphaned children came to our door, hands in the air, pleading for eggs and rice balls, wearing tattered clothing, their bare feet bleeding from the flights they'd taken from flaming villages, falling bombs, and buried mine explosions. They came with stories that made all of us weep.

Many families were destroyed by the war. Fathers died. Mothers died. Brothers and sisters were torn apart. We also saw many new families being made in the process. An old couple whose children had abandoned them took on a young soldier as their adopted son. When the son fell in love with a neighbor's widow, the old couple got new grandchildren. My own mother invited the young men and women who came through our house to join our family. Even as food became more scarce in our village, the number of people around our table grew. This is how my two older sisters met their husbands, both soldiers from the Lee clan who entered our home from faraway journeys, who arrived with not only guns and bullets, but also words of admiration and offerings of love.

My mother did not try to stand in the way of her daughters. She understood that her children were growing up. She watched as my sisters were married and cried as they left our village to start their lives with their husbands. Far too often young women ran into the village in torn, bloodied clothing, their long hair covering their faces, their hands shaking unceasingly. They told stories of massacres during the day and ambushes during the night. Some of them would begin stories and then put their shaking hands over their mouths, unable to let out the words they had lived through into the world. All of my brothers but Eng, who was too preoccupied with the war and its imminent dangers, met young women and fell in love. They offered the protection of their arms and our family's size. By the late 1960s and early 1970s, there were few Hmong families who were intact. We were one of the lucky ones.

In 1975, my family could no longer stay in Phou Khao. The Americans had left. The Communist Party had taken over the country. General Vang Pao and his high-ranking soldiers had disappeared with the Americans. Phou Khao and other villages in the Phou Bia mountains were now known as enemy sites. The Pathet Lao and North Vietnamese soldiers entered the small villages and began transporting truckloads of Hmong men and boys. The soldiers said that they were to be reeducated, but the men and boys never returned. When the worries of their wives and mothers grew loud, the remnants organized search parties. They found the bodies on the damp jungle floor, lying across the fallen leaves like broken logs. We knew it was only a matter of time before the Hmong who had been in contact with the Americans would be killed. The Hmong warned each other across the war-torn villages of Phou Bia. My brothers gathered with friends and relatives and whispered urgently of guns and bullets. All over there was talk of defending family and homes. All over there was talk of defeat and death. In May of 1975, there was news that a truck was coming for the men in my family. My older brothers felt that our only option was to flee into the jungle.

$$\diamondsuit$$

It was 1978, three years after we had left our village. I was nineteen years old. She was only sixteen. We met in the jungle. My best friend and I were out hunting for wild game. She and her mother were on a search for bamboo shoots. It was late afternoon. The air was heavy with humidity. The sunlight was filtered by the green canopy of tall trees. Tunnels of golden light slanted across the deep foliage. The birds cried from different directions. The wind whistled softly through the leaves. It was a still, shady moment when I first saw her. She had her hair in a high bun. Around the bun, she wore a strand of white beads. Most of the women and girls I knew kept their hair tucked beneath stretches of dirty cloth. Strands of her long hair had come undone. The shorter strands clung to her neck. Her pale skin, an anomaly among the women in my life, glistened in the humid day. I saw the rise of her high chest. I made note of the tapered waist. Her feet were small. She wore shoes. I thought her feet must be soft, clean. My own dirty feet had hardened with calluses years ago. My one pair of good shoes was long gone. Some people tried to wrap their feet in bits of fabric. There were no bits of fabric for my feet. Our meeting was a matter of seconds. I don't know what she saw of me, but I saw so much of her. I imagine that as we passed by her mother called out the customary greeting, "*Mus zoo neb os me tub.*" (May goodness travel with you, son.) If she did, I did not hear it.

Both our families were in the jungle, with different groups of people, hiding and foraging for food. Her group was smaller than ours. They had fewer children to look after, fewer mouths to feed. They had done a better job of holding on to their things. They were less poor to begin with. Neither family approved of our short courtship.

I remember hearing her laughter for the first time. Like a well-mannered Hmong man, I paid my respects to her family camp. I visited under the guise of befriending one of her brothers who was close to me in age. I saw her immediately when I walked into the camp. Her people had set up temporary shelter in a banana grove. She was doing the wash by the edge of the camp, dunking a few articles of clothing into a metal pail full of water, again and again. I spied her brother by the fire and made my way there to announce my presence. I made small conversation with her brother for a short period, and then I made an excuse to approach her. I had asked around and learned some things about her. She was known for being haughty. She was very good at shutting out young men. She didn't like to talk very much. Unlike her younger sister, she did not like to babysit. She preferred to work with the older women. She had gone to school before her village fell apart. She could read and write. In fact, her nephew had told me, she had been at the top of her class and a favorite in her family. She was many things that I wasn't. It made me like her so much more for having skills I didn't, abilities I had lost, a position I had never known. I wanted to have a conversation with her. I wanted to learn more about her from her. I walked her way, but she didn't look my way.

She was squatting on the ground, rinsing pieces of clothing in her small hands. When I was but a few feet away, I coughed a little to get her attention. Still, she didn't look up. I stood beside her and tried to appear confident. I cleared my throat. There was just the sound of the clothes going in and out of water. I could feel the flicker of embarrassment grow inside of me.

I said, "I'm not here to pursue you. I just have a story to share."

The noise of the wash grew quiet. She turned toward me. I leaned against a banana trunk. I began to talk softly but persistently, to the air she occupied, until my voice surrounded her. I told her a true story I had heard from my brother Eng. I couldn't remember all of it so I made up some of the parts and used the first person so that the story could grow strong in my voice.

✧

I was a young boy. The old man was well respected for his ability to raise healthy chickens. My father used to have me go to his house to fetch eggs whenever we had visitors. I was on such an errand when I saw the bald little rooster. He had no wing feathers. It was a strange sight. In a yard full of fallen feathers, in the run of black-winged creatures that raced to and fro, this chicken stood very still. I thought he was sick. I could see his reddish skin through the thin spread of fuzz over his body. I thought that perhaps he was dying. His head was bent toward the ground. I pointed to him in the yard and asked the old man when the chicken would die.

The old man looked at me and said, "Boy, when you raise chickens as I do, in the same yard, year after year, you learn that every few years there is a rooster born this way. He is as he should be. He is not sick, not old, just an unfeathered friend. The female hens don't like him, so he doesn't chase them."

The old man said, "I prize him. He is a good one. He has not isolated himself as many roosters like him have done, starved himself with loneliness. This one stands in their midst."

I started looking for the bald rooster every time I visited the old man's house. The sight of him became reassuring. I'd just nod my head to him in greeting or goodbye. I didn't move close or try to touch him. Each time I spied him standing in the yard, he would just look up at me slowly before training his gaze back to the ground.

One day, I couldn't find the little bald rooster anywhere among the chickens. I asked the old man where my friend was, and he pointed to a thin tree on the outskirts of the yard and said, "Look."

I saw a wild chicken, in full plumage, more peacock than hen. She was emerald green, a green deeper and shinier than any leaves on the tree. When she turned her head away, and I could unlock my gaze, I saw the little bald rooster by her side. I said, "How?"

How did he reach the tree limb? Featherless roosters do not fly. I have never heard of a chicken that could climb.

The old man smiled and said quietly, "Shhh. Just look."

I watched the beautiful creature from the treetops of the jungle turn to look upon the bald rooster with his featherless wings, her eyes little marbles of glistening black. I saw her head bend and her long, graceful neck turn to entwine with his. I watched her feathered wings spread wide and then circle him. It was my first love story.

I came home and I told everybody who would listen: my mother and father, my brothers and sisters, Shong. They listened, but the magic of the moment could not be communicated. They were happy for my experience. They had not experienced it with me.

I visited the old man again and again. I never saw the beautiful wild chicken again. I saw only the little bald rooster, by himself, no longer in the middle of the chicken yard but at its edge, looking hopelessly toward the treetops. I asked the old man if she had returned. He shook his head sadly. I asked if the bald rooster would now die from loneliness. The old man said he hoped not.

One day not long after, there was a voice of excitement at our door. It was the old man, my friend. He said that I had to come quickly. My mother asked why but he was in a great hurry, so all he could say was, "Eng will tell you when he returns."

I didn't even grab my flip-flops. I just raced with the old man, as fast as he was moving, to his chicken coop. There, at the edge of the coop, beneath the spread of the thin tree, was the bald rooster. He was not alone. Around him were six little chicks, not the black little furry balls that I recognized as Hmong chickens but green, gold-streaked fluffs. I said, "What?"

The old man shook his head, his face a collection of broken wrinkles. He said, "I don't know. This morning I came out here to feed the chickens and I saw him sitting at the base of the tree. I worried he was sick so I walked over to see. When I approached he moved and I couldn't believe what was before me. I wanted you to see it with me."

The old man and I watched over the bald rooster and his little chicks. The days turned into weeks, and the fluffs flew away and in their place grew long-feathered emerald wing feathers.

One day, we saw the wildness enter their veins one by one, and the birds lifted off the ground. We marveled. Their father, unable to follow, looked on helplessly as his children flew up to the tree limb that had housed his love. He cried for them on the ground, but they did not return. The old man told me that all the chickens slept on the tree limb that night while their father rested on the ground beneath them, refusing to return to the coop.

I visited the next morning to find that all the wild chickens had flown away with the rise of the sun. They had taken off in a line over the tree's edge and into the expanse of the jungle. Only one remained. The one that had not flown away was with his father on the ground. He was larger than his father. His emerald feathers gleamed in the early morning sunshine. He saw me approaching with the old man. When we got closer, his father shied away, but the wild chicken stood tall on his thin legs and turned his head in our direction. He stared at me with the round, black, glistening marble eyes of his mother. His blue lids did not close. The old man clucked his tongue, once, twice, three times. The creature, as majestic as his mother had been that day on the tree limb, walked toward us. The old man was careful when he wrapped his thin arms around the bird. He held him close for a moment, and then handed him to me. The old man said, "Boy, this one is yours."

I kept the wild chicken for two years. I kept him as my wild bird. At night, he slept on the tops of the village trees. In the day, when I went looking, he would sweep down and land close to my feet. I fed him balls of cooked rice, sometimes a handful of corn kernels. We were friends without language. He would stand still so that I could wipe down his long feathers with a brush of my hands. My brothers and sisters admired our friendship. They were astounded that I knew the sound of his song and he knew the call of my voice. They asked if I would ever eat him. I said I would never do such a thing to my friend.

When the bombs started falling in our village, the wild birds scattered. In the smoke and the fire, feathered plumage fell to the jungle floors. One day, my wild friend and I watched as a canopy of jungle trees fell in the distance. We heard cries from afar. There was a rise of winged creatures. My feathered friend danced about my feet, and then his gaze met mine, and I knew it before it happened: his wings unfurled and his feet lifted off the ground; he flew up to a tall tree. I called for him but he did not look back. He did not respond. I saw him surface from the tree's green dome and fly in the direction of the wild birds. I watched as the emerald plumes of my wild friend dimmed in the distant sky and grew small in the wash of smoke and clouds.

In the days after, I waited for his return, but I saw no emerald in any sky, no sign of my friend anywhere.

✧

I was looking far off into the trees as I finished Eng's story. I heard the young woman's laughter before I saw it. She was still crouched close to the ground, the laundry dangling in her hands. I looked for maliciousness in the eyes that shined up at me. I checked for a hardness of heart I would not be able to bear, a flicker of fun at my expense I did not want to see. Her gaze did not waver. Her eyes did not shift. There was only delight. She liked my story. The look in her eyes said she might like me.

She said, "My name is Chue."

She had the same name as one of my older brothers. I didn't care. I thought it was the most beautiful name coming from her lips.

I said, "My name is Bee."

Both our families felt that we were foolish for choosing marriage in a world fraught with danger and death. I had no dowry money. How were we going to make a life, running from one cave to another, from one fallen tree to another?

In the face of our families' disapproval, we grew unsure of ourselves. I approached Shong for guidance. Shong asked me several questions to which my responses were: I have never thought of marriage before I met this woman; if I die tomorrow I will die happier because I lived with her today; I am intrigued by her approach to the dangers of the world we live in, a reference to the fact that Chue did not run from the bombs that rained on us. She believed you couldn't run from death or through life. I could see that Chue's thoughts on life and death gave Shong pause. Shong was quiet as he listened to me rationalize Chue's fearlessness as a reason our marriage would work. I was prepared to talk as long as Shong would listen, but then Shong held up his hands for me to stop.

Shong said, "Bee, there is no wrong time for love to flourish. Perhaps now, when so many men and women have learned to hate and fear, is the most perfect time of all, for each of us to be reminded of a lesson in love."

Shong silenced the protests of my family. He helped me

borrow the dowry money to pay for Chue's bride price. He was the negotiator, master of ceremonies, and spiritual guide at our small wedding gathering. In 1978 my wife and I got married under the auspices and care of Shong.

✧

That same year our family left Shong, his wife, and their three children behind in the jungles of Laos. There was an early morning ambush. Families scattered in different directions. Shong was running with his little boy strapped to his back. The two-year-old boy was cowering behind his father, using his hands to protect his head from the branches scratching at his face and the bullets flying in their direction. Shong knew that something had gone terribly wrong when he felt the boy's head fall heavily on his shoulder and his hands drop on either side of his body. Hot liquid began to seep between the child and himself. He couldn't stop to check. He couldn't stop running.

It was not until after the smoke had dissipated and the cries of the fallen were silenced by the enemy's guns that our family met in a designated cave. There, Shong released the child from his back and everyone saw what had happened: the boy's head had been hit by a bullet. There was a hole through the side of his head. Blood was seeping from the wound, turning thick and purple, clotting over his face and the back of his head. His chest rose and fell in exhausted waves. His breathing was shallow. He had grown pale and still. My mother thought that death was near. My older brothers said that the whole family had to pack up and run. Everybody said Shong could strap the child onto his back again and make the trek. It wasn't safe to stay. They could all help carry the child as far as the boy would hold to life. The soldiers stalking us knew that too many had escaped the ambush.

Shong was silent in the face of our reasons to run. His wife sat quietly holding the child in her lap, rocking as his blood seeped into her clothing. Their other two children huddled close. When Shong did speak, he spoke so softly that we had to strain our ears to hear his words. He said that his child would die if he ran with us. He said there was no point in his being alive if his child was going to die. He told all of us, his brothers and sisters, to run with our families. He said that his family would stay and give the child rest. If the child made it through the night, he would come looking for us. No matter what stood in the way, he would find the road that would take him to the family, across a river or an ocean, across the chasm between life and death, into the land of the ancestors and beyond. If his child did not make it through the night, then Shong told the family to proceed knowing that we had loved him well and that our life together as brothers and sisters had been a good one.

We understood that there was no changing Shong's mind. His wife said nothing. We knew that faced with the same situation, we could each of us make the same decision. In the last few years we had seen many other families make equally hard decisions. At least we had a chance to say goodbye.

The sound of guns started again, and from the mouth of the cave we could see bursts of flame and smoke in the distance that brought down entire groves of trees. My mother cried and tried to pull Shong and his wife up from their little boy in his pool of blood, but they could not be pulled. When the sound of voices neared, my brothers and I, along with our families, got up and we took our sobbing mother with us out of the cave, down a ravine, and into the dark jungle foliage. Shong and his wife did not look up as we left, each of us brothers placing our hands on their bent heads, stooping to hold their children close for a brief moment.

I will never forget the look on Shong's older boy's and girl's faces as they watched each of their uncles leave. Their tired, scared eyes followed many of us, follow us still, across the wide ocean of space and time, the far distance of years.

Shong, his wife, and their three children were captured by the Pathet Lao soldiers who found them in the cave. They were taken to a small Communist-operated village. Shong's wife and children were sent into an open shed close to the edge of the jungle. Two of the men in uniforms brought them water and balls of rice on chipped white enameled steel plates. Shong was dragged into a split-bamboo hut. His struggles were futile; a small middle-aged man, he was no match for the young men with guns and knives.

The soldiers left the door open so that Shong's family could see them tie him down to what looked like a wooden table. With her feverish little boy in her arms, Shong's wife sat shaking on the small bamboo platform. She had cried herself hoarse. The muscles in her throat felt slack and heavy. Her other two children huddled by her side, each holding a fistful of fabric, straining the thin cotton of her shirt. Her numb fingers tried to pick the dried, crusted blood off her baby's head. The only parts of her body that seemed to be working were her ears and her eyes. In the open shed, she could hear the soldiers yelling questions at her husband: Where are your brothers? What direction did they go? Will they come back for you? Are they worth the lives of your wife and your children? She heard Shong's muffled responses, too short to be an answer to any of the questions.

She saw one of the soldiers, a figure in the shadows of the enclosed hut, grab a large stick of firewood and slam it across Shong's middle. She felt the tightening of his body, the smashing of his muscles, and the cracking of his ribs as she heard his cry of pain.

One blow and then another. At first, Shong grunted, but as the blows kept falling all she heard was his whimpers of pain. Although the day was hot and humid there was a fire burning in the torture hut. She saw another soldier walk to the fire, retrieve something small from the orange flames, and take hold of Shong's arm. Shong screamed when they inserted the red-hot needle into his vein. The hands of her children clenched and unclenched on the fabric of her shirt. She felt the shirt grow damp. She did not know if it was from her sweat, her children's, or their tears. She could see her husband twist and turn on the bed, his whole body rigid. He yelled and he screamed. He cried, and then he started begging. The soldiers asked him to point in the direction that his brothers and their families had run. There was a small stretch of silence. His loud breathing quieted. He shook his head. They beat him some more and then they inserted more hot needles into his veins. Shong's family watched from their open hut; too afraid to yell or cry, the heat of the day gone, they shivered as blood and sweat turned them cold.

Shong was tortured for two weeks. In that time, the little boy with the bullet wound grew quieter, his sleep more restful, and his moans softer. His mother soaked the tail of her shirt in the clay water barrel each morning and wiped the cool fabric across his brown face, down the bony chest that rose and fell with each staggered breath. She used her fingers to trickle water into his open mouth and wet his parched lips. Each day, she grew more confident of his survival. His brother and sister sat close to each other, not moving, listening very carefully to the conversation of the soldiers, a blend of Vietnamese, French, Lao, and Hmong. Each day the two listened for clues of what tomorrow would bring, but each day they had no more idea than the day before. Shong's wife tried to tell the children stories to occupy the long hours of waiting, but it was a futile effort. None of them could be distracted from the men who stood guard.

The soldiers wore old fatigues. They were casual men. They smoked their cigarettes without hands to help, just a balancing act of thin lips. They used their sharp knives to carve into pieces of wood that they had debarked. The children watched, expecting familiar shapes to emerge out of the blocks in their hands, but no recognizable figure ever did. At the end of each day, the men would toss the pieces of wood onto the ground, disgusted and frustrated. Each man carried a gun; some were strapped to their sides and others slung behind their backs. The family could not tune out the grunts of pain and the sounds of torture that came daily from the little hut.

In the two long weeks, the family did not see any of the soldiers bring food or water into the hut. It seemed Shong just lay there, quiet and broken, day in, day out. He made noise only when the soldiers questioned him and caused him pain. One day, the family heard a moan of pain give way to silence from the hut. The three soldiers who had been with Shong walked out in a line, shaking their heads in disgust. The familiar soldier who had been stationed to guard the family told them they could go bury their father. Shong's wife told her two children to stay on the platform to watch over their wounded brother. She braced her weight on a bamboo pole to help her stand. It seemed the muscles in her leg had gone soft. Each step was too small, too stiff, too scared. She swallowed hard. The distance from the open shed to the doorway of the hut was not far, but Shong's wife felt the earth shake under her feet. She felt a great need to stabilize herself. Why hadn't she picked up a stick to help her walk? What example was she setting for her children? She wiped the long strands of hair that had fallen from her tattered wrap away from her face, smoothed the torn shirt down her front, focused on her dirt-stained feet, and ignored the trembling in her heart.

When at last she reached the door, Shong's wife gripped the frame with both hands. The sun was behind her. Her tall shadow touched upon the figure of the small man. She hesitated before entering, looked behind at her children, and then took a deep breath and went in. Her eyes adjusted to the dark hut, a simple room with a fire pit near one wall, a clay barrel of water at one corner, a wooden shelf beside it with a few metal plates stacked. The hut was quiet and still. The floor beneath her feet, pressed dirt, felt firm. The stench of raw flesh rose from the wooden table where her husband was strapped. She inched closer toward his body. She reached out her hands to steady herself on the table. She narrowed her eyes to focus her vision. She saw his feet twitch. He rolled his head weakly from one side to the other. His shirt was ripped open. His bare arms, chest, and legs were crusted with blood. His face was a swollen mass of bruised flesh. He made an effort to raise his hand toward her, but he had no strength so the arm fell heavy onto the wooden table.

Shong went crazy after the torture. The soldiers left him and his family in the small Communist village. They said they had more important business to attend to. They told the family that they had news of a big capture of important Hmong attempting to cross the Mekong to the camps of Thailand. They spat on the ground and walked away. In their wake, Shong's wife begged the old village men who had emerged from different thatched huts to take a closer look at the family and help build a hut for the children. The men agreed. From the village women she got handfuls of seed. A kind couple shared their gardening hoes. Shong's wife began a small garden with the help of the two older children. In a short time, the tips of green onions surfaced on the fertile ground and little sprigs of cilantro grew taller every day.

Shong's wife taught her oldest son how to plant tall twigs by the green beans to serve as guides. She taught her oldest daughter how to weed the garden patch and thin the Hmong cucumbers and mustard greens where they were growing too heavily. The little boy who had been shot grew strong again in body but his mind could not recover. His words couldn't surface despite the effort on his face, the twist and turn of his mouth muscles. His play was no longer what it had been. He struggled with his walking. Each time he got up, his legs would shake and then crumble. He crawled along the walls, sitting close to the shade, to watch his mother, brother, and sister work in the garden each day. Shong looked upon his little disabled son and tears fell from his eyes but he, too, had no words. Like his child, he was no longer who he had been.

Shong started taking fences apart and climbing roofs. He recoiled from the touch of his wife and the affections of his children. He never said he didn't want them near, but he stopped himself from being too close to them. When they ate at the table in the center of the hut they had made into a meager home, he huddled in a corner by himself with his bowl of rice in hand. Instead of sleeping with his wife on the bamboo platform, he made a bed for himself using an old blanket alongside the wall of their hut. When village folk asked whether he had brothers or sisters, he would not say. When people asked him what was wrong, he would not answer. Instead, he cried wordlessly and dug into the earth with his hands, pulling at grass where there wasn't any.

The year 1978 passed without celebrations or feasts. The old folk called out for ancestors to protect families. There was no spirit calling for a return to homes that no longer existed. The younger adults shushed the elderly, warning of ambush and unwanted attention. They were too busy looking out for danger, too tired carrying hungry children, too depleted worrying about death to care about the year's end or a new one's beginning. Many of the children, too young when the country fell apart, had no recollections of how the Hmong had celebrated the coming of New Year's at all, the feasting and courting rituals that the young and old participated in. They didn't know that for centuries their ancestors had marked the New Year as a time for joy and laughter, days carved out of the long months for love and family and food.

In 1979, my brothers and I crossed the Mekong River into Thailand with our families. Across the border, we registered as refugees of war with people from the United Nations. Uniformed guards took us to first one refugee camp and then another, Ban Vinai Refugee Camp, where we would stay for the next eight years. In the camps, we learned of what had happened to Shong from scouts who had passed through the small Communist village on their way to Thailand. Those who had known Shong before the upheaval cried tears of regret as they told us of what remained. They said, "He is not at all the man he had once been. What happened in Laos has happened inside of him. Like the country, he is now a collection of open pits, broken trees, and burnt houses. It is better to remember him as he was."

My brothers and I cried openly to each other. On scratched cassette tapes, we sent words of apology to Shong and his family. We shared memories of when we were still together. We recalled the songs of birds long gone from our home village, the particular taste of the small fish we'd once netted from the cold river nearby, the feel of the dew and the fog in the gray mountainous dawn. We did not tell him how our own lives were in the camps, of the children who died because of bad food, bad water, and disease. We listened as our mother wept into the old tape recorders, pressed her wrinkled hands to its microphone surface, and said in a voice laden with pain, "My oldest son, how I miss you, how I miss the life we shared, how I beg your father to take care of you each day, to send your worries far and your memories away so you may live the remainder of life without the heartache and pain of having been left behind by another mother who could not stay with you or take you with her."

Shong's wife sent us cassette tapes in response to ours. She told us what had happened after we left them, again and again, in every tape she sent. The details were painful. She cried. There was no judgment, just hurt. There was so much hurt she could not hold it inside. There was no one to listen to her in the village where they'd been taken, the village they called home. On some of the tapes, she asked Shong to say a few words to his brothers. We heard muffled sounds we wanted to recognize as his voice coming close and then growing dim. There were no messages of love, no words of understanding.

In 1987, my brothers and I flew on one-way tickets with our growing families to the United States of America as refugees from America's Secret War in Laos. There was no life for us in Thailand. We knew that if we wanted to give our children a chance to live beyond the fenced confines of the camp, we needed to take our chances once more. On the planes, we leaned our heads back against the tall headrests, closed our eyes to what we had known, and imagined futures for our children—not for ourselves, because we knew that we were too old to start anew and filled with too much sorrow, too many regrets. We tried to still the fluttering in our hearts as the plane made its way over foreign lands, the mystery of an ocean.

In America, we lived in cement housing projects in Minnesota, walked between walls of frozen snow, huddled in jackets that did not fit, shoulders hunched high against the bitter cold as we made our way to the loud, jarring factories. In America, we lived in cramped shacks and falling-down houses in California, worked in the expanse of green fields, walked beside irrigation canals full of murky water, our weathered feet in flip-flops and our callused hands gripping the ends of gardening hoes. Our children went to school. Sometimes they sat at the table, heads in between their open hands, tears soaking the open books before them, exhausted and beaten by words they could not understand, formulas they could not figure. The saddest, though, is what happened to our wives. They took off the sarongs of Southeast Asia. Many cut off their long hair. They clipped the silken strands away from their haggard faces each day, made their way to work alongside men and women who yelled at them to hurry up, to meet the quota, to quicken the pace, to unfurl their cracked fingers and stand taller on their broken heels. In America, brothers and sisters lived apart. They called on telephone lines stretched across the wide continent. As far as the eye could see, a person could trace the tall poles, the lengths of fiber in between, the silent songs of love and yearning carried across endless miles.

Every few years, we received news from Shong's two sons and daughter. The son who had not been shot wrote the letters, telling us, his uncles in America, how their mother had died, and how their father, with each passing year, degenerated further. He lost his memory. He gathered fruits from trees he didn't own. He climbed high on those trees. He sat on the tree limbs for hours. He wept the whole while. He forgot to come home. He forgot his children. He forgot his grandchildren. Shong was getting into trouble with the villagers. He was destroying public property. When confronted with his actions, he would simply nod and await punishment. Unsure of how to punish him, his children struggled to keep him contained. When Shong did speak, he spoke his single, continuous wish. In moments of rare lucidity, Shong asked his children if he would ever see his brothers and sisters again.

✧

Every few years, I dream of Shong's father, my only uncle. I never met this uncle; Shong's father died years before I was even a possibility. However, in the dreams, I know that it is my uncle speaking to me. He tells me updates of where he is on the long road to justice. In each dream, Uncle says he is getting closer and closer. He says that more and more people from the other clan have died. The courtroom is filling up with many of the people who had been present that fateful day many years ago.

In the dreams, I always ask, "Do you regret going to argue that case, knowing as you do now that it would result in your death and leave your son an orphan?"

In each dream, Uncle answers the same way: "My son has

continued my fight for family. His death will be like my own, unavenged, and the search for justice destined to continue on the other side of life."

$$\diamond$$

In 2003, our big brother Shong Moua Yang died three weeks after our mother passed away. Big brother Shong was not our birth sibling. He was the son of our father's youngest brother; he was our first cousin. After his death, all my brothers and sisters and I waited for dreams of Shong. There were none. No figure of a small, muscled man with the wide-legged black Hmong pants and the shirt secured in front with a safety pin. No words of wisdom. No tender goodbyes. In the dark nights after his leaving, we talked of hope. We hoped that on the other side of life there is a place where justice is not delivered in a courtroom but around the hearth of a home.

Love Song

I learned how to sing love songs long before I learned how to love. I knew the love of a mother, of brothers and sisters, and the continual turns that good friends take through years of being together. When I married Chue Moua I was bathed in a torrent of desire to love and be loved by her. Throughout our nearly thirty-seven years of marriage, I have told her many times of my love for her, but I have never spoken of the moments in which love bloomed in my heart.

I sang songs of finding love, of losing love, of loving through the ages, of loving through different lifetimes. I have been unable to sing the one song of how love found me, how love never lost hope in me, of how love taught me to grow up, and how love is helping me grow old, Chue.

When we were young, it was the narrowness of your waist, the rise of your breast, the smooth strands of your long, black hair, the clean curve of your cheek, the gentle turn of your head, the feel of your small, soft hand in my own that pulled me, one day at a time, toward the possibility of us. This much, you know. I've yet to tell you all the things that you don't know.

◇

I loved you when the Pathet Lao soldiers came into the jungles of Laos with their guns and their shouts, their threats and their warnings. We had been married for just six months. To save the women and children, the men had to run. We couldn't afford open gunfire. There was no time for goodbye in the hustle to part. You and I stood beside a stand of bamboo trees. The wind blew through the fine leaves. We stood beside each other, holding hands beside a big bamboo truck. You were carrying my child in your belly. You were wearing my one spare shirt. You would not let go of my hand even as the sound of the soldiers approached us from all sides.

I loved you when I pulled my hand free and saw the look of hurt on your face, to be replaced by fear because the soldiers had discovered we were there. I will never forget running away from you into the jungle after my brothers, leaving you behind with my mother and my sisters-in-law and their children, and those soldiers running toward you with their guns high in their hands. You looked young. You looked lost. You looked so brave. You placed both your hands on top of your belly, spread your fingers wide to protect our child; and you watched me run for a moment, and then you turned toward the soldiers and you faced them.

I loved you when I found you again, thin and pale, with our child strapped to your chest, your hand curved around the small globe of her dark hair, supporting the fragile neck. When I stood in the mouth of that mountain cave and I took our child into my arms for the first time, unburdened you from the weight of her during the months of your captivity, felt her warmth and smelled her breath against my cheek, felt softness I had never known, and held something I could never own, I knew I loved you. You, who had carried her so far, to share her with me. You had given her a name to live by, Dawb. Her name was the color of white in our language, white like the clouds on the mountaintops or the flowers that perfumed the air in the cool months of the New Year.

I loved you when I heard you cry in the middle of the Mekong River because the silver necklace your mother had given you had slipped from your neck and you could not free your arms from our child to grab it in the strong current. I heard you cry on the banks of the Mekong River with the baby in your arms. In the months it took to get to the river, she had turned from a chubby baby into a small burlap sack of skin and bones. In the crossing of the river, her head had fallen beneath the surface of the water. She had stopped breathing. Her arms and legs dangled limply from her small, bloated belly. You clutched her close to your body, you rocked on your heels, and you stared not at the dawn or the new world around us but at the world in your hands. I watched your chest rise and fall, and your heart hammer in your throat, as you breathed life into our child, one breath at a time, your body swaying with the weight of a war lost, a country left behind, the future at its end.

I loved you during our first night in Thailand, sitting in the United Nations compound, our child strapped to your chest, when I heard you whisper, "When we get to the refugee camp, I want papaya salad. I want the taste of spicy and sweet, of sour and bitter in my mouth. I want papaya salad when we get to the camp. I want the taste on my tongue." I saw you shaking with hunger. I watched as your thin frame bent over our baby, our baby who hung on to life only because you refused to let her go. Your breast was infected and you were so thin, you had no milk for the baby. You extended your hand out of the shed overhang, your fragile wrist white and delicate, the thin blue vein throbbing with the beat of your heart, so you could catch the rain drizzle. You dipped your wet fingers into the mouth of our little baby, again and again, the long night through.

I loved you when we walked into Ban Vinai Refugee Camp and all you owned was the sarong around your waist, the torn shirt on your body. You walked with a limp because your little feet were so badly torn. The infection in your breast hadn't gone away. You couldn't hold the baby close to your breast because of the pain. You held our little baby strapped to your back. Your hair was swept away from your face, tied back. Your spine was straight. You held your chin parallel to the ground, the way I will always remember you in our weakest moments. Your eyes were trained ahead even as mine swerved to look behind, tried to find the mountains that had been our home, the country across the river, the family you left behind so you could be with me and mine.

I loved you when we had our second daughter, Kalia, in Ban Vinai Refugee Camp and you were scared of her because the night of her birth she cried each time one of us made a move to turn off the precious oil lamp. You were so exhausted, your head against the shirt we used as a pillow, but you looked at her the whole time, the small bundle of red and white in your arms. I couldn't sleep the night through because our older daughter, Dawb, was only a year and nine months old and she had never been separated from your warm embrace in the dark of night. I remember her reaching for my breast, pulling at my nipple, on the brink of sleep, whimpering. I saw you looking at me as

I offered her my breast, a poor substitution for yours, and allowed her time to suckle, held her in my arms so that she could find sleep in a night that offered no rest.

I loved you when you had your first miscarriage. We were so excited about the pregnancy, about the possibility of a son. You woke up in the early morning. You left the door open so the dawn could stream in on us. I was holding the girls close against the morning chill. You were on your way to the garden, to till the rows of green onions you had nurtured in the dry, hard soil. You wanted to haul water from the well so you could water the few rows of cilantro before the hot sun grew strong. You were four months pregnant. Instead of getting up and going with you, or telling you to stay with the girls while I attended to the chore on my own, I allowed my eyes to grow heavy and the warm breath of our daughters to lure me to sleep. I can still hear the screams of the women, the sisters-in-law, each in turn, as they called out to me to run fast. You were at the garden. You said you felt cramps. You were on your way to the toilet sheds when you fell. Blood seeped through your sarong and pooled in the uneven earth. You cried for help. You reached for the women who ran toward you. Your first words were for me.

I loved you during the second miscarriage. I heard you poke me in the night, and the shortness in your breath as you whispered, "The bleeding won't stop." I felt the thick wetness of warm blood between us. The girls slept their deep sleep by the wall. You said, "I don't want to die on the bed with my girls." Your voice broke. I grappled in the dark for you. I felt the tremor in my legs as I lifted you up from the bed. Your head went limp on my shoulder. I started screaming for help. Voices from the sleeping quarters around us: "What's wrong? What's happening, Bee?" Footsteps rushing our way. The door into our room rammed against the split bamboo wall as lanterns were raised. I saw you in my arms, your pale face, your eyes closed. I heard your labored breathing. I heard my mother say, "Bee, you are covered in blood." My heart jerked, and I ran with you to the water wagon. I pushed you the distance to the camp hospital. I stumbled on rocks I couldn't see. I lifted the wagon across the sewage canal, and my heart was hammering so hard against my chest, all I felt was its beat, not the water, the waste, the cold of both in the night.

I loved you during the third miscarriage when I stood beside you on the single bamboo bed and watched as the doctor and nurses circled us. I was helpless as I saw you wince in pain when the needle went into your arm. The nurses struggled to find your small veins. The doctor yelled, "She needs an IV. Now!" Your gaze was trained on the bedpan on the tray. Our baby was laid on the cool metal, on his side, six inches long, eyes closed, mouth open slightly, thin arms and legs, little red fingers and toes. You looked without blinking. I wanted to put my hands over your eyes, to block what you were seeing, to stop the gasps that you expelled. Your eyes did not blink and your gaze did not waver until one of the nurses noticed and took the baby away. You blinked. You blinked again as if you were in a dream, waking up for the first time. You turned toward me, you raised your hand a little, but it fell back on the bed. I saw your hands fisted tight, your knuckles white against the hospital sheet.

I loved you during our fourth miscarriage when I helped you home along the dirt road, your light weight against mine, your feet directionless, your eyes on my face, and the words you kept on saying: "I'm so sorry, Bee. I know how much you wanted this baby. I tried to be so careful. No matter what I did, I felt the baby slipping away. I tried not to open my legs. I tried not to squat. I tried everything, Bee. I'm so, so sorry." All I wanted you to do was be quiet. All I wanted you to do was stop apologizing to me for the pain you just went through. All I wanted was to be the person for you to rest on, to trust to lead you home again.

I loved you during our fifth miscarriage when the little baby was the size of a Coke bottle, its head round and pink, and you kept on screaming and screaming, and crying like you had never done before, deep from your belly, bellows up to the sky. I tried to hold you still but you fought me, in your wash of blood, you struggled away from my arms, moved toward the corner, put your knees up, and put your arms around your knees, shaking so hard. You would get tired, and when I thought you'd given up, you'd start again until your voice grew raspy and your screams were just muscles of the mouth and throat moving. I told you then, "We stop trying. This is our last time. I don't want you to have to go through this again. We have two girls. We will be fine." I told you, again and again, "This is our last time"—until my voice grew hoarse and I lost the energy for words.

I loved you during our sixth miscarriage when we thought it would be our last, and all I could do was bury my head in my hands and cry by your side at the camp hospital. I heard the scream of a mother in pain and then the cries of her baby being born. All I wanted you to do was reach your hand for mine, but your hands were cold and they held your belly, and your eyes looked up at the ceiling fan, and the only reason I knew you were in the room was because streams of liquid flowed down either side of your cheeks. It was you, then, who said, "This is our last time, Bee. I'm not going to try again. I can't make it through this again."

I loved you in the early morning when you got up to stoke

the embers from the night fire, blow into the red lines in the burnt wood, and wave your hand in front of your face to ward off the smoke.

I loved you late at night when the sound of the crickets grew fierce and unafraid, and we could hear the scurrying of mice along the floor, but your head was on my shoulder, your hand was on my heart, and the smell of your green Parrot soap wafted up to my nose and invited me to play in a garden of fresh flowers lush with rain, to swim in streams warmed by the day's hot sun.

I loved you when you set aside the thigh of a chicken for my mother at dinner, spooned the softest part of the rice from the metal pot onto her plate, and made sure she had a bowl of broth by her side to help her swallow down the food we shared.

I loved you when you bathed our girls at the small well on our side of the camp. You hauled buckets of cold water up from the dark depths. You told the girls to close their eyes. You poured the water over their heads. You used your hands to create suds from our soap. You washed their hair, made them giggle with the tickle of your soft hands on their scalps. Your gentle hands ran over their arms and legs, brushed the expanse of their bare backs, slapped at their bottoms. You washed inside their ears, under their necks, in their armpits, everywhere, the crooks of elbows and knees, in between fingers and toes. You held the bowl of water high over their heads and you created a fountain of love for their growth.

I loved you when you refused to let me sleep so that we could talk about a journey to America. I told you that my mother wanted us to stay together in Thailand, that losing Shong in the jungles of Laos was too much already, that we couldn't lose each other in a journey to a country whose language we didn't speak, whose people we didn't know, whose work we probably wouldn't be qualified to do. But you just kept on shaking your head; you said if we left, then so would the others and eventually my mother would have to agree. You said what happened to Shong was a consequence of war, and that we would lose our children to poverty and a life of fear if we didn't take this chance with our fate. You said we were young, still, and that in America even if we never mastered the language, we would learn enough to survive. You said if we never got good jobs in America, at least we could get jobs that allowed us a chance to educate and raise our children so they might one day find good work. You said so many things that when I closed my eyes and my breathing evened out, your words led me into dream worlds where you and I ventured far and grew brave and fearless, we went to a place where buildings shone and walkways were paved, lived a life where there was food on the table the long week through and cars to drive whole families from one place to the next.

I loved you when you did not cry as we boarded the orange bus for America. You sat straight in the seat and you held Dawb in your arms, and when you looked at me there was no fear in your gaze, only a determined focus on the future. You showed me in that moment the heart and the hope that allowed you to walk away from your own mother to be with me, the courage that I lacked but have always loved.

I loved you when we arrived in Phanat Nikhom Transition Camp to America to find ourselves encircled by barbed-wire fences taller than grown men, beneath watchtowers guarded by men with guns. You held the hands of our daughters and stood by my side as we both turned toward the gray peaks far away and breathed our last breath of captivity in a country that could never be ours. Late at night, on the hard cement floor with just a cloth spread on the ground to buffer the cold, we slept with our girls between us. The cloth walls that separated our sleeping compartment from other families' billowed in the night wind. The open entryway beckoned our eyes to the stars in the black distance. Our feet touched in the night and I felt the cool softness of your skin. I knew we would walk from this long night together.

I loved you during the hot, endless days of preparing for life in America in classrooms of people our age, men and women, with hands covering mouths, practicing American words slowly with stiff tongues: "Hello. How are you? I am fine. Thank you. Goodbye." We said the words again and again to ourselves before taking away our hands and slowly repeating the words to each other. Your eyes glittered with fearless mirth as you said the words while I struggled to find the laughter in our situation.

I loved you on the plane to America when your new shirt from Thailand began soaking up the blood of our youngest, Kalia. She leaned into you on the seat, across the hand rest that separated you two. Her head rested against your side, the tail of your shirt clutched in her hands, as she wiped at the blood that dribbled from her nose. I took her from you so you could rest. In my arms, her eyes grew heavy with sleep. The red on your shirt dried to the color of rust, and in the dark chamber of our flight across the heavens I watched your fingers scratch at the dried blood, trying futilely to remove the stain. I watched you hide the stain in the fold of your fingers.

I loved you when we stood up on the bridge overlooking Highway 94, side by side, in our American clothes. We wore jeans from the thrift store. We had on sweaters whose sleeves bunched at our wrists. The church-basement jackets were too big and too long. We stood without words, looking at the cars that rushed below on the fast highway. The sky was a layering of dark clouds. The rain drizzled lightly. Half the trees that rose high from the walls on either side of the highway were bare without leaves, arms reaching hungrily toward the gray. The other half carried brightly colored leaves in yellow, orange, crispy brown, shades of pink, some of them still clinging to the last of the summer green, all a sharp contrast against the day. A brisk breeze blew. We had no words for each other or our new lives. You kept both your hands in your pockets. Strands of your long hair flew across your face, and I knew you would cut it soon, and I could not ask you to stand young beside me for longer than I could stand young beside you. We knew we would age in America.

I loved you when you asked me, "When are we going to get a washing machine now that we are in America?" I hadn't expected the question. We'd walked through Sears and I had seen you touch the tops of the washing machines with their matching dryers. I had seen you flip price tags and look at numbers. I hadn't expected you to ask me that question in the car. The children were loud. They grew quiet. I tried to focus on the road but everything was blurry for a moment. My throat grew tight. Words were hard. All I could do was swallow my hurt and my pride and tell you what you already knew to be true: "I am sorry I cannot get you a washing machine, even now that we are in America."

I loved you when you were pregnant with our little boy, Xue. Your stomach hadn't been growing much. You had been bleeding. You felt pain. I couldn't believe we would have a baby and I chose not to believe it even after the ultrasound. I loved you when you gave birth to Xue. I couldn't believe he would be in our life until the moment he cried up at me, his head all bruised from the vacuum, his little face suffused with purple. His hands were in fists and he punched up at my unbelieving eyes. He was angry because I had not dared to accept him as part of my reality. He was angry because the journey to us was so long. The look in his brown eyes, so fierce and focused, worried me. For the first time, I wondered if I could be a good father to a son. I felt my own reservation and fear in the wrestling of his fist against my hold, the soft fragility of fingers I wanted to fold into my own. I looked at you, exhausted, hair mussed, eyes closed, sinking into the hospital's pillows, and I knew you would leave this for me to figure out, my son and my relationship, leave it to our own making. Your trust in me then and now scares and reassures me.

I loved you all those years we worked every hour we could to feed our children and clothe them and the young ones kept on coming, and our hearts were full of love but our heads hurt trying to work around budgets that never balanced. I loved you on the cold dawns when we dropped off the younger children at my brother Chue's house. We scurried in the dark, up their icy walkway, tinkered with the lock—all in the shadows of night. We sat the children down and took off their jackets and snowsuits. We turned on the television set and placed them in front of the flickering screen. We propped bottles nearby. We watched Xue hold Hlub as Hlub sat close to sleeping Shell, as they waited for their cousins to awaken into the day, for their aunt and their uncle to gather them close in the morning light. Each day you whispered to the children that it was your last day of work, of leaving them. I had to nudge your arm to get you to move. I had to be the one to open and close the old brown door. I had to watch as the Minnesota cold stung your eyes and its icy wind bit into your face, as you tried not to cry for the three little ones and yourself. Each and every day, those long years through, feeling but unable to do a thing to alleviate or help the sorrow that grew and grew inside of you for the time you could not give the children, the gift you could not give yourself, my love for you grew.

I loved you when you said we couldn't get up at three in the morning anymore to go to work away from our youngest children, and you wanted me to change jobs, to get work that would allow me to take care of the children during the day. I wanted to tell you that we were assemblers who did not speak much English in this country. I wanted to ask you who would drive you to work in the mornings and back home again when your shift was through. We only had one car. You were afraid of cars. I wanted to tell you that I was scared to go looking for a job and come home without one. I wanted to tell you that I was scared to go to work without you in the same place with me. Who was going to help you move the heavy boxes of machine parts to the stacks when you'd filled them? What if something went wrong in the factory? Who would hold your hand and run with you outside? How would I ever work in this country, raise the children, without knowing that you were beside me? You were the only reason I felt we had a chance going forward as a family and you were asking us to part our days for our children. I loved them too much to speak to you of my fears, so I said I would look for a job, even at lesser pay, on a different shift, so that I could take care of the children, and we wouldn't have to part with them each morning for work before the light of the sun could comfort them from the dark.

I loved you through all the years when we couldn't be together because we worked different shifts in different places.

Each day, you continued our old routine. You woke up at three in the morning. You brushed your teeth, cooked food, and then dressed. You pulled the front door behind you and the key turned in the lock by four. By five you were at Phillips & Temro Industries in Eden Prairie. I took care of the children until you got home at two in the afternoon. My shift at the new company started at three. We had the minutes in between to say hello and goodbye. I didn't get home until midnight. The only light in the house that was on each night I came home was in the kitchen. The small, moldy house was fogged up by winter and our efforts to stay warm. The house was quiet because you and the younger children were already asleep. The older girls looked up from their homework at the small dining table, called out greetings, made an effort to get up and come give me hugs, but I always thought about their safety first, I always told them not to come close. I was working as a polisher in a machine factory and I didn't want the residue of the chemicals and steel particles I worked with to get on them. I knew that it could cause cancer. I said, "After I shower, I'll give you hugs." Each night, I showered and then I kissed my older girls good night, and then I made my way to our room, where I clung to my edge of the mattress, the three younger ones in between us, their even breathing my song in the night. Rest never came until you woke at up at three again, and I could scoot the children over, closer to your vacant place by the wall, and sleep on my back.

In those years, it was only in my dreams that we were together. There, you reached out to me and you held my hand across the heads of our children. There, you spoke softly and asked me how I was doing with my new work. There, you held me close and told me that I was doing a good job right alongside you, but our life wasn't like my dreams. I never asked you what your dreams were. I was scared of them, as you were of mine. On the weekends, we were shy and angry, tired and exhausted, too happy only to be with the children, unsure of how to be with each other, our voices colliding, crashing, silencing, pleading on the weekends when we shared the same house, the same children, the same life.

I loved you when you said we had to move because our little girl Taylor had gotten lead poisoning in the small, moldy house, and there was no room to breathe. You pushed the air from my chest with your fervor and your fearlessness. Financially, nothing added up. We were barely making ends meet. The house we lived in we bought for $36,500. We were on a thirty-year mortgage. You said we had been in America for sixteen years. You said we had lived in the McDonough Housing Project, in a haunted Section 8 house, in a two-bedroom apartment, and in this rotten house for eight long years. You said you wanted more than nine hundred square feet. You wanted more than one bathroom. You wanted more than two and a half bedrooms. You wanted more for your six children and yourself. You wanted more for me. I looked at you, chest heaving, your short hair touched by gray, and for the first time since we came to America, I saw what our life here had done to you.

I saw your trembling hands, hurt by carpal tunnel. I saw the turn of your head, ear angled toward me, your loss of hearing because of the loud machines. I saw the heavy curve of your shoulders, once clean lines of flesh and bone, muscled and toned. I saw the force of poverty that pulled you down, the gravity that sucked you close to the ground. I saw you trying to rise up in life, one more time, perhaps the last time. I worried about you, and I said, "I want a house like the one you want. I want a house with a big yard where my children can run and I can have chickens." Then, we began smiling, tight at first, rigid with fear, and then we began laughing, crazy and loud, and the children noticed, and the young ones danced around us in joy and celebration. But they said, "We don't want to move. We love this house. We want to stay here." We turned to each other, perplexed by their love of a house that had destroyed so much of our health, and we called in our crazy laughter and reined in our fear, and we said, "We are moving to a better place where we can be together more often. We don't know how we are going to do it, but we will figure it out as it is being done."

I loved you in 2003. In 2003, our oldest daughter was at Hamline School of Law. In 2003, our second oldest graduated from Carleton College and was on her way to Columbia University in New York City. In 2003, my mother died.

In 2003, I realized you stood with our children in the place my mother had stood with me. She was alone in the fight to feed and clothe us. I started worrying that I had left you alone for stretches of the fight, that you alone had been the engine for the journeys of our family ship, as my mother had been in a life without a husband to help.

In 2003, I lost all the songs inside me because I had not written them down, and when my mother died, my heart grew weak and could no longer hold the songs intact. For the first time in my life, I had become an orphan, this person I had always felt I was but had never really been. I looked at our children and you and I knew that even without me, you would raise them to adulthood.

In 2003, I realized what I had done to your life. I married you when you were only sixteen years old. I took you far away from your family. You never saw your own mother die. You had been an orphan for a long, long time. As we buried my mother in the frozen earth, all I could feel was the empty space inside where once my songs had been. My mother had told me to bow down toward the rising sun on the morning of her burial. She said what I needed would come. My mother died on February 18, 2003.

On November 26, 2003, nine months after my mother died, you gave birth to Max, a little boy with an American name, a little boy I didn't think we could handle and had said maybe we should consider not having, a little boy who looked up at me with almond eyes, who smiled my smile. Max was a surprise. Nearly nine years after our youngest daughter had been born, long after we said we were done having children, long after I had tried my hand at being a father to a son and was beginning to feel I had failed, out of the blue, cloudless sky a little boy traveled into our life on the wings of my mother's death.

In 2003, I realized I had never written you a love song.

Cry of Machines

The flower dropped her seeds into the currents of a rapid river, and the Hmong brothers and sisters found themselves beyond the mountains and valleys they called home.

Where once he was a man, he is now tethered like oxen, the stretch of his rope lets him traverse the hard folds of frozen earth. His children live in tattered clothing. The woman he loves moves by the turn of the clock, rushes when her name is called.

Where once his heart remembers a time when the water tasted like the wine and sour greens turned into seasoned meats because his brothers and sisters were by his side . . .

 . . . now the ox is tethered.

The refugee is an orphan.

In Ban Vinai Refugee Camp, most of the jobs were for non-Hmong people working with the international agencies that focused on refugee resettlement. For the Hmong with English-language ability and education, there were a few positions available as intermediaries of culture: Hmong persons selected by non-Hmong individuals, whose work involved conveying messages and rules, laws and regulations, ration details and medical reports to the Hmong who could not speak English, French, or Thai.

I was a Hmong man without much formal education. In Laos, I was making my way through secondary school when the war came to us. For most of the Hmong people in the camp and me, work was what you created for yourself beyond carrying water from the well, scavenging for dry twigs to supplement small fires, taking care of your children and your wife as best you knew how on the crowded bit of dried earth designated for the life of refugees.

There are pieces of paper, stamped with aging red and blue seals, that carry Chue's and my name, in Thai and English. The paperwork says that Chue and I both volunteered our time with different relief agencies. I worked in a laboratory helping doctors, nurses, scientists, and other professionals with simple tasks like transferring vials of blood, cleaning up spills, and learning about the importance of Western hygiene, the dangers of bacteria, the deadliness of diseases, and the costs of illness. Chue took a course in sewing and spent time sewing Hmong ornaments for an organization that gave her a certificate of assistance. We both took the classes that were available on different aspects of Western culture and Western ways of living. There is a photograph of my classmates and me sitting on chairs, tying ourselves with pieces of rope, preparing for a life of safety belts in America. There is a photograph of Chue and her classmates, mostly men, standing beside their Thai teacher, a woman in a white tennis shirt and white shorts with huge, round glasses, smiling because they've just finished a course on American greetings and good-byes. Both Chue and I took the classes gratefully because it freed us from the endless waiting, the turmoil of the jobs we found ourselves doing to survive.

Hmong women are renowned around the world for their embroidery, but not many people know how many backs have been bent permanently for the beauty and the bounty of a story told in cloth. In the camp, Hmong women sat on low wooden stools close to the ground. The ones with babies held their babies in the spread of their sarong skirts between their wide-spread knees. The women sat with curved necks and narrowed eyes. They settled in groups of three or four in the early morning, worked through the hot afternoon, until the light dissipated from the sky and the cries of the night crickets sounded. Each woman held a needle between her thumb and her forefinger and she picked at the white fabric strewn across her lap with her needle and her thread, telling the stories of her people, drawing the animals of her past, envisioning the way life could be again—if we could return the bullets to the guns, suck out the craters from the earth, stop the bombs from falling in the sky and the planes from flying overhead, and if we could stop time and tragedy from happening to the Hmong. The long pieces of thread, bright pink, neon green, and deep blue, rested in crumpled plastic bags by their sides. Without looking up, the women swatted at the black flies that came close to their children every few minutes. Occasionally, one stopped to heave a sigh in the midday heat, to stretch the tight muscles of her neck. When mothers got up at the day's end, we heard the cracking of weary backs. When they reached out to the older children for steadiness, the young boys and girls stood still and grew as solid as they knew how so that their mothers could blink away the blur in their gazes, gain stability with their help.

The children watched in the spread of the long, hot days the white fabric on their mothers' laps grow full of embroidered images of faraway villages, of animals they had never seen, of people they had never known, and of a life they could only imagine far back in the recesses of a war where they were the lucky ones. Each time a mother finished a piece of embroidery, she would hold it up to the sunlight, search for spaces where the light could penetrate, and fill them up with color. Chue was one of the mothers, Kalia in her lap, dozing away the day, while Dawb played and then hovered close at day's end to provide a shoulder for Chue's hand to land on.

The children watched with wide, curious eyes as many of their fathers tried to make a living and hold on to their lives by following the orders and dictates of the Thai men with guns who needed and wanted the transfer of illegal drugs. For a time, I was one of those fathers.

I don't know if my children have nightmares about that part of our life in Thailand, the unspoken realities that we adults faced when they were sleeping or looking away. I don't know what they can or cannot remember. I have tried hard to forget. I tell myself that my memories of that time are clouded by nightmares. In my mind, the first time the Thai men approach me, it is like a movie, a story of fear, a song I cannot sing.

✧

The Thai men approached in the gathering dusk. There were bulges in their pockets but no guns in their hands. The girls laughed and played in the compound yard around us. They smoothed the dirt with their small, bare feet. The sun was hanging like a heavy pomelo in the far western sky.

I stood with my hands at my side. I knew I had nothing but my fists to protect me. I understood that the children would see everything. I did not want them to hear a thing.

The Thai men stood with their booted feet planted wide apart. They smoked cigarettes. They blew the smoke into my face. I tried not to cringe.

The Thai men had a task for me. It was a simple job: they wanted to bring me goods and they wanted me to take them to certain individuals in the camp in the cover of night. They would give me a cut of the profits if I agreed or they could cut me up in front of my children.

They disappeared into the ending day—only the sight of the flickering cigarette butts they'd thrown to the ground, close to my feet, remained as markers that the men had been there.

The girls continued their games in the compound. I stood until the sun had descended fully into the hills and the western sky was illuminated by its last glow, a spectrum of orange and pink that filtered the dust the children danced upon and quieted the world.

I felt as if a bomb had just exploded and I was at its center. I walked toward my girls. I could feel the pebbles beneath the fine dust, rolling beneath the soles of my feet, the rubber of my flip-flops small protection against the reeling earth.

✧

Late at night, Chue stayed awake. She sat on her haunches on the bamboo platform we used for a bed. She turned her head toward the door at the cry of a cricket, the shifting of a mouse. Her hands around her knees, her long hair falling around her— as if the girls were not in the room, as if on the other side of the split bamboo walls there weren't brothers and sisters-in-law snoring away, babies turning in their sleep. Chue's hair shielded her face. She sat in the place where I was supposed to sleep, waiting for me to come home.

Even then I knew Dawb and Kalia had heard about the Thai men killing Hmong men and boys. The men and boys were killed for a variety of indiscriminate transgressions, from searching for wild mushrooms beyond the campgrounds to, in the case of a husband and father whose arms were full of clinging children, failing to move fast enough to obey some demand, some direction, some call for attention.

In the moonlight of Chue's watch, I did not know if I would return alive or dead. I had told my girls ghost stories of fathers who had died tragic deaths away from their families only to return hungry and hopeless. They had asked me if the ghost father would still smell the same in death as he had in life. Would he carry the scent of deep earth or the stink of rotting sardines? They had wanted to know what he would look like. A stiff soldier or a stooped refugee? A man or a boy? The person they knew and loved or someone else altogether? Their questions filled my head as I thought of the girls each night I was away doing the bidding of the Thai men.

My daughters felt the cloud of loneliness around their mother's still form but they did not dare reach for her. They knew that she was in a place only my presence could touch.

Sometimes, if the girls stayed up late enough, they could hear my whistle as I walked the planks on the patio to our sleeping quarter. I liked to hit my knuckles on the split bamboo walls to create a beat for the rhythm of my walk, the melody of my whistle. It was my song at night, and it had the power to pull forth the breath from their mother's lungs and push her into action: a flurry of movement in the yellow light of a steady moon. She rushed to the door and opened it a crack. When my shadow stepped from the night, she opened it wide enough to let me in. When I entered the room, the world became a whispering place, her soft voice sounding again and again, the run of words slurring through her lips, "Is it enough? Are you okay? No threats or blows tonight?"

All the while, my girls looked at me from the bed. When I moved to hold them, I could feel the stiffness in their bodies. I could see the fear in their eyes.

I have never answered their unasked questions. What was there to say? I transported opium for the Thai men with the guns. Every time they called me, I faced them with rocks in my pockets, my only weapon in the event that they fired their guns, hoping to return to my family alive. In the dark of night, I ran between the shadows of the camp houses among the abandoned dogs, delivering opium from one uniformed guard to the next. Each time the thin men took the package from my hands, they thanked me as if I were doing the deed of my own accord, doing a nice thing, bringing an anticipated gift. Each time, I saw their guns and I said, "You're welcome."

The days and months and years passed in the camp and the late-night excursions became as weak as bad dreams in the light of day. I knew that what I did was the work of staying alive but I could not control its power to take from me my ease in the world, my belief in a man and his choices—the place in my heart where innocence hid.

Time cannot erase my memories of fear and shame. It has been over a quarter of a century since we left Ban Vinai Refugee Camp and there are things that I still cannot speak of. I am not afraid of Dawb and Kalia asking me whether I carried illegal drugs to make money or to avoid death. I am afraid of them seeing the shame on my face, shame on a face they know as good, a person they know as true, a man who teaches them scruples and honor, decency of heart, and fearlessness of mind. They have never asked me and I have never said. When we see reminders on television about the dangers of a life caught in crime and corruption, I know my face crumples in compassion. I, their father, who speaks of the world in terms of right and wrong, who tells them that each heart, no matter the circumstance, must do what is right, disappear, and in my place is a man they've only seen through the shadows of memory, of nightmares past, a man who has nothing to say.

◇

Still, none of the work I did in Ban Vinai Refugee Camp prepared me for what America would bring. My life in America has been a series of days spent within the confines of factories. For the last twenty-two years, I have worked with machines. Since we came to this country I have worked for three different companies. I was an assembler at a company that made coolant systems for cars. I was a general machinist for a second company that made wooden plaques and metal awards. With the most recent company, I was a second-shift polisher for different components that are used in industries such as canning and oil drilling. There have been moments in each of these jobs when my supervisors said in different ways, "Bee, you are not here to talk to me. You are here to talk to machines."

In America, my voice is only powerful within our home. The moment I exit our front door and enter the paved streets, my deep voice loses its volume and its strength. When I speak English, I become like a leaf in the wind. I cannot control the direction my words will fly in the ear of the other person. I try to soften my landing in the language by leaving pauses between each word. I wrestle with my accent until it is a line of breath in the tightness of my throat. I greet people. I ask for directions. I say thank you. I say goodbye. I only speak English at work when it is necessary. I don't like the weakness of my voice in English, but what I struggle with most is the weakness of my words.

In Hmong, my children hear so much of my words that sometimes I know they become heavy with the meaning I want to impart. I tell my children that my work in America is not important, but I work hard so that one day their work will be. I tell them that my big dream is for one of them to become an international human rights lawyer and bring justice to stories and lives like ours. I want one son or daughter to cross over the petty barriers erected by nations and states and stand firm for those who do not belong to these definitions. I try to prepare them in the ways I know how. I tell them to watch CNN and MSNBC with me. I turn on Fox News sometimes so they know that life is full of difference in opinions and ideas. I tell them to look at the world around them, but always to hear it first. I tell them so much that they grow tired of hearing my words, my dreams for their future lives and their future jobs, their future selves.

Sometimes, I see the exhaustion on their young faces. I find myself wanting to fast-forward to the future to see where they will one day be. I think that seeing them happy and safe and successful will give me energy to get through one more day and that that day will turn into years. Except I know that the price for the future is the present, and I am much weaker than they believe me to be: as I was in Thailand before the men with guns, I am in America before the men in suits.

I am not proud of the jobs I have done. I have never invited my children to visit on "Bring Your Children to Work Day." My children ask if they can come to work with me. I tell them no. I tell them that the jobs I do are not in spaces that are safe for children. I tell them that they are not the kind of workplaces that I want them to ever know. They say that I cannot hide my world from them. They are right.

◇

Kalia drove into the parking lot of the big gray building I worked in. She tried my cell phone but I didn't pick up. I had told her many times that I was not allowed to use my phone while working. Kalia left me a message. She had brought me lunch, spring rolls and an aloe drink; she wanted to put it inside my car, but she didn't have the key. She said she would hide the food under a bush or beside a tree except there was no greenery in sight. I worked in a concrete lot. Even the buildings were cement, painted gray. A six-foot-tall chain-link fence separated this parking lot and building from the others. Kalia said that she would figure out what to do.

Kalia must have noticed that the entry door to the company was open. She had never been inside a factory before. She must have been curious.

Kalia opened the front entry to find herself in a small space with two glass doors opposite each other. She saw that the door to the left led to an office area with a reception desk, the place where management worked. The door to the right led directly to a space the size of an elementary school gymnasium. The ceilings were high, the walls were bare, and the area was well lit. Large machines the size of Dumpsters, dining tables, and large furnaces were stationed throughout the space.

I had been working at this place for nearly a decade. It was the largest manufacturer of hard materials in the world. I was one of forty-one thousand global employees. I had been working for a small Minneapolis tooling company but in 2004 the bosses sold it to the international corporation. When the ownership changed, there were new rules for us to follow and new people were flown in to oversee us. The company sent men from Europe and South America. The new management asked no questions about us, the fifteen Hmong men on the second shift, a small percentage of their large workforce.

The hardest rule for me was the introduction of work uniforms. I could no longer go to work in my jeans, safety-toe boots, and button-up shirts. When the big company took over, I had to wear blue-lined shirts that said whom I worked for. The company name was stenciled into the shirt and underneath it in small black letters was my name, Bee, followed by the word "Polisher." The uniforms differentiated the factory workers from the office workers. The office workers could wear suits and ties. The secretaries continued wearing their turtlenecks and sweaters. Only my friends and I, the factory workers, had to wear the uniforms.

The big company sent a photographer to take a picture of the second-shift workers. When I showed Chue the photograph, she placed it on the refrigerator, next to the children's school pictures. In the photo, I am standing slightly apart from the group of men. My hands are on either side of my body. I am almost smiling because I had to rush from my station to get outside for the photograph, and the energy of the run and the fresh air had made me happy that day. It was a reprieve from the continual hum of the machines. In the photograph, my shoulders are straight and I am raising my head at a high angle. There are about thirty to forty people in the photo, but I and my Hmong friends get to stand in front because we are shorter than the rest. All of us are wearing the blue-lined shirts and the dark blue cotton-and-polyester-blend pants. Our pants are bunched up at our ankles because they are too long for us. In the sun, most of our balding heads are gleaming. It is our favorite part of the photo.

My friends and I know each other well. We have a thirty-minute meal break every evening (our shift runs from 4:00 p.m. until midnight). We gather in the company's break room, a sterile cement and glass enclosure in the middle of the high-ceilinged factory. In this room, the company has set up a few tables. We sit close to each other over coolers full of Tupperware dishes. All the men, except for me because I have asked Chue not to pack me a meal, bring dishes of steamed rice and an entrée, usually greens with pork, beef, or chicken. Some of them, the hunters, bring more delicate dishes of carefully seasoned squirrel, bear, venison, or duck meat. The aroma of lemongrass and hot chili with caramelized onions and garlic heating in the microwave makes each of the men hungry, particularly me and the conscientiously healthy ones who look upon bowls of clear broth and blanched greens. Mealtime is the moment in our work shifts when we get to bring pieces of our homes to work. Through the food we bring, we show how well we are treated by our wives and children and how much we are loved.

I rarely have anything to show from my home. I tell Chue that I don't need an evening meal because I have to lose weight. I have type 2 diabetes.* The truth is that I don't want Chue to

---

* On November 9, 2000, Acting Secretary Hershel Gober announced that the US government would pay for the treatment of type 2 diabetes for US veterans exposed to Agent Orange during the Vietnam War. Research has shown that exposure to Agent Orange and type 2 diabetes is linked. My father and many of the Hmong men who currently live with type 2 diabetes are not considered veterans of war, so they manage the diseases as best they can on their own despite

pack me any food because she no longer cooks the more delicate and time-consuming Hmong food we both enjoyed. She suffers from carpal tunnel in both hands and is in a long recovery from shoulder surgery after years of working in a bank vault pushing heavy carts, carrying banker's boxes, and shelving and pulling mortgage loan files; Chue can no longer stir, cut, or use both her hands without feeling pain. There is also the fact of Chue's personality. She has never been the type of woman to invest time in the kind of battle that my coworkers wage against each other using food from home. She says the search for leverage in the world using Tupperware containers is futile and pathetic. Other than the rare meals my daughters drop off, usually a few items from an Asian deli, I go to work with fruit if there is any in the house.

Although most nights I have no food to eat with the men, I sit with them at the tables. The men make jokes and laugh at each other. They compare pickup lines from long ago. (One of my coworkers won the affection of his wife by saying to her, "I think you are so beautiful that when we die, I want to be buried underneath you so that your life juices can drip down on me.") They also talk more seriously about all the things that are happening in the world. Many of them listen to the local news. A few of them know how to use the Internet to find international radio programs in languages they can speak well, Thai or Lao. There is always a great deal to talk about. We reminisce about the past, nostalgically recalling the lives we lived in Laos. Many of us carry memories of fleeing from our homes, dodging

---

the fact that many of them were exposed to Agent Orange during the war as children and as US soldiers.

bullets and bombs, and growing hungry and thin in the jungles. Sometimes, when things aren't going well at home, we counsel each other on the best options for going forward. Many of the men come to me for my advice. I love many of the men I work with; they make the hours beneath the bright lights of the factory and the fall of carbide particles bearable.

Each night, we are careful to take off our uniforms, get into the factory showers, and scrub with lava soap before going home to the wives and children who wait for us. We all know that we work with carbide particles. We know that carbide particles cause hard-metal lung disease. Each of us is aware that the glittering particles in the air of the factory are dangerous. The whirling fans that spread the shine do not help our odds. We are confined by the knowledge: every job kills you eventually. Some jobs kill you with a single carefully weighted bullet, while others kill you slowly by floating the pieces and particles of metal over time.

I don't talk with my children about the dangers of the flecks of metal that float around me—just as I don't talk about the dangers of the job I did in Thailand.

The only reason the children know about the carbide particles is that several years ago, I was asked to report to work early every day. I came home with a cough that wouldn't go away. It lasted for months, a dry cough that caused my body to spasm, both during the day and through the night. I drank different cough syrups from the store, but nothing was helping. Chue made me herbal teas but they didn't work. Finally, we decided it was time for one of the kids to take me to the doctor.

At the doctor's office, he wanted to know if there were any factors in my life that could be causing the cough. Through Kalia, I told the doctor that I had been going to work early, and at work, because the first-shift workers were still in their positions, I had to polish metal on a table without a vent or a fan. I explained that I had been breathing in the carbide particles directly. The doctor was surprised by my work conditions.

He started to ask a question, but instead he said, "There's nothing I can do for the cough. You have to have your children write the company and request the installation of a vent."

I told Kalia to explain to him that I had spoken to my supervisor about the situation. The first time the man had waved me off, saying, "Bee, just work." When the cough would not stop and the family grew concerned, I tried to speak to the supervisor again. The supervisor walked away as if he had not heard a thing.

I coughed so much telling the story that I grew embarrassed before the doctor. I didn't want to make him uncomfortable. I used my hands to cover my mouth, but I noticed how the deep lines in the cracks of my hands looked as if they had been dipped in chalk powder against my skin. It was not only that I was embarrassed; I didn't want my daughter to be embarrassed by me.

The doctor shook his head at my story, suggested we get a humidifier for the house, and said that there was no medicine for the problem we were dealing with. He said it was beyond the reach of medicine.

At home, Chue told me to take better care of myself at work. She suggested I turn away from any carbide particles I saw in the air. She told me to try to breathe through my nose only, to remember to close my mouth the whole time I was polishing. She offered to go buy me a mask like the ones the people in Asia were wearing on television during the bird flu epidemic. I told her I would be careful. I told her that a mask would interfere with my vision and that would be even more dangerous than the coughing. Chue patted me on the shoulder like a sympathetic friend.

After the doctor's visit, Kalia did not say much to me. She went down to the basement to the little closet room that the children used as an office. The room was big enough for a bookshelf and a desk. We had the old Sony desktop in the room, the first computer we ever bought for the kids. Ten years old and it was still working. Surrounded by peeling wallpaper, old blue flowers that bubbled in odd places, sagged, and drooped, Kalia did research on carbide particles.

When Kalia came upstairs, Chue and I were sitting on the back patio, looking over the prairie grass and catching the evening breeze. She interrupted us and told us what she had found out about carbide particles and hard-metal lung disease. She talked about the increased rates of lung cancer for workers around the world who worked in the metal industry. I could see Chue get more and more agitated as Kalia went on. I tried to interrupt my daughter, but to no avail. Finally, I said, "Enough."

She said, "You have been working with metal for the last twenty-two years in America, Daddy."

Kalia handed me a letter and told me it was for the company's human resource team. I asked her what it said. She explained that it was a letter outlining the situation and a request for the company not to ask me to go to work without the proper vents and safety precautions. I didn't know if the letter would work but I took it with me and gave it to the supervisor and told him it was for HR.

The company responded quickly and swiftly the next day. A fan was brought in to help direct the flow of carbide particles away from me. The supervisor came with a sheet of paper and asked me to sign on the line saying they had solved the problem. I signed it.

I brought the company's letter of response back to show Kalia. I was happy that my daughter had helped me. I was hopeful that perhaps now that the company knew that I had daughters who could write letters like that, they might be more careful in how they treated me. Kalia's eyes scanned over the letter, but she did not look pleased by it.

In Kalia's silence, I told her about how my coworkers and I were initiating a program to potentially get lucky in life.

Each week, most of us Hmong men pooled our dollars to buy communal lottery tickets. We do Mega Millions for fun but we prefer Powerball. The numbers are always automatically generated. The men who buy the tickets make copies of the lottery tickets so that we each know exactly how many tickets have been purchased and what the numbers are.

Each week, I came home with pockets full of lottery tickets and asked my children to check the winning numbers online. I always began by saying, "Just in case our lives are going to change."

The children accepted the black-and-white printout of lottery tickets from my hands. The full-size sheets of paper were folded and crumpled from being in my pockets. They smoothed them on the dining table. They went on the Internet and checked. Sometimes I could tell they didn't want to. Sometimes they told me that the lottery system is a ruse to win money from the poor and the hopeful. They were not willing to see that poor and hopeful is exactly what their father was.

Kalia stood on the outside of the glass door to the company where I worked. She knew I didn't want her there. I guess she wanted to breathe the air that I breathed. She wanted to know the place. Perhaps she was tired of imagining the space. Kalia turned the handle, and the door opened.

Kalia walked into the big room. She saw the dark hair of familiar men, men like her uncles, men like her father, standing beside tall machines. Each was in his uniform, performing the duties specified for his position. Kalia walked into the room and a few of my coworkers recognized her. I had shown them the photographs of my children I carried in my wallet. The men greeted her with quick hand raises, quick smiles, and quick motions of the shoulder toward my station. None of them were in a position where they could stop the machines and show her where I was. They helped her helplessly.

How Kalia must have seen me: an aging, bald man standing beside a machine the size of a small SUV, staring intently at a laser beam. The man was positioning light on metal. He was concentrating so hard that he didn't notice her until she was about ten feet away, standing still, watching. The machines were loud. She could hear gears running, pistons working, pressure being released. From somewhere behind her a piece of metal fell to the ground. The man did not look up. He finished his task. She could feel the air in his chest, the heat of his focus. The man straightened, he looked up and around. When he saw her, he put up his hand, protected his eyes, adjusted something inside, and then walked toward her. He stopped on his way. The machines hummed around them.

For the first time, she saw me the way I see myself: much older than she wanted her young father to be. My eyes looked blurry, the milky growth that covered the brown of my pupils seemed bigger, and the red veins that fanned across the white of my eyes were thick.

I saw the wash of liquid in Kalia's gaze. I had not wanted her to see how I worked and what I worked with. I had not wanted her to see me this way.

My right hand went to my nose, an unconscious gesture for Kalia not to breathe in the air.

Song for
My Children

Kao Kalia Yang

Doctors and Lawyers

I have not been the father my children have wanted or
needed me to be.
I have been, at my best and at my worst, only the father I
imagined for myself.

From our earliest days in America, my father has said, "Every family needs doctors and lawyers. Doctors heal what is broken in the human body. Lawyers protect the rights we've never had enough of."

It was 1989. Dawb stood in front of the large gymnasium. Her mouth was pressed in a straight line. Her almond eyes peeked out from the black fringe of her bangs. She was short for a nine-year-old—even among the Hmong girls her age from the refugee camps. Dawb stood only as high as her teacher's waist. She was a third grader. We had been in America for two years. Her teacher, a tall, slender woman with the green eyes of a cat, beamed down at her. Dawb was the winner of the North End Elementary School Spelling Bee.

The principal announced her name, "Dare Young," but we knew she was calling for Dawb Yaj.

Dawb got fifty dollars as a prize for winning the spelling bee. In front of our classmates, their parents, and the adults in the school, the principal held a black microphone to Dawb's mouth and asked her what she wanted to do with the money. Dawb looked across the crowd until she found our father, standing in the back of the gym with the other parents. She said into the microphone for all to hear, "I want to use the money to buy my father a pair of shoes that fit. Thank you very much."

My toes curled inside my walking shoes. I felt self-conscious. Our mother had gotten our father's shoes from a church basement. They were too big for him. They slapped the ground when he walked. At parent-teacher conferences, our father held our hands in his and made sure that we all walked carefully and slowly in the wide hallways because he did not want the slap of his shoes on the shiny floors to echo in the classrooms.

When Dawb won the spelling bee, she changed the way our father walked in America and raised his expectations for us.

Instead of saying every family needed doctors and lawyers, my father became more specific. He said, "Our family needs a doctor and a lawyer."

✧

American lawyers needed to know English. Dawb was well on her way. Daily Oral Language was a breeze for her. She came home with new words like "foul" and "impudent." The first time I heard Dawb use the word "foul," we were playing kickball with our cousin Xwm in the front yard at the McDonough Housing Project. Xwm and I thought Dawb was making up the word. We argued with her until she nearly cried. It wasn't until

Dawb ran inside to retrieve the old *Webster's* dictionary that my father had laminated with packing tape to last forever that we conceded. The first time I heard the word "impudent" Dawb was speaking to a neighborhood friend named Ye about me. I loved it. I thought it meant that I was unpredictable.

I wasn't unpredictable. Nor was I impudent. I was seven years old. I was a selective mute.

The lightbulb in the bathroom had been flickering for days. During our hot showers, the flickering bulb made the foggy bathroom scary. I complained to my mother until she decided we would go get new bulbs.

Our family went to Kmart, our favorite American store for new things. My father and Dawb waited in the car while my mother and I went inside.

My mother and I entered the big, boxy store. The lights were bright. The air-conditioning kept the summer heat at bay. My mother held my hand as we walked up and down the aisles. She said we were "window shopping." It didn't make sense because we were not looking at windows, but I didn't ask questions or correct her. I enjoyed the smell of the brand-new clothes as we passed by the circular racks of T-shirts and shorts in color-ful patterns. The shoe section was filled with leather sandals and plastic jelly shoes with tiny heels. There were lovely inflated balls of varying sizes in a huge cage at the end of a toy aisle that my mother did not take me down. I struggled not to look too long at any one item because I knew we had no money. In the household goods section, we walked between plastic mops and brooms, big and small cleaning sponges, buckets of different sizes. We took our time reading the labels of dishwashing liquid and detergent bottles. We passed through an aisle full of white plastic and wooden hangers, plastic hampers, and boxes for organizing things. We searched for lightbulbs as we passed each section, but we could not find any.

My mother worried we were taking too long. I was enjoying the window shopping, but I knew my father would grow impatient. He hated shopping. He didn't like us to be surrounded by things we wanted but could not have. My mother tried to find someone who worked in the store to help us.

At last, we saw a woman with a Kmart name tag filling a cart with empty boxes. We approached her. She noticed us as we got close.

My mother said, "Excuse me."

The woman said, "Yes?"

My mother pointed to the high ceiling.

She said, "Where is the thing that makes the world brighter?"

My mother did not have the word for lightbulb. I was too shy to speak up. The Kmart person listened. She frowned. My mother cleared her throat, trying to rid herself of her accent.

The woman said, "I can't understand you. I don't know what you want."

She was annoyed. Her feet were tapping the floor. Her lips were pursed.

I had never seen my mother embarrassed before, but she was in front of the busy Kmart person. She couldn't find the English words fast enough. She looked down at her feet.

The Kmart person said, "I don't have time for this."

My mother and I watched as the Kmart person pushed the cart full of empty boxes away from us. I was angry. I watched the woman's back until she turned the corner with her cart. I hoped she would wheel the cart into an aisle and make a big mess she would have to clean up.

The floor, the lights, the store were still bright and shiny but I didn't want to be in it anymore. I looked to my mother for a cue but she wasn't moving. She just stood there. I hoped the Kmart woman would return. I hoped she was on her way to get one of the young Hmong workers who could speak both Hmong and English to come and help us. Perhaps my mother hoped for the same thing, because instead of holding my hand and walking away, my mother stood in place. We waited for long minutes. The woman did not come back. When my mother accepted this, something changed inside of her, and I could feel it in the tense hand that reached for mine.

I decided that if the world did not need to hear my mother and my father, it didn't need to hear me. We left the store without buying anything. In the car, my mother told my father that we couldn't find the lightbulbs. She told him to drive us home. I was angry. I was angry because I was secretly hoping to get a package of orange-flavored Tic Tacs at the checkout lines, because I knew my mother had been disrespected, because I knew the word for lightbulb and I had not said anything.

Dawb became our outside representative in English. She was the interpreter every time there were English words at the end of a phone line, a non-Hmong person at our door, behind a counter, at a desk. She helped our parents schedule dentist visits. She interpreted at school conferences. She went with our father to go to buy registration tabs for the car. Dawb was going to be our lawyer.

Dawb and I grew up doing our homework together. At home, we shared the dining table. In between meals, we did our schoolwork: reading, writing, mathematics, sometimes art. Whenever I got stuck in whatever I was doing, Dawb helped me. She did not enjoy doing it, because there was no smiling or joking, but she did not complain. She took it as a matter of duty. Whenever she got stuck on her work, which hardly ever happened, she grew frustrated trying to figure things out. I could only observe from a distance; I didn't know how to alleviate her emotions or provide useful assistance.

Our mother and father felt bad when Dawb was stuck in her schoolwork.

They said things like, "We are sorry we cannot help you. It will be the men and the women in the classroom who will show you where you stand in a larger humanity."

They said big words that could not comfort Dawb.

Our father resorted to stories. It was his way of encouraging us to do our work. At the dining table, we heard about caterpillars and butterflies, grasshoppers and birds, little things that grew and transformed. He created conversations between the winged insects and the beautiful birds. He showed us that he cared through his stories. He fortified our hearts with words. When we were young, they were enough to distract us, to compel our questions and interest, and to spark our imaginations and fire our hearts, but we outgrew most of the characters he created, the narratives he wove, by the time we were in junior high school.

Then, our father took us to the houses of Uncle Chue and Uncle Hue, his more educated brothers, so that we could hear their stories.

Uncle Chue and Auntie lived on the west side of St. Paul, in an area full of decrepit houses. Their house, a government-subsidized four-bedroom, was a two-story wooden structure. With its high ceilings and hard, scuffed wooden floors, the place was cold, even in the summers. The dusty light fixtures dangled from the ceilings, the metal chains on some of them old and rusty. They moved to and fro at the slightest touch. In the dining area, there was a built-in buffet made of dark wood, its back mirror so tarnished that the images it reflected made swaying children look like mermaids underwater. In the living room, like in ours and those of the other Hmong houses we visited during the family gatherings to call in newborn babies and cure sick spirits, there were several used couches, covered with old floral top sheets from church basements and garage sales. In the center of their living room, there was a big plastic mat from the Asian grocery store for us children to sit on. In the corner of the room, there was an old color television set, but it was hardly ever on. Whenever we visited Uncle Chue and his family, we children spent most of our time whispering to each other and listening to the stories the adults told of life back in Laos.

Uncle Chue spent many hours telling us how he became the first person in our family to get a formal education. Sitting on one of the couches, he spoke seriously about how he started school at the age of twenty. His thick glasses glimmered in the shadows of evening as he spoke, his eyes traveling to a different version of himself, a different man in a different time, far from his life in America as a once-educated man debilitated by war.

"It was 1957. The Americans had infiltrated Laos, the French were leaving. A new school was being built in our village. Finally, there were enough children to fill a schoolhouse and get a government teacher. Neither my mother nor father had ever been to school, but they understood that education was important. The country was changing, and more and more news of what was going on in the world entered our village on folds of paper. In our village of Phou Khao and the two villages nearest to us, there were only two individuals who could read, and only one of them could write. Each time a piece of paper entered our village one of the men had to be found.

"Nhia was already married so our parents did not offer him the chance to go to school. It was the beginning of a new year. The harvests had been brought in. The festivities had just ended. It was a typical night. The day was done. We had gathered around and washed our feet in the bowl of cold water by the door. We were all sitting close to the fire, drying our feet before the flames. It was our father who started the conversation.

"My father was a slow speaker. He would start a sentence. You would think he was lost within it, searching from one word to the other. He was thoughtful that way, patient, so very patient with himself and others when speaking. He said, 'Chue and Sai, as you know, a schoolhouse is going up in our village. Your mother and I, we only have money to send one of you to school. The other is needed in the garden. We don't know who to choose for the different paths. We know where the road to the garden leads, a life not so different from ours. This journey to school, it will be a road far from the one we have taken. You two think carefully and then let us know.'

"I was thinking carefully as our father had asked. I sat there in the firelight thinking about every person I had ever seen with a pen in their pocket. I saw the white of their shirts, the buttons going up in a fine row. I saw the hair parted to the side. I saw the shoes with laces. I saw the government officials and the high-ranking military men.

"I watched Sai in the flickering of the flames. His square jaw, the sharp rise of his nose, the brows slanted up. My younger brother with the defiant face. Would he be the one to lead us on a path we had never traveled? I kept my thoughts inside of me. Neither Sai nor I had ever held a pen or a pencil, felt a piece of paper or a book. The garden hoe was our friend. I would honor my brother's decision.

"My mother did not say anything, but her eyes were on mine. I turned my gaze so she would not be able to read the yearning in them. I had always been her most obedient son. The silence stretched around the fire. Around us, the younger children sang their night songs. I could hear the cry of the crickets, the call of the mating frogs.

"Sai cleared his throat. He looked from my mother to my father. He turned to me. He cocked his head. He shrugged his shoulders. The gravity I was feeling in the moment evidently did not weigh on him so heavily. He said, 'I'd rather tend to the fields than the books.' He laughed. He said, 'Let me marry in the next year. Start a family. I am ready for all that. I want to be in the world we are part of, not some imagined place in the future, people we've never been. We will leave the schoolroom to Chue.'

"Sai's decision made mine.

"I started school a week after our family conversation around the fire. I was the oldest student at school. There were a few students who were men already, although they were younger than me. We found ourselves in a classroom full of six- and seven-year-olds. Our teacher came from the provincial headquarters. He wore button-up shirts and Western pants and a belt. He carried not one, but two pens in his front pocket. He had a long ruler. He tapped on the board with the ruler as he recited the lessons. He was very direct and sure of himself. He said that our job as students was to memorize the Laotian script, practice writing it, practice reading it, and then to learn how to write numbers and do simple mathematics. He asked if we understood the concept of an education. The young children looked with wide, open eyes, soaking in his words with no inclination to answer. I tried to find an answer. I tried to relate education to gardening. If we garden so we can have food in the seasons to come, why are we in school? To garner the lessons for the long years ahead. I couldn't say that out loud. I gripped my pencil so hard that first day, my fingers ached into the night.

"I was not an especially smart student, but I was a hardworking one. After each class, I would come home and practice. Afraid to waste the lead in my pencil or the pages of my book, I practiced the lessons of the day on the dirt floor of our home with a twig. I'd write and write and then erase the words with my feet and practice again until night fell and I could no longer see the lines I was making in the earth.

"By spring, I had passed the first grade. The following year, I passed two more grades. My father died during my third year. His death and my mother's grief halted my educational journey briefly, but by 1962, I had traveled as far along in my studies as I could. By then, the men who were younger than me in class had all dropped out. Many of them were married. They joked with each other, saying if I continued to work so hard, by the time they had their first babies, I would be ready to teach them. The idea was born in their laughter. I decided to become a teacher.

"There was a government program to train teachers in a town about two days' walk away from our village. It was a two-year program but in 1962, it had been collapsed into a single year. There was no tuition. All I needed was enough money to buy the soap to wash myself and my clothes so I could stay clean. Meals were provided. Breakfast was coffee and a piece of bread with sweet condensed milk. Lunch and dinner were full meals with rice and a dish of greens, a little meat. All the students lived in a long wooden house with beds along the walls. It was too great an opportunity to pass up. I had learned that teachers were salaried. The idea of constant, predictable income—money not dependent on the shine of the sun and the fall of the rain, the balance of the soil, or the long hours of bent backs—lured me.

"I told my mother what I wanted to do. I did not ask for her permission. By then, I was nearly twenty-six years old. I knew it would be difficult for her to let me go, but with my father's death we had both learned a lesson about life: the futility of holding on.

"I signed a ten-year contract with the Royal Lao Government. I started my first appointment as a teacher in 1965. I was told to choose three places where I would be willing to work. I knew few teachers wanted to work in the rural provinces and the small villages. I thought that I would end up in Xieng Khuoang, my home province. I was wrong. I was placed in a small Laotian village in Luang Prabang. When the village folk found out that a Hmong teacher was coming to teach their children, they were not happy. My boss got a letter questioning my qualifications to teach Laotian children a language and a history I had learned as a Hmong man in an obscure village in the mountains no one had ever heard of. My boss laughed as he read the letter he wrote back to them. It said: 'Every teacher I train is qualified to teach any child of Laos.' I was determined to do a good job and justify his words. I fulfilled the terms of the contract I signed with the Laotian government.

"It was May of 1975 when the Americans left Laos and the Communist Party took over the government. All teachers' salaries were suspended. Genocide was declared against the Hmong for helping the Americans. I lost hold of my pens as I took up a gun to protect my family."

By the time Uncle Chue got to 1975, his voice had diminished. The initial energy was gone. He was tired.

There was no suitable response. We did not have the words to console our beloved uncle. "Congratulations" made no sense for an achievement that could not translate into the life we shared. "Sorry" was not our word to use for a war that we had nothing to do with, a reality that we had been born into. Still, we could feel the weight of gravity pushing on us in Auntie and Uncle's house. With each Hmong family we visited, a relative or a neighbor, we were reminded of how unpredictable life can be, how harsh it can be.

In the wake of our silence, the rest of the adults, our father, mother, and aunt, tried to distill lessons from Uncle Chue's story. They reminded us how lucky we were to be starting school as children, to begin at the beginning line and not have to catch up. They talked about how wasteful we children were in America. They told us how they hated to find half-used pencils discarded around the house as if pencils were like twigs, a matter of going outside and walking beneath the tall trees, the shrubs and bushes. They spoke of how we could salvage the unused pages from our unfinished notebooks and bind them together to make new ones for the new school year. I sat there listening to the adults, thinking about how notebooks were only ten cents apiece at Walmart during the return-to-school sales.

Our visits to Uncle Chue's house to hear the story of how he became the first person in our family to become educated always ended with words we knew were important but did not know how to feel.

But he then dispelled the mood of the room by unleashing a deep breath and saying, "While we are poor in America and many of us have no jobs, in a different country, underneath a different sky, we had nothing to be embarrassed about. I was a teacher, someone who stood at the head of the classroom, not just someone who looked in from the windows or walked by the doors. You must remember this."

After the visits to Uncle Chue's house, Dawb and I would return to our studies at the round dining table with its rickety legs. Sometimes our father walked by with the big, taped-up *Webster's* dictionary in his hands. He did not sit down with us but he'd open the book to a random page between us and say, "Look at how many words there are in the English language. If you learned one a day, imagine how many words you will have in a few years, or in ten and twenty years. Imagine what the words can do together."

Our father loved words. He believed in them. He was hurt when people didn't live up to them, and his words for us and our future were big ones. As much as we loved his words, we were scared of them. What if we failed to become doctors and lawyers? What if we didn't even graduate from high school? Some of our cousins struggled to pass the competency tests for the high school diploma. It took many of them numerous tries. One of them, after a series of failures, had to ask someone else to go take the test in his stead. Another relative who was smart but not handsome got a beautiful girl to marry him by tutoring her on her competency test and making her promise that if she passed she would marry him. High school graduation was a hard accomplishment. When a Hmong family had a high school graduate, the elders would often refer proudly to the graduate as someone who had "completed" his or her education.

Dawb and I were worried about our own abilities to complete not only high school but college. We had no idea what graduate school was then. Few Hmong families did. When our father dreamed of us becoming doctors and lawyers, we wished he were less talkative, more like our Uncle Hue.

Uncle Hue had never been much of a talker. He was the quiet uncle. Whenever we visited Uncle Hue and Auntie's house for his stories, there were few words. We had to use our imaginations to fill in the young man he must have been and visualize the educational journey he had taken. Being with him was like having the television on mute. There was always action but it forced a different level of engagement. Most of the time, Uncle Hue just sat by quietly while our father and other uncles spoke of his high marks in the village school and then his eventual placement at the American university in Vientiane, the capital of Laos. Through them, we learned that in Xieng Khuoang Province, Uncle Hue was one of two students who gained admission to the university by the merit of his test scores alone, not through any external connections. Uncle Hue would have been the first person in our family to graduate from college if not for the declaration of genocide against the Hmong; he was in his final year then. As our father and uncles told us of his brilliance, we saw Uncle Hue looking out the window, making the occasional scan of the room.

At the end of their stories, Uncle Hue said things like, "The English that I know today, I knew coming from Laos."

We all nodded at Uncle Hue's words, accepted this bit of information in the way that he had delivered it as a matter of truth.

Auntie Hue added, "When I first met him, he walked so straight and quickly, like a student with places to go. There was a sense of purpose and urgency to his every step. Your uncle is not like that anymore."

We acknowledged Auntie's words, the same as we had Uncle's, but we had no memories of our uncle moving in the past and our experience of students in America was not necessarily of young people full of energy and purpose.

I tried to imagine Uncle Hue as a young man in motion by recalling images of the leading actors in 1970s Hong Kong productions, romantic stories of poverty and love: healthy, good-looking men with ballooning bell-bottom pants and tight-fitting button-up shirts, heads of dark, thick hair parted to the side, young, handsome men smiling slowly in the sunshine with their bright teeth, frowning pensively, furrows across their foreheads, walking purposefully up and down the cement paths of faraway universities, beautiful music accompanying each step. Although I knew that my uncle was too slight to be cast as a leading man, he had the eyes for it, heavy-lidded, intelligent eyes that assessed the world carefully and quickly.

More important, in the reality we shared, Uncle Hue was still our fastest-moving uncle, a man who worked for himself, not others.

Uncle Hue and Auntie owned a small cleaning service. They had bought it from someone else. The business had a single white minivan with the company name on it, Kristina's Cleaning Service. No one knew who Kristina was, but we all agreed it sounded American enough. None of their customers ever asked for Kristina. They just assumed that Kristina was Auntie and Uncle's boss. When the clients called, it was my cousins who picked up: "Hello, this is Kristina's Cleaning Service. How can we help you today?"

My cousins spoke English just fine and each of them sounded

very professional on the phone, not at all like the cousins we had shared ghost stories with on hot summer nights. It was a fun, necessary ruse, part of our life in America. The same child who picked up the client calls was usually the one who later comprised the janitorial team for the assigned house. No one got paid individually. It was a family business.

Together, Auntie and Uncle and their children cleaned the houses of wealthier folk in the suburbs, the occasional group home for adults living with disabilities, and a few local businesses. They had a client who wanted to know their names and once took Auntie Hue to a co-op to buy organic vegetables. Auntie was impressed that there were people who could afford to pay for watermelon by the pound—unlike any of the grocery stores we frequented. They cleaned a group home where the caretakers had its residents sleep on mattresses so thin that the metal coils stuck out and tore the sheets. Uncle Hue wanted to call the police because he thought the condition of the home bordered on abusive, but didn't because he was afraid that the man and woman in charge of the home would retaliate and kill the business. After conferring with his brothers, Uncle decided to give up that customer so he would not be part of the probable abuse. For the most part, though, their clients didn't care who they were so long as they cleaned the houses and buildings quietly and efficiently. To be quiet and efficient, Auntie and Uncle and their children worked mostly at night. The important part was that they worked for themselves, unlike our parents.

Our mother and father yearned for the opportunity to work for themselves, but they did not believe they could; instead, they believed that one day Dawb and I would. We had Uncle Chue's story to remind us that a person didn't need to be born with education; it was a position in the world each of us could work for. We had Uncle Hue's story to tell us that college was not something new or impossible for our family; it had almost happened, if not for the outcome of the war.

Dawb and I spent many hours listening to our mother and father dream of a future where we would be educated and become doctors and lawyers with specialized skills that garnered respect. Each time we passed a private clinic or law office on the old avenues and streets of St. Paul, our parents pointed out the car window, drawing our attention to the bright flower baskets that hung from the porches and awnings of the wood and brick buildings proclaiming proudly: "Lor Law Office" or "Thao Medical Clinic." I looked at the blooming flowers and the solid doors. I couldn't imagine myself inside them. If I tried really hard, closed my eyes to distraction, I could imagine Dawb walking up one of those sidewalks on a sunny day in the future, opening her leather briefcase, taking out a pair of keys, unlocking the front door, and going inside. Sometimes, I could even hear the door closing behind her.

After winning the North End School Spelling Bee, Dawb skipped the fourth grade at Como Park Elementary School. When she graduated from sixth grade, she won a scholarship to a local Catholic school, but our parents decided against it. They did not want to separate me and Dawb. She was disappointed by their decision, but she understood that I needed her help. Instead of the private school, our mother and father enrolled Dawb at Washington Junior High School to ensure that we would be in the same public school system.

From the outside, Washington Junior High looked like an old hospital. It was a three-story brick building with white trim around the many windows and the doors. An American flag flew from a pole near the front entry of the school. It was on Rice Street, a familiar stretch. Dawb and I had grown up visiting the public library there. We got our drinking water from Tiger Oriental Grocery Store, farther down the small-business corridor. The scent of fried garlic and hot oil emanated from the Chinese restaurants and buffets with their red-and-black letters. But Washington Junior High looked lonely, set apart from the places we knew by a huge, fenced-in grass yard. The school seemed closed. The windows of the old building did not open. The big double doors were locked. We could not hear the bell ring. We were familiar with the playgrounds of elementary school and the voices of young children running around; this empty yard and serious-looking facade did not feel welcoming, but it was the next step on the educational ladder.

Dawb said, "If life is like a ladder, I am the first tier. You'll be the second."

After going to Washington for a year, Dawb assured me that continued educational success was possible but that it was not going to be as easy. There were so many Hmong kids that it was easy to get lost in the crowd. In the classrooms, the teachers tried to teach technology but the lines to the computers were long. Few students got a chance to actually engage with the Apple computers; most just learned by listening and watching. Dawb said that all one needed to do to succeed was show up and be quiet and get As on papers and tests. While Dawb made a few friends and appreciated the teachers, she thought we needed a different educational environment to foster our lawyerly and doctorly possibilities (although I was not brave enough to say I wanted to become a doctor, by a simple process of elimination it was decided by my family that doctoring was a good dream; I didn't fight the conclusion because I knew myself as a descendant of shamans and liked that healing was part of my history).

Dawb discovered Murray Junior High School in a conversation with a high school recruiter who visited Washington. The recruiter said that each school was designed to meet different educational needs. For example, while Washington focused on technology, Murray focused on math and science. Dawb transferred herself to Murray so that she could prepare for me, as the sciences would help me toward my goal. Also, she felt we could get a better education in a school farther away from the commotion of Rice Street. Murray was a small school in a residential area of St. Paul with huge trees and quaint, well-kept homes. It was predominantly white but had decided to open its doors to the influx of Southeast Asian refugees. At Murray, we Hmong students became the bused-in kids. We did not stay after school. Our parents did not go to open school nights to meet our teachers. We didn't participate in extracurricular programs. We did the classroom work and sat together at the same tables during lunchtime: heads of dark-haired children whispering over trays of free and reduced school lunches.

From Murray, Dawb took us both to Harding High School, on St. Paul's east side. She felt we were ready to return to the bustle of a neighborhood school, one where the Hmong students constituted 51 percent of the population. This time, we were at a school with some Hmong kids who were newer to America than ourselves, students with even more brothers and sisters to take care of at home, mothers and fathers who were older or younger, who didn't work, who spoke less English than our parents; we were also at a school with Hmong students who were born in America, who were part of the middle class, whose parents worked as secretaries at dentist's offices and as school counselors. Dawb and I were part of the biggest Hmong demographic at Harding: kids whose parents spoke limited English and worked in the factories and fields, kids who received reduced school lunches and had no older siblings in college but aspired to one day go. In high school, Dawb signed herself and then me up for the International Baccalaureate program and other college prep classes. By the time she was sixteen, Dawb decided to leave high school behind to be part of the Postsecondary Program at Hamline University. At eighteen, Dawb was already a sophomore in college. It all happened fast. She was not distracted. Dawb applied the lessons we learned in school directly to our life: the shortest distance between any two points is a straight line.

Our family could not afford to do without Dawb at home, so she was a commuting student. Our mother and father had saved up enough money to buy another car for the family, a used black Toyota 4Runner with a red stripe across the doors. Each day, Dawb drove the car to college and back. Whenever any of the younger children got sick or needed extra care, it was often Dawb who picked them up at school. Sometimes when she had to, she even took Taylor, our baby sister, to classes with her. Our parents' jobs had little flexibility. Taylor spent many days at college with Dawb. At three years old, she was already sitting in regular lectures. Dawb joked that Taylor was a good student; a quiet child, she would listen to Britney Spears songs on her headphones and draw pictures in a coloring book. Our mother and father were concerned that bringing Taylor might be against the rules, but Dawb assured them that unlike their workplaces, the college couldn't kick her out. There was no refuting Dawb's statement. Together, our whole family was working hard to make sure that life in America was possible. At the forefront of our efforts was Dawb.

At home, across from me at the family dining table, Dawb read her books and wrote her papers. She often tied her black hair back in a thick ponytail. She wore a big sweatshirt with the words Hamline University on it. Her hands flipped through heavy communications philosophy textbooks respectfully. Her gaze chased the words on the page. Her nails, painted with a clear coat of varnish, glimmered as she tapped her fingers against the top of the table to a rhythm in her head. When she came across a good idea or a nice line, she called for my attention. Sometimes, it bothered me because I, too, was doing my homework or thinking about doing it, but I knew it would hurt her feelings if I didn't look up and ask, "What?"

Dawb told me about people in the world who ate from silver spoons. She saw it on *Masterpiece Theatre*. She took our parents' silver coins, gifts from Grandma for their old age, and placed one on my tongue so I would know the taste of silver in my mouth. I was surprised by how soft the silver felt, how malleable it was to my bite. Dawb told me that acting happened in life, not just in the movies. One of her teachers, Mr. Graham, was an actor in the local community theater. He read dramatic lines from *Hamlet* and *Othello* to them in class. The first time Dawb discovered eating out in an American restaurant with some of her Hmong friends, at Perkins, she took me the very next day. We ordered eggs Benedict for dinner and were blown away by the hollandaise sauce. When I turned seventeen, she used a hundred dollars from our parents' checking account and bought me my first real diamond ring from a jewelry store in Maplewood Mall, a speck of shine set in fourteen-karat gold. All my life with Dawb, she has struggled to give me the best of what our lives could offer and afford.

Dawb was the child born in Laos, the last one in our

extended family to be born in the old country. She crossed the Mekong River at little over a month old in the arms of our mother. She nearly died in the crossing. On the banks of the Mekong, her small, starved body was shrunken like a wrinkled burlap sack; it was only the fluttering of her eyelids that told our mother and father that she was still alive. She had grown so weak that her chest no longer rose or fell. Her mouth was a sunken hole in the dark of her struggle to hold on to life. The fact that Dawb did not die, and the strength with which she pursued life, humbled our mother and father and, through their stories, the younger children and me. None of us saw trouble coming.

It was a weekend. The day was bright with autumn sunshine, but the weather had started getting colder. The leaves on the big tree in our front yard were turning away from the green of summer. While it looked like the color was being sapped from some of them, others turned fierce yellow and orange. There were leaves that had begun to resemble ripened apricots hanging off the old branches of the aspen trees along the highways. Other leaves on other trees turned pink like budding roses in springtime. Many of the oak leaves began browning around the edges, crinkling up, dry as burnt paper. In the mornings when I walked to the bus stop, white clouds of moisture rose up from my nose and mouth. It impressed me how warm and wet my breath was, and how moist the core of me must be.

On this day, the family was together inside the house. Dawb, Xue, Hlub, and I were reading by the front window, lying on our bellies with books in front of us or sitting down with books in our laps. Shell and Taylor, too young to do homework, sat in front of the television watching an *NSYNC music video that Dawb had gotten them, singing along to each of the songs, occasionally getting up and swaying, left to right, left to right. Dawb and I both had books in our hands, but we weren't reading them. Instead, we were talking about a fishing trip we wanted to take to Lake Red Rock in Iowa in the spring. Other Hmong families had gone and they'd returned with stories of how anyone could catch fish there. Friends and relatives talked about white bass that leaped at empty hooks. Our mother and father sat close to the younger girls on the sofa, talking to each other.

Our father had taught us how to fish at a young age. When we first came to America, it was what the more established relatives took the newcomers to do in the summers for fun. Before we could afford fishing poles, we fished with empty soda cans; we wrapped fishing line carefully around the body of the can, tied on floaters and hooks at the ends, and cast our lines by gently flicking our wrists toward the lakes. While the cans were no good for sizable fish, they worked tremendously well for the little sunnies and bluegills we caught at Como and Phalen Lakes. Our father had taught us about fishing as our uncles had taught their sons. By the time Dawb and I went to junior high, our father had gotten us fishing poles and we were quick and efficient at stringing them, securing bobbers, sinkers, and hooks. We felt no qualms about hooking wiggling worms or slippery minnows to the ends of our fishing lines.

At the beginning of each school year, our father promised us fishing trips in the summer if we got good grades. Dawb always got good grades. I did fine. We knew that doctors and lawyers were not made overnight, and so it was that we went from one year to the next dreaming of the fishing trips we would take.

That autumn day, Dawb and I were loud in our talk of

fishing. The house was full of the comfortable chatter of a big family in close proximity. The scent of jasmine rice from the rice cooker lingered in the air and created steam on the windowpanes. The windows made the bright world outside fuzzy with light. The electric flame of the heating unit in the living room licked at the air with its blue tongue.

Our mother and father were talking about a Hmong woman they knew who was dating a white man. The white man and the Hmong woman had gotten into a fight and he had beaten her up, badly. Our parents were so engrossed in the conversation that they did not notice when Dawb and I grew quiet in our talk and started focusing on theirs. Our father said that the woman should have never been with the man in the first place. It was dangerous to cross cultures and to pit a Hmong woman's small fists against that of a much larger white man's.

I thought the conversation was interesting. Dawb did not.

Dawb's book closed. She slammed it against the carpet. I watched as she got up and moved toward our parents. She pointed a finger at our father's face.

She said, "Racist."

Our father slapped Dawb. The sound of flesh on flesh hung in the air. The force of his hand turned her head. In the seconds it took for Dawb to turn her head back toward him, my mother was in between them.

Our mother and father hardly ever resorted to physical punishment. When it happened, it was restricted to the occasional rubber band across the butt, and usually only when one child had purposely done something hurtful to another or something dangerous to themselves after a series of verbal warnings. There was a process in our family. We gathered as witnesses. There was a conversation. A parent asked, "What part of you do you want the rubber band to hit? Do you know why I am using the rubber band? Are you going to do that again?"

This time there were no rules of engagement. Dawb and I had stopped getting punished for our actions years ago. We were part of the adult world. We interpreted for our mother and father. We took care of the children. We had access to their bank accounts. We bought groceries. No one expected Dawb to respond so fast to a conversation we were not part of; no one expected our father to respond so painfully to Dawb's voice breaking into our parents' talk.

Before this point, education had always been a path full of light, the direct road to becoming doctors and lawyers. In the past, we had shared things we learned with our mother and father—Christopher Columbus, slavery, the Civil War, and affirmative action. It had all made sense, the American story that we were entering, the place we were in. Never before, though, had the lessons in school penetrated so deeply and been applied so emotionally in our home.

The problem of education had entered our lives. Uncle Chue had not talked about it. Uncle Hue had said nothing about it when his brothers told the story of his academic success. No one had told us that education could change the way you felt about the world and the people in it, that it could give you words to use, and actions to take, not in support of those who love you but as a response to them, that education in America would make our father and mother less educated in our eyes.

Even then, I recognized my father's action for what it was. It wasn't an effort to discipline. It was an unmediated reflex, an instinctual response to Dawb's finger in his face, her one word and all that it implied: you are ignorant, uneducated, and wrong.

My mother stood between them. She had a hand against my

father's chest—although he wasn't moving. His heavy breathing. Dawb's breaths were as rampant as his. She did not pull back or put her hand to her face. Dawb glared at our father, daring him to do more. Our mother could see that our father was holding Dawb's gaze. Neither one was backing down. Our mother started crying. She told our father to calm down, this minute, right there and then, for both of them to stop immediately. She turned to Dawb. Our mother put her arms around Dawb. She turned to glare at our father.

Our father sank into the sofa slowly, like an old man with stiff legs. We could hear the squeak of the sofa as his weight fell into it. He placed his head in his hands and leaned over his knees.

The sunlight was leaving the day. The sky had turned gray. The temperature was dropping. A light drizzle of white flew in odd directions in the growing wind outside our window.

Our father said, "I did not send her to school so she can come home and call me out on the things I have not learned, judge me on the comments I make in my own home."

Dawb walked away from Mother. She walked past all of us. The children and I stood in hushed silence. I wanted one of them to reach for her, to remind her that we were there and looking, to help her remember to act like our role model. None of us did a thing. Dawb didn't say a word. She started moving fast. She grabbed her backpack, stuffed her books inside, sat down by the front entry, pulled her walking shoes on, ran to the key hook on the wall, and grabbed the keys to the Toyota 4Runner. The front door slammed shut after her.

Our mother called for her, "Dawb, *me naib*, Dawb, my dear!"

The engine of the Toyota 4Runner growled into motion. We

heard wheels on the pavement. The children and I got to the front window in time to watch Dawb step hard on the gas down York Avenue, the exhaust coming out of the muffler in a sputtering of gray smoke.

Our mother has always said that Dawb and our father carry the same heart. She has his dark fire, his defiance, his disobedience. Our mother hates their short tempers, their bad attitudes, their restlessly high expectations of each other, and their violence. She cannot understand how two people can be so much alike and point to each other as inaccurate and wrong.

The children and I did not go near our mother or our father. Instead, we gathered the books and cleaned up the living room. I turned the television off. I didn't turn on the lights. We sat in the shadows of evening. There was nothing to look at on the dark screen but the reflection of our father, shoulders down, head in his hands, on the sofa.

None of us had anywhere to go. Our house was nine hundred square feet—two and a half bedrooms, a small bathroom, and then the kitchen. We watched each other.

It was dark when Dawb came home. Our mother looked up at the sound of the front door opening and, at Dawb's appearance, asked if she had eaten yet. Dawb shook her head. The normal chatter of our house had resumed in her absence. Dawb stared at us as she walked past. Her backpack looked fuller, heavier than when she had left the house. We wondered what was inside, but none of us asked.

Dawb stopped speaking to our father for the rest of the school year. At mealtimes, I noticed how our father made a special effort to call her to the table. He used his softest voice. We all knew he was sorry he slapped her, but Dawb did not care. She walked to the table at her own pace, as if he had not called, ate at her own leisure, looked out the window at the old house next door when her gaze wandered from her plate. Dawb acted like she did not see or care that our father was at the same table. In a room, she walked out whenever he entered.

When our father was not home, I heard our mother beg Dawb to speak with him. She told Dawb how much our father missed her. She told Dawb how sorry he was. She explained how in hitting Dawb he had slapped himself. She said that all parents who hurt their children feel the blow in their hearts. She could not say what she was only beginning to see, that the educational paths they had urged us to walk, and cheered for us to run, were full of treacherous holes they could not help us navigate. Dawb listened to our mother with no emotion on her face. Our mother got angry.

She said, "I have heard many stories of parents raising children and I have seen many parents raise their children, and I thought I knew the hardness of the work, but you, you are the most rebellious, hardheaded, hard-hearted girl I have ever known. What kind of daughter points a finger in her father's face? What kind of daughter walks around, month in and month out, living as if he was dead?"

Our mother cried. She had fallen in the rift between Dawb and our father. Without their help, she didn't know how to get up.

When Dawb was not home, our mother talked to our father, reassuring him that Dawb still loved him.

She told him, "Bee, she is your daughter, she is like you. She loves you as you love your own mother."

When we were alone, the children and I asked Dawb to forgive our father. I said it was wrong of him to slap her. I knew she was hurt. I told her that she was carrying her anger and hurt too far. I couldn't believe that she could just stop loving our father like that. She shrugged her thin shoulders at me and pulled one of the younger kids close for a hug. Neither Dawb nor I could talk about the loneliness that grew inside us with every new idea we loved, every new place in the world we wanted to visit, every drink we thirsted for, every dish we yearned to taste beyond our home. We were supposed to become doctors and lawyers and everyone would celebrate at the end; we didn't know that we would have to become those things alone.

Outside, the heavy snow came. At first the snow was white and it made the crumbling neighborhood we lived in nice and clean. Even the dying, diseased trees looked dressed up in the white spread across their peeling limbs. The line of lilac bushes between our house and the abandoned house next door became a magical entry into another world. We made tunnels in the snow. It was great for the first month or so and then the snow got dirty and the winter winds got fierce, and the time we spent outside waiting for school buses to come in the mornings became bitter with cold.

Getting up in the morning for school became an uncomfortable chore. Everything felt damp in the small, moldy house. In the mornings, we lined the heat fixtures with our socks so they could warm up before we put them on. When we breathed deeply, we could see our breath turn to fog in our very own home. Our father tried his best to make us feel better with his words, but that year he had more trouble than usual. Whereas once he'd tell us wonderful tales of little flowers freezing in winter, only to come alive in spring and summer, all he could manage that winter was, "I'm sorry the cold is so fierce. Come close."

By winter's end, the snow had grown dirty and heavy with

the sand and the salt that the city trucks released on the streets and highways. The little brown birds stopped pecking at the snow; instead they sat hunched in balls of feathers on the electric lines in the continual gray. The tall remains of summer grass poked out of the snow in the abandoned yards, a standing reminder of seasons past. The world had grown dull and heavy with cold, sharp ridges of frozen ice. We harbored hopes of spring, but latent with winter, we shivered through one cold day at a time, closer to each other to keep warm. As the cold eased away, we found ourselves all growing gentler to each other, including Dawb and our father.

When spring finally came, there was a collective sigh in our home. Our neighborhood came alive with the warm days. The line of lilac bushes unfurled their leaves, then opened their fragrant blooms, and the air grew sweet with their scent. The yellow dandelions popped up in the beds of green grass. The squirrels raced down the big trees and stood like prairie dogs on the garbage cans before the garbage trucks made their morning rounds. Children filled the streets after school. The African American neighbors took to the rocking chairs on the porch. The old Hmong men and women gathered in their tiny gardens. Laughter and talk floated in through the open windows late into the night as teenage boys and girls played their music loud and moved to the rhythm beneath the streetlights.

Our father and Dawb's relationship, like the coming of spring and the diminishing of the cold, came naturally. There was no drama, no deep conversation that I knew of, just the expiration of the tabs on the Toyota 4Runner.

Our father said, "Dawb, let's go buy tabs for the Toyota 4Runner today so that you don't get a ticket."

Dawb said, "Okay, Daddy."

They left the house together. They returned later. Eager to accept the peace, we did not make a big deal out of the truce, and thus the loneliness in our educational lives grew as a normal consequence of our dreams and went on beneath the surface of our family as we journeyed deeper and further into becoming doctors and lawyers.

That summer, our mother and father rented a minivan and our family went fishing at Lake Red Rock in Iowa. We left the house a little after midnight. Our father and Dawb took turns at the steering wheel on the four-hour drive. The children slept most of the way. My mother and I took naps. In between sleep and wakefulness I could hear Dawb and our father talking of family, of school, of doctors and lawyers.

We arrived at the lake in the early dawn. As the sun made its appearance into the day, the family found places beside each other along the lakeshore. The fish did not leap out of the water. The bugs flew into our faces and we batted them away with our hands. Our father and mother reminded us that the best fishermen were the most patient ones. We battled each other to be patient.

The day was long and exhausting. The sun grew intense. The lakeshore became crowded with other Hmong folk who had heard stories similar to ours. Every few hours, there was a shout of excitement: someone got a fish. We left our posts and scattered close to the lucky person to admire the white bass the size of children's feet. We had Kentucky Fried Chicken with sticky rice for lunch. The balls of glutinous rice in our hands had never tasted so good. We licked the oil from the chicken on our fingers despite our mother's pointed looks at the napkins in our laps. We drank soda, which we rarely bought because it was too expensive and sugary. It was our first and best vacation, if only the fish had really leaped out of the water onto our empty hooks, and the stories we'd heard were true.

As the sun made its descent over Lake Red Rock and into the line of green trees behind our backs, the wind blew its cool breath and brought on the evening clouds. There were patches of yellow and white wildflowers in bloom around the shoreline and they attracted the winged insects. Tiny little lavender butterflies flittered and fluttered about. The small creatures flew in solitary patterns around the patches of flowers.

Dawb and I stood side by side, watching as the water grew strong in the evening breeze and our bobbers moved in the push and pull of water. The lake became more menacing in the coming night. Old stories we knew by heart of dragons who entered villages looking for beautiful girls made their way into our consciousness, but we dared not talk of the dragons lest they lived in America, too. Instead, we talked about the boy Dawb had a crush on and the Thai actor who would perhaps one day marry me, thoughts of becoming doctors and lawyers far, far away.

The whole world was perfect then, on the shore of Lake Red Rock. Our mother and father, brothers and sisters, were close by. We breathed in the summer air. We watched as the first stars grew visible in the night sky. With each breath we took, school became more distant, the weight of books and ideas, the things we spent the school year carrying on our backs, lifted a little from our shoulders. It was enough to be Dawb and Kalia, the oldest daughters of our mother, Chue Moua, and our father, Bee Yang. We were happy. We needed to be no more and no less than what we were in the moment: young girls fishing.

The Son Must Rise

Where is the moon?
Where is the sun?
I am blinded by the light of the bombs.

At an event, I heard a Native American man tell a story about a young man named Xue.

The man said, "This boy, Xue, comes up to the reservation. He is a Hmong kid. We don't see them much up there. A few days in, my son comes and tells me, 'Xue is cool.'

"What is cool anymore? These young folks, they take a word and they change its meaning and they use it left and right. So I don't know what cool is. I see no harm in cool so I don't say anything much about it.

"Xue has been with us for a few weeks and it is duck-hunting season. My son really likes Xue. He tells me one day, 'Dad, Xue really wants to go duck hunting with us this year. You mind if I take him along?'

"What's a father to say?—I say, 'Okay.' Xue comes along and he is this young man, heavy on the walk, quiet at our first meeting. He shakes my hand and I shake his hand. My grandson

wants to come along. Our tradition says if a boy wants to journey with his father and his grandfather, then it is their job to
take him along. So, we got to the woods. The little boy runs
ahead with his father. Xue is walking between us through
the trees. I am an old man. I run out of breath. I slow down.
I lose sight of my son and grandson. I never lose sight of Xue.
The distance between us does not change. I realize at some
point that Xue is keeping my pace, waiting for me. 'Cool,' I
think to myself.

"We are on the canoe in the lake and my son is spotting
ducks left and right. I am sitting, calm on the water, staring at
the sky in the liquid depths around us. My grandson, he is only
seven. He sits and he plays with the water, runs his hands into
its silvery surface and he leans in. I get worried and I am about
to yell for him to be careful, then I notice—the whole time,
Xue has a hand on the boy's shirt. Xue's hold is not so tight
that the boy even notices in his play, but it is tight enough that
a grandfather can sit back and marvel at the picture of the clouds
in the mirror of the water.

"'Cool' is a word that I still do not use easily or well. I worry
that I misuse it. It has been many months now since I've known
Xue. I love that boy. His tread is heavy on the earth, full of the
weight of too much going on, but his hold is gentle, his step is
firm; it does not dig into the surface of the earth, it turns the
ground firmer. Xue is a good man.

"I am sad to know that there are systems on earth, powerful and mighty systems that can overlook the coolness of such a
young man as Xue. What kind of world are we living in when
a man's deeds—the goodness of Xue—cannot translate into a
résumé or a job? Xue was sent up to the reservation because he
did not fit into the system. I question that system here and now."

I shared the story with our father because he has a Xue, too. His Xue's coolness, too, cannot be translated into good grades, a strong résumé, or a good job. The Xue the Native American man is talking about could easily be ours.

Our Xue was born on September 19, 1989. Other than the day we got to America, July 27, 1987, Xue's birthday is the only date that our father remembers.

On the day that Xue was born, our father called all his brothers and sisters, who had sons already. There was talk about how Xue was our mother and father's first American. There was talk about how Xue was the one who had made it safely to life with us when six other boys had tried but could not. Over the phone our grandmother told my father, "Bee, you finally have a son. I have been eager to love him with you."

Xue was a small baby. His head was twice as long as it should have been and it was shaped like a pimple. He had been sucked out of the birth canal by a machine. Instead of being reddish or whitish yellow, he was bruised like an eggplant. His delivery into the world was a tough one. No matter how much my mother pushed or how many incense sticks my father burnt to our ancestors, how many times he pleaded with the spirit of his father, Xue could not be propelled out of her womb. After nine hours of pushing, my mother had no more strength to push. Her body sagged into the hospital bed despite the waves that caused her round belly to grow hard as a rock. It was her doctor, Dr. Wessler, an old woman with gray hair and a firm hand-shake, who said it was time for an intervention. In the end, it took Dr. Wessler's strong grip and a vacuum machine to get the baby out. Our mother and father worried about Xue's life from the moment of his birth, but they also marveled at his resilience.

As a baby, Xue did not sleep at night or feed well. Our

mother and father took turns sitting the night through with him in their arms, rocking him back and forth. Late at night, I stared at the dark ceiling in the room I shared with Dawb, listening to Xue's urgent cries, wondering when they would ease up, trying hard to find any hint of exhaustion in his voice. There were no such moments. Our father said that Xue could sing song poetry like no other baby he'd ever heard. Some nights Xue's endless cries bothered me so much that I'd get up, go into the hallway, and voice a complaint: "Xue is a crying machine with no Stop or Pause button."

Our mother and father simply nodded their heads in agreement.

Our father ushered me back to bed, saying, "Go to sleep; pretend his cries belong to the night insects. Instead of the fall, pretend we are in the depth of summer. Let warm thoughts help ease your body into sleep."

He'd look at Xue and sigh and say, "Go to sleep so your big sisters can sleep. They have school tomorrow."

Our mother, though, would only give me a soft, tired smile and tell me to close the door to the bedroom firmly so that it would dim his cries. I'd pause to see how, her hair clipped back from her face, she cuddled the tiny bundle of cries in her arms, shifted him close to her neck, breathed into his tuft of light brown hair. Despite the lack of sleep and the hard labor, Xue's birth gave my mother a softness that made her beautiful. Her skin looked creamy and her eyes glowed with a gentle light. Unaware of me watching, she offered Xue words of love: "Shhhh. Don't cry. Why does my son cry so much? If I knew what was hurting you, I'd make it go away. Hush, my little son."

In bed once more beside Dawb, I still heard Xue's cries through the closed door. I could not hear my mother's slippered steps on the hard tiles of the floor but I caught her soft words billowing to cushion Xue's crying. I knew it had been nine years since she'd held a live baby of her own close to her breast. I knew that she never got to hold the little ones who had died in Thailand. The more I thought about the gift that Xue was in her life, the less annoying his cries became. Eventually my breathing evened out, his cries sailing me to sleep on the winds of summer, and it would be his cries once more that would wake me up to the cool of the autumn mornings.

In those early days, deprived of sleep, our father said things like, "Either Xue has a lot to say to the world or he is trying to unload all the rainwater he carried from the clouds so that he can lighten up for life with us."

With Xue in his arms, rocking back and forth, my father sang baby songs, Hmong words set to melodies from ceremonial chants: "*Ua neeg tau los tau, nyuam nyuam quaj tsis tseg . . . ua neeg tau los tau, nyuam nyuam quaj tsis txaus.*" (The shaman's rituals won't stop the baby's cries, the shaman's words can't quiet the baby's cries.)

The sound of our father's voice would calm Xue down. I'm sure it was because Xue didn't understand the words about how healing ceremonies can't calm crying babies. As our father sang, Xue's crying would cease. Eventually, he would fall asleep and his small open mouth would close slowly. Occasionally, his pink tongue licked at his chili-red lips and allowed for glimpses of pale gums. When he woke from his naps, his eyes were round beneath the light whisper of his brow. His misshapen head had a soft spot the size of a quail's egg on its top. The skin on his face was so soft to the touch that I worried I would leave fingerprints when I pressed a little and saw a small island of white in the sea of red.

Xue was precious.

When Xue was nearly a month old, our mother and father had a family gathering at our house to call his spirit home. They spent six hundred dollars on a cow and bought a hundred-pound bag of Kokuho rice. It was the first cow we bought in America at Long Cheng's butchering house. It was the first big party we had in America. Family and friends came at dawn to help prepare food in the backyard on propane stoves. There were vats of sweet-smelling rice and huge pots of hot, boiling meats. Folding chairs, borrowed from the houses of cousins and neighbors, aunts and uncles, were set up outside the small yard. It was all Hmong style.

The day was busy with people I knew and didn't know coming and going. Our father held a crying, angry Xue in his arms as loved ones vied with each other to tie white cotton strings around his small wrist and wish him a long, healthy life filled with good health and prosperity. There were so many strings that they climbed both Xue's arms up to his elbows. We feasted on trays of seasoned laab, beef that the young men in the family had chopped with Hmong knives on huge chunks of smooth wood that we used as cutting boards and cooked up quickly in large pans over the hot propane stoves. Everyone present agreed that the laab was rich in the flavors we loved: mint and cilantro, Thai basil and fresh chilies, lemongrass and Kaffir lime leaves, roasted rice powder, and a perfect blend of salty fish sauce and sour lime juice. We ate the laab with chunks of sticky rice and bits of lettuce and cabbage. We ate bowls of rice noodles rich with chicken pieces, coconut milk, and spicy red curry sauce. The children slurped down cups of sweet tapioca dessert with tiny bites of fresh cantaloupe and durian fruit from jars. The food was fragrant and robust—as was our newest family member. Our aunts and uncles and cousins stayed late into the night to help with the celebration of our mother and father's first son.

After the more distant relatives and guests had gone, a few of my aunts and uncles lingered to help with the cleaning up. Xue had fallen into an exhausted sleep. I volunteered to watch over him. A young cousin offered to help. We all went upstairs together. My father placed Xue on an old flat pillow on top of the special blanket that Grandma had brought from California. It was a furry blanket with a "Made in Mexico" tag on it and it carried the image of a large yellow-and-black-striped tiger. Grandma had told Dawb and me that the tiger was powerful enough to scare away nightmares in the dark. We loved the blanket. I was happy to share it with my little brother. My father positioned Xue's head on the heart of the tiger.

The dark hair on Xue's forehead formed a small V. His closed lids were so thin I could see the movement of his eyeballs beneath their veined surface. The cotton cloth that he was wrapped in rose and fell with his breathing. I was careful not to wake him when I covered his head with my hand. I felt the softness of the hole in his skull.

My cousin and I got bored of looking at the sleeping baby. We decided to have a concert. We sang songs in Hmong and English. We sang songs we created. We sang songs that we had learned from school. We could hear the buzz of the adult conversation from downstairs.

Soon, the singing grew boring. We decided to add dancing to the mix. We decided to dance on the bed. We started jumping on the bed. It became fun fast. We jumped higher and higher. Our laughter drowned the conversation downstairs and the words of our songs.

When the baby flew off the bed and flew to the floor, his

head hit the ground first. There was a juicy, soft sound like a melon falling and cracking open. At first, both my cousin and I were paralyzed. There was a moment of silence. The baby did not cry. We watched from the bed as his little face turned blue. My cousin began to whimper. I jumped off the bed and stood over my little brother. I watched him turn white. I screamed, "Mother! Father!"

My mother and an aunt were the first to enter the room, followed by my father. The women made noises when they came into the room and saw the baby on the floor. They said no words, just made exclamations. They moved to the baby in what felt like slow motion. My mother went on her knees. Her hands were trembling so hard she could not pick up Xue. She reached out and tried, but she couldn't wrap her fingers around his little form, just empty scoops of air. My aunt helped gather the baby from the floor. Xue looked limp in her arms. She handed him to my mother. My mother held him in her arms, close to her heart, and started rocking.

She said in a whisper, "My baby, my baby, my baby."

She didn't look at me or my cousin.

My mother stood the small bundle up in her arms. She placed his face against her neck. She started cooing to him. One of her hands started patting his back. His face turned red.

We heard a small hiccupping sound, and then Xue's cries erupted with sputtering hurt; small, white bubbles welled up out of his mouth.

My father had been frozen by the doorway. Xue's cries allowed him the freedom to move from the door into the room. He came to us, my cousin and me.

He said, "What happened?"

I started crying hard as I told the adults what had happened.

My cousin started to cry with me. Soon, it was me, my cousin, and Xue all crying in the small room. My father shushed us. My mother and my aunt admonished us and said we were not careful enough. Everyone knew that it was an accident, but they reminded us that accidents could kill.

✧

The grass in the yard of the abandoned house next door was wild. Xue walked ahead of me. It came all the way up to his thighs. It scratched against my knee with each step I took. I was fifteen years old that summer. Xue was six. He pushed the grass away from both sides with his hands to make a path for me to follow.

He had been asking for days. "Will you please go grasshopper catching with me?"

Finally, I had conceded.

I said that grasshoppers were disgusting. I said that their butts were too long. I said that their butts were shaped like poop. The grasshoppers reminded me of caterpillars, which both Xue and I and many Hmong children feared. We had grown up hearing stories from our mother and father about how caterpillars back in Laos and Thailand sometimes latched onto the breasts of unwary men and women and sucked them dry of milk and blood, and eventually life. We knew that healthy people could become cocoons in the hold of certain caterpillars.

That summer, Xue had a miniature rooster that he loved. Usually, the rooster ate grains of rice and stale bread crumbs but Xue wanted to catch grasshoppers to give him more nutrients. I agreed to the venture not because of probable nutrition for Xue's rooster, but because Xue, my only brother, was lonely. He was too young to run around with the neighborhood boys, who traveled in groups of five or six, armed with slingshots and other hunting essentials. They walked the streets looking for little swallows and squirrels, hoping for a shot, talking of dinners for the family.

It was hot. The earth beneath my flip-flops transmitted heat through their plastic soles. It had been a dry year, and the grass was thirsty. Sapped of green, the leaves were nearly baked through. The earth was cracked in places where lines of ants gathered with tiny grains of sand.

The neighborhood was empty. Most people were inside their homes. Many of the houses had their curtains pulled shut to keep the rooms cool. Even the neighborhood boys were absent from their usual posts at the different corners, beneath the big trees that lined our street, York Avenue. I imagined the whirl of fans in darkened houses, exhausted bodies sleeping off the heat in sweaty beds. Dawb and the younger children were inside the house. The younger girls were painting on paper plates. Dawb was watching television. Our mother and father were at work. The house was abuzz with the wheezing of a new window air conditioner that Uncle Chue had helped our father install because the baby, Taylor, was getting heat rashes underneath her neck.

The house next door had been vacant since we moved in. Its white stucco walls were cracked and the paint peeled like old, dried scabs. The jagged cracks on the walls looked like the bottoms of Grandma's feet, filled with dirt from long ago. The windows were boarded up and initialed with symbols and signs in red and blue by the rival gangs that lived in our neighborhood. There were words in black paint that we knew but our parents forbade us to speak.

My long hair was pulled back in a ponytail. I felt the hot

sun on the back of my neck, on the top of my head, heating my scalp. Xue's spiky head of hair was wet with sweat, but it was so thick that not even the weight of the moisture could pull it down.

Xue looked back at me every few minutes to check my progress through the tall grass. There was a smile on his face, half-pleased, half trying to please. He wore an old forest-green polo shirt and black soccer shorts. I had on an old summer dress my mother had gotten from a church basement years ago. We both wore Cockatoo-brand flip-flops from the Asian grocery store. Mine were green and Xue's were blue. I waved him back to the work of catching grasshoppers.

Xue had finagled a stick from a nearby bush and was using it to whip at the tall grass on either side. I followed the small path he made in the tall grass. All around us, grasshoppers leaped and flew. Many of the grasshoppers had grown large and strong. Some had wings so formidable that in flight, they took on the appearance of butterflies. We jumped in the direction of the winged insects. I caught them in my cupped hands as they landed on stalks of suspended grass, and called to Xue in an urgent whisper. I hated the smear of brown butt juice that the grasshoppers left on my hands, its scent a little spicy. When Xue joined me, we carefully switched hands, his cupped palms where my hands had been, so that he could catch the grasshoppers and put them in the old soda bottle we'd made holes in for the express purpose.

Xue and I stayed outside until the hot day soaked through the back of Xue's shirt and streaks of dirt and sweat dribbled down his face. There was exhilaration and fun I had not expected. It was like fishing, the same familiar wait, the same rush of excitement, the satisfaction of a catch. We moved from one patch of the lawn to the next. My ponytail came loose and tendrils of hair stuck to my face. The sun was no longer high atop our bent heads by the time I felt the discomfort in my neck and noticed Xue slipping and falling into the grass as he hobbled after the large grasshoppers.

The absent neighbor's house had a sunken garage. Built into a small rise, its tiled roof was broken in the middle. Half the roof was covered in thick ivy leaves, yellowing because there had been so little rain. Exhausted from our grasshopper hunt, we decided to climb on top of the roof.

The crumbling tiles were too hot for us to sit on. We stood on two high points of the garage roof, the break between us. Xue held the bottle full of steaming grasshoppers and shreds of grass. I held on to Xue's stick, which he had given me for protection against the occasional bee that flew among the flowering weeds.

Xue said, "One day, we should climb the roof of the abandoned house."

I said, "Okay."

Xue said, "Catching grasshoppers was fun, wasn't it?"

I nodded.

Xue said, "We should do this again next summer. Maybe we can catch grasshoppers every summer."

I said, "Maybe."

But for us, there were no more grasshopper summers. I never found enough energy or interest to go into the burning sun and scratchy grass to look for grasshoppers again with my little brother. Xue stopped asking me after I said no too many times. He started looking to the boys in the neighborhood for friendship and fun.

✧

Xue was nine years old when I left home for college. He wrote me a letter the first year I was away. I believe it was Xue's first letter to anyone. I believe it may also be, to date, his only letter:

> Dear Kalia,
>
> I miss you. We are all doing okay. I know that maybe I'm too big to write this but when I think of you, I think of me as your Red Ranger. I will always be your Red Power Ranger no matter where you are.
>
> > Your Mystic Warrior,
> > Xue

Home from college, I attended parent-teacher conferences for the children with our mother while our father was at work, doing his evening shift.

On conference nights, when our father came home from work, and after he showered, our mother, Dawb, and I sat around our rickety table with him to go over the children's report cards. Different animals from different calendar months stared down at us from the walls. Our mother had cut out the pictures from the free calendars we got from our car insurance agent. She said the pictures were art; we didn't need expensive paintings to see that the world was full of beauty, just reminders of all the creatures who occupied it with us.

The images are now ingrained in my mind, yellowed by wear: long-feathered pheasants flying from wintry cornfields, tall bucks with chandelier antlers standing behind copses of birch trees, blue skies with the geese flying high, emerald-feathered loons sitting atop silver lakes.

Dawb and I pointed to the carbon copies of the report cards and directed our mother and father's attention to the little boxes with Xs or check-marks. We reviewed the numbers that stood in for grades.

Xue's report card was always the last one we looked over. The girls were doing well at following directions, getting 3s and 4s on everything. Their teachers felt that they were making good efforts. Xue was getting 2s and 3s for schoolwork. His teachers were not satisfied with Xue's effort. While he had surprisingly high test scores, which meant that he understood the material, his actual grades suggested that he wasn't trying his best. As we talked about Xue's grades, we could feel our father's tension grow. Both our parents were not happy about Xue's academic performance, but to our father Xue's performance was a reflection of his fathering.

At the end of the review session, our father called all the children to the kitchen. In a line they stood around us. The girls were doing well. Xue needed to do better. The girls could go play. Xue needed to stay and talk.

Xue stood before the four of us. He wore a striped black-and-white T-shirt with green basketball shorts in a slippery fabric that shone in the light. I looked at Xue's thick feet, a younger version of our father's thick, wide feet, on the stained carpet of the kitchen floor. Xue's toes, pudgy and innocent as a baby's, curled against the rough fibers of the once beige carpet. I looked at the bruises on his shins. His chubby fingers were clasped in front of his belly. I did not want to meet his eyes, round and intelligent, nervous. I felt a push to protect him from our father's words. I knew it was a mistake to interfere with our father demanding more from Xue, but there was a sadness about my brother that called to me.

Xue was alone. As much as he was with us, he stood before us by himself. His eyes were downcast. His huge front teeth bit on his bottom lip. His face grew red. He waited for our father's words. The minutes ticked by on the old clock.

I have never been able to understand Xue's patience with our father. Perhaps it is restraint that I am calling patience? Xue, fairly short-tempered like most of us, has never responded to our father in sheer anger, or expressed his frustration or been cruel.

Xue had a hard job to do as our father's son. He belonged to a man who had grown up yearning for the love and support of a father, believing that the sadness and disappointments he has had to live with were a particular consequence of his father-lessness. Our father wanted to give Xue all the things he had missed in the high mountains of Laos: a father's continual presence, his guidance, and his love. He believed that he would have turned out a different man, a less lonely man, a better man, if our grandfather had been around. Xue was our father's chance to find out if this lifelong belief was true; Xue, who had already shown his resilience in making the successful journey into our lives when six others hadn't made it. Our father was raising a boy who he believed could become a man far greater than himself.

It was hard witnessing the talks when Xue disappointed our father.

To our father, Xue is "*me tub*"—my son, the same thing his father had called him—with all its love, its unfulfilled promise, and its yearning complexity. Our father began with facts. "*Me tub*, you are not doing your best in school. I want you to try harder. I would not ask this of you if I didn't think you could do it. Your father loves you. I want you to have a life that is better than mine. A good life in America for you is only possible through school. Why aren't you trying harder?"

Xue raised his eyes. A shadow grew in their gaze, not of dark, smoky anger but something more complex, an emotion like regret and a look of apology.

Xue had been apologizing for disappointing our father for a long time.

Xue was five years old when he lost the house key on his way home from kindergarten. At the dining table, when our father asked, "Who is going to protect your sisters now that anyone can open our door?" Xue had answered, "I'm so sorry." That night, once our mother and father left for work, Xue set up a small stool by our front door and held a bread knife in his hand for hours. Dawb and I had tried to get him to go to bed, but he had refused. It wasn't until he grew so tired that the bread knife fell from his hands that we could maneuver him, half-asleep, to the sofa, where we told him he could still protect us from danger.

The old clock continued to tick.

Our mother, Dawb, and I did not want to hear Xue's words, but they came anyway.

Xue said, "I am sorry, Father."

Xue has never called our father "Daddy."

✧

When I was twenty-one, our mother and father moved the family to Andover, Minnesota. The decision to leave the moldy house on York Avenue was one of the biggest our parents made in America. They were moving from our 900-square-foot home with its tiny yard on the east side of St. Paul to a 2,300-square-foot home on 2.69 acres on the Minnesota prairie. The new house was forty-five minutes away from the familiarity of St. Paul. We were excited about the new house but worried about our new neighbors, the new schools, and a community full of white people who had little exposure to Hmong folk, unlike our east side neighbors. The children loved the St. Paul public schools, where Hmong students comprised the biggest part of the population. In Andover, they became the only Hmong kids in the classrooms for the first time in their lives.

Xue was fourteen years old at the time of the move. Dawb enrolled him at Andover High School, about three miles away from our house. The girls were placed in the elementary and middle schools. We asked how Xue felt. He shrugged his shoulders and told us, "It will be fine."

It was not fine.

The first incident happened shortly after the move. The family was rejoicing over the birth of a little brother, Maxwell Hwm Yang. Nine years younger than our youngest sibling, a surprise that came nine months after our grandma's death, he, we knew, would be our mother and father's last. Born in a new house, underneath a cold November sky, at the peak of the noonday sun, Max was Xue's big wish: the brother he had been waiting for.

We believed that Max would help Xue balance the work of being my father's son; he would set forth different possibilities. We were happy there was another boy, but no one was happier than Xue. He walked around with Max in his arms, smiling at everyone. The sadness in his eyes lifted and in its place was light.

Xue had gone to school early that morning, after kissing Max goodbye. He was in shop class, working with nuts and bolts. He was stationed at a table with four white boys. As Xue was working, the table started shaking. At first, he said nothing. Each time Xue tried to put the nut on the bolt, the table would shake again. Xue asked a tall boy with brown hair to stop moving the table. The boy laughed. His friends chuckled with him. The table shook harder. Xue stopped what he was doing and asked again, this time his words slow and quiet. In response, the shaking grew worse. The group of boys at the table stopped working entirely and laughed some more.

I can picture Xue's scowl growing stronger, his body becoming tense. The hands I love curled into fists. The table continued to shake. Xue channeled all his fierceness into his face and stared at the boys. Perhaps he hoped that the look on his face would be enough to stop them. It was not.

The brown-haired boy said, "Go back to your homeland, fatso."

The other boys snickered.

Xue stopped what he was doing. The nuts and bolts were still in his hand. He unleashed his fists into the air. The metal objects flew. Xue's frustration traveled in seconds. The boy's hands flew to protect his face. The nuts and bolts made contact with the skin of the boy's hands, bits of his arms.

Xue was sent to the office. He was sent to see one of the assistant principals. There was paperwork to be done. Xue was suspended.

Our mother and father were angry at Xue when they learned what happened. They yelled at him. Did he not understand any of the stories that they had told him about their lives in the refugee camps of Thailand or the years of running through the jungles of Laos? Did he not hear of the Hmong people who had died? Children too young to run, old men and women, too frail to escape, friends and strangers, loved ones, who hadn't seen the bullets coming? All of his life, they had taught him about the dangers of power, the consequences of hurting, and the long road we must walk together in order to heal what had been broken in the Hmong heart, the Hmong life. Had their lives' lessons been for naught? Our father paced in front of Xue. His love of language, the freedom with which he allowed his words, the air they floated in, fell away. Now his words felt metallic, hard and cold, sharp enough to cut. Our father spat them out like they were poison. He said, "You. Violence. There is no room for violence in this house."

There was a pot of anger boiling inside our father. The bubbles burst and burst from his mouth even without words. They were fanned by flames we could not see, their outcome a desperate heat that showed in the red of his face. A fire burned inside our father as he stared at Xue. Our mother pulled him away.

Later, we heard our father, much calmer, say to Xue, "People's words can't kill you. It is guns and bullets that kill. Your life was not in danger. You didn't need to endanger the lives of others."

Xue made no excuses. He was silent in the face of our father's disappointment. He told our parents that he would try harder to control himself. He said he would work harder to ignore the boys at school. Xue said he was sorry.

We were not convinced that it was Xue's place to apologize, but our mother and father knew that their son didn't have parents who could go to school and speak up for him, demand respect. How could they do it for him when they couldn't even do it for themselves? At work white men said "fuck" and "shit" and "hate you people" regularly to both of them—whenever a part wasn't perfect or the assembly line halted. Each time the dirty, hateful words were spoken, our mother and father pretended they hadn't heard, pretended to be sorry, just to get by.

In the night someone sprayed our mailbox with the words CHINK, GOOK, FUCKS.

In the day, our mother and father drove to Ace Hardware and bought spray paint and painted over the words.

When they came home our father told Xue that he needed to find a way to bear the burden of his race and his people in America without violence. They pointed to the African American experience, the things he'd learned at school about slavery and endurance. Our father turned the television to a special about the teaching of Mahatma Gandhi and nonviolence. He pointed to Dr. Martin Luther King Jr. and said, "You will never be as smart as he is, but you don't have to be to stand in his legacy. He is the example in our world."

Our father repeated to Xue the words he had told Dawb and me long ago, that we were the oldest and that education was our only path forward. He directed Xue to lower his head and look away. He said a middle finger in the air can't kill anyone. He told Xue how words such as "chink" and "fatso" and "go back to your own country" mean nothing to us because they are not born in our hearts, language, or experience. Our father said the most important thing that each of us has to remember is that it should be the words and actions of those who love us, like our mother and father, brothers and sisters, that should enter our hearts and spur its beats, not those of people who are out to hurt us, out to silence and diminish us.

Xue returned to school once the suspension had been lifted. It was his first day back. In the afternoon, Xue found himself in an empty hallway. He had just closed his locker. He started walking in the direction of a classroom when he turned the corner to see the brown-haired boy and his friends waiting. They approached Xue, surrounding him. They moved in close. They towered over him and started pushing him. Xue punched.

Xue was suspended again.

Xue walked through the front door of our home slowly, his backpack in one hand. Underneath his jacket, his shirt was open. The buttons were missing. His undershirt was torn. His cheekbones were swollen. There was a purplish bruise around the side of his mouth. Someone had scratched his neck. Our mother was the first to reach him. She had never seen Xue beaten like this. None of us had. It was the first time we saw our brother bloodied from a fight.

Xue said, "I'm okay, Mom."

Our father, like the rest of us, leaned against the railing along the stairs. Our father's mouth was a taut line. He raised both his hands, palms up. It was his gesture of surrender. He shook his head. He shrugged his shoulders, but they were raised high. It was as if he, too, was preparing for a blow. He was tense. It was difficult to discern the emotions on his face. There was anger, there was pain, there was frustration, there was giving up, and then there was more, there was fight. Did he want to fight Xue? Did he want to fight the boys? Or the world he was raising Xue in? He said nothing.

Once Xue was cleaned up, the family talked. Xue did not have much to say. He had no excuses to offer, just a short narrative of what happened.

Our mother and father asked why he pulled that first punch. Xue just looked at them and said, "I don't know."

We all knew the truth: he could not run. Like our father in that moment on that road of boyhood, sometimes a boy had to stand and fight. Besides, we knew there were no places to run. Each of us had done our part, big and small, to raise a man who would not run; it was enough that our mother and father had run so far to get us to America. From the moment we arrived here, they had told us this would be home.

In the night, someone drove by and took a bat to our mailbox. They hit so hard that the metal caved in and the mailbox was unusable. We heard nothing—just the lonely whistle of the trains on the tracks.

The next day, our mother and father drove once more to Ace Hardware. This time, they bought a new mailbox and took off the old one. They bought shiny gold stickers and posted them on the side: 14655.

Our mother and father became more persistent. They talked and talked to Xue about how we could all survive if we worked hard together, focused on what was important, and let go of the things that weighed us down. Xue promised them that he would no longer fight.

Xue crawled through the ninth grade and into the tenth. He did the minimal work he needed to do to pass his classes. He did not participate in class discussions or ask questions. One or two teachers saw his potential. Most did not. Xue started smoking. He carried around a tin box with CDs of hip-hop artists, rappers who were angry at the system, trying to make ends meet, dreaming big dreams but living on the streets.

When the girls got to high school with Xue, they told us that he had a group of friends, the outcasts in the school. Xue's friends were the kids the other students pointed at and whispered about. In the lunchroom, Xue sat at a table with a small group of multicultural boys; many of them lived in group homes. They had designated him as their unifying leader. Xue started wearing big hooded sweatshirts with pockets full of stuff we didn't ask about.

Our mother and father spent late nights arguing about what was best for Xue. We could hear them through the thin walls and the vents of the house. Her voice and then his. Discord. Disagreement. Disaster.

I'd die in his place.

And you think I wouldn't?

During the day, our mother and father watched Xue intently and worried in whispers. It was clear that Xue had stopped fighting. He stopped talking about school entirely. He put on weight. We heard the girls talking among themselves about how the white boys at school made fun of Xue. The girls said that Xue never answered but sometimes he growled deep in his belly, low in his throat, like a bear. Hlub wanted to fight the boys. Taylor, who was only in elementary school, said she would help Hlub fight anyone who fought Xue. Shell told both of them that if they got in trouble, too, surely our mother and father would go crazy. She said there had to be other ways of working at the bigger issue. She identified the problems in Andover as a product of ignorance and fear. She and Hlub agreed to join the multicultural group at the school, in the hopes that they could build a friendlier environment for their big brother.

Dawb and I watched from a distance, busy with our respective educations and the tasks of taking care of the family: applying for free or reduced school lunches, scheduling appointments with doctors and dentists and specialists who gave cortisone shots so our mother and father could continue at their jobs; we watched as our mother and father winced at the pain from carpal tunnel and bone spurs and still continued to go to work, day in and day out. Dawb and I tried to have conversations

with our brother in our spare moments, when we weren't helping the girls with their homework or attending to our own, but
he was silent. When we talked to Xue, we missed a version of
him we couldn't locate in the young man who sat opposite us,
the sullen body, the heavy, heavy walk.

I tried hard to find the laughing boy with the bottle full of
grasshoppers, but I couldn't. During those years in Andover my
family missed St. Paul, a forty-minute drive away, but much
farther than we knew how to return to.

In the night, someone drove a car into our mailbox. They
ripped the thick, wooden post that the new mailbox was on.
They threw the mailbox with the shiny numbers in the ditch.

In the day, our mother and father drove once again to Ace
Hardware. They bought a new post. They picked up the mailbox from the ditch and cleaned it. They nailed it to the new post.
They bought cement, dug around the old hole, and cemented
the new post in.

In eleventh grade, Xue learned the word "insubordination"
from an adult whom many of the students of color disliked.

Xue had been sent to detention for being late to class once
more. In detention, he started doing his homework. The over-
seeing adult did not want Xue to do his homework. She wanted
him to reflect on his tardiness.

Xue looked at her and said, "You are not even a real teacher.
That's why you don't understand the value of doing homework."

That day, we received a phone call from the school admin-
istrator outlining Xue's insubordination. Our mother and father
had always told us to show our teachers respect and to give the
adults in our lives the honor of their age and experience. There
were no excuses as far as they were concerned. No reason big
enough for Xue to say those words to an adult who worked at

the school. Our father's anger toward Xue grew deep and dark and frantic. When Xue came home from school, our father looked at him from the living room sofa. He could barely wait for Xue to go to his room, to take off his jacket and backpack. Our father met Xue in the kitchen. Xue was about to pour a glass of water. With the empty cup in his hand, he stood still as our father's words boiled over.

"You are lazy. You are no good. You are living like an empty weight on the earth. You, you do not understand the world we live in.

"It is not what they do to you that makes you who you are. Don't you understand that I am your father? Your mother and I made you who you are!

"You are better than your actions have become."

In the heated current of our father's words, Xue's shoulders, which were already sagging, fell lower. There was a look in his eyes that recalled the commercials of hungry children in poor countries, children from refugee camps, children starving and dying, orphaned and alone, afraid. I saw what the world we lived in had done to my brother and our father.

He asked Xue, "Have I wasted my time in trying to teach you? Have I wasted my love in raising you?"

Dawb and I pushed ourselves between them. Our mother wasn't home. Our father's shirt was damp with sweat.

Xue stood, as he had always stood, with his head down. This time, the wash of liquid in his eyes gave way to tears that fell on the old linoleum floor. His shoulders shook. He did not answer our father. He did not offer to try again. He did not say sorry. He simply waited.

I heard my father take deep breaths and felt how his muscles grew soft.

Our father pleaded.

He said, "Xue, promise me you will stop smoking. Xue, promise me you will stop hanging out with the kids no one wants. Xue, promise me you will go to school tomorrow and try harder. Will you promise me to try some more?"

There was no sound. Xue's shoulders shook so hard they rocked his body. If our mother had been home, her heart would have broken with Xue's, but she was not, and so the breaking was his own. Our father looked away from all of us standing there. He walked the darkened hallway to the room our parents shared. He closed the door.

Later, when our mother came home and we told her what had happened, she went to Xue. She wrapped her arms around him and cried. She asked him to try harder, for her, for himself. She said in the end, all that mattered to her was him. She didn't want Xue to let his whole life slip away because some kids were calling him names at school. She told him she loved him so much, more than herself even, and that if she could, she would stand in for him and go through the hurt.

Our mother had always been the one to find the words of love to soothe Xue's cries. But her love, all our love, could not bandage what was broken in Xue.

It was the last semester of his high school career. Graduation was coming. We were starting to believe that Xue would hold on long enough to graduate. In quiet conversations, Dawb and I, and our mother and father, dreamed together of sending Xue off to college, not one of the selective colleges, but someplace where he could have friends who were Hmong like himself, boys his age who were striving for their lives, who'd somehow survived the statistics and the realities of growing up poor and different in the urban and suburban centers of America.

It was a cold, clear day when Xue came home and told the family, "I am not going back to school anymore. I can't do it. I am not like my sisters. It is too hard for me."

We all argued with him. He didn't argue back. Instead, he went into his room and closed the door. Somehow we had become like the rest of the world, expecting and demanding what Xue could not deliver. He had become a disappointment.

In the mornings, our mother and father pounded on his door.

They shouted, "Get up, get up, Xue! You are going to be late for school."

His door did not open. Their shouting went unanswered.

Away from Xue, in the Honda CR-V, the family talked about him.

Our father said, "I have fought against Xue to make him better. He is so stupid because he doesn't know what is at stake. I am so stupid because I do not know how to help him."

The girls nodded. They had seen more than they wanted to. They had heard more words from our father, thrown at Xue, than any of them knew what to do with. Our mother was often silent during these talks. She stopped looking at our father when he talked of Xue.

Sometimes, he challenged her openly: "You think I am a failure as a father. Is that why you can't look at me?"

She never did respond to him, but away from him, she said to us, "This has nothing to do with your father. It is about my son."

In the car, hands hard on the wheel, he said, "I love him more than I love me. I love him more than perhaps our relationship as father and son."

Our father's eyes, dry and irritated from the vents at

work, from the chemicals he used on the hard metals he polished, from the carbide particles that flew as the lasers did their blinding work to smooth jagged edges, grew wet with moisture.

We knew that sometimes our father spoke of his love for Xue so he would remember the father he had dreamt for himself, the father he was struggling to be. None of us needed to hear his love for Xue; we knew it, except perhaps Xue, who was not present at the moments when our father cried for him.

The old Honda CR-V swerved in the traffic lane next to the big trucks and SUVs on Highway 10 going west, in the direction of the setting sun. We girls tried helplessly to comfort our father. We talked of institutional racism and discrimination against boys and men of color. We struggled to show him via the things we'd read and witnessed at school that Xue was not the only one struggling, failing to find a fit in school. Dawb and I wished out loud for a world that would be gentler on boys and men like our father and our brother. We watched as our father struggled to still the fluttering of his heart so he would keep the steering wheel steady and somehow blink the tears away so he could see the long road before us.

Sometimes our father asked us questions: "Do you have any ideas on what might help Xue survive in this country?"

We could not offer good answers. We could not stop the white boys at school from hurting Xue or change the rules and protocol of the school district to take bullying and racism into account; we could not undo a system that was as old as this country we were told to call home. It all felt much too late.

The newspaper articles about the culture of fear and the suicide epidemic that would break the silence of the Anoka-Hennepin School District hadn't yet been written. It was only

2003. It wasn't until 2012 that Dawb and I read *Rolling Stone* magazine's piece about the bullying that was killing kids in Andover and other cities in Anoka County and shared it with our mother and father.

All we had was Xue, who was bullied at school, who had struggled to fight for himself. But we had told him to stop fighting, and so he had done as we had asked. Xue was now hiding from the world. We had become a part of the world that he was hiding from.

In the car, as night fell upon the exit off Hanson Boulevard, we listened to our father's struggle to breathe, clearing his throat against a stickiness in his lungs, fighting against the explosion of coughing that grew uncontrollable when his breathing deepened. We listened as he made resolutions: "I am going to try one last time to get through to Xue. I am going to get my son to turn around, to walk toward education and life in this country with us."

Our father could not do it, not by himself, not without a father's example to lead. The situations in which he had seen Uncle Shong stand up for his family, the words of wisdom he had cherished for many years, didn't translate easily to the hard lessons of raising a first-generation Hmong boy in the whiteness of Andover, Minnesota.

That spring we had no graduation to go to. Uncle Hue had a son graduating from high school. Uncle Chue had one. We shared in their joy. The uncles shared in my father's frustration.

We focused on breathing in the warm spring air. We saw green shoots of young grass rise up beneath the tall, dried stalks from summers past, grass that the cool of fall and the cold of winter had killed but somehow the earth had preserved. Our mother began work in her garden. Our father started to mow the lawn. We watched Xue, home day after day, looking out the window to the nearby tracks, waiting for the sight of the long trains going places.

On a dark, rainy night, our father called for one more family meeting. He presented Xue with two choices: Xue could return to school or get a job and leave home.

Our mother sat on the sofa beside our father, far enough so that she didn't touch him. She held pieces of tissue in her hands and pushed them up to her face to cover her eyes as our father spoke. She contained her tears. She did not contain her mouth. She had listened and she had loved and the years had grown too long and the words she had wanted to say to our father had stewed inside and all we could do was watch as our mother fought our father for our brother, who he, too, was fighting for.

Our mother said she would rather Xue be safe at home than thrust into a world that would not welcome him. She said that our father could blame her for being too soft on Xue if he wanted to but that she was not going to let Xue alone take the responsibility for what had happened in Andover. She said our father could blame himself if he wanted to because a father has as much to carry as his son. She said what our father did at work was no different than what Xue did at school. He was just pulling through and the only reason he didn't quit was because unlike Xue, he had children to feed. He was no more of a success in America than Xue, his son. Did anyone give him ultimatums, tell him to leave?

At first, our father tried to speak over her, saying that the meeting wasn't about him, or their relationship, but Xue. It was for Xue. It was about Xue. But our mother would not be quieted. She couldn't stop. She had her hands over her heart. She ripped the tissues in her hands into shreds, yet her voice did not crack, the words did not slur or slow down, and at last she said, "I'm so tired of loving you both so much in America and seeing you fall into yourselves instead of standing up for the men you are."

The more our mother spoke, the smaller our father became in front of her. The air he breathed in so he could be big for us leaked from his body with each statement she made.

It was Xue who came to his rescue. Xue raised his hand at our mother, a stop sign. He tried to speak, but no words came out of his lips. He gestured toward Max. He didn't want to leave Max, who adored him. Max was only four years old. Xue looked at Max sitting by the stairwell. Max looked back at him.

Our father said, "I do not want you to be an example for your little brother Max on how to survive in this country as a Hmong man."

Perhaps our father thought his words would motivate Xue? We watched them slice our brother apart.

Max heard our father's words. He snapped his head in our father's direction. He had been sitting by the stairwell to block Xue's exit should Xue make the decision to leave. When Max heard our father's words, he got up.

Max said, "Xue is my brother. He cannot leave me. Life without Xue is no life at all. I would rather die than live in America without my brother by my side."

Max locked his gaze with our father's. He tilted his chin up. Max walked to our father and held on to his arm.

Our father moved away from Max's hold. He stood up. He paced in front of Xue. He couldn't keep his pacing even. He walked with a limp. The balls of his feet burned with each step, the flesh tender and abused by the long nights beside the tall machines at work, the stretches of standing and walking, carrying iron and steel. He walked the small stretch of the dim living room into the light of the dining area and back again.

He said, "This is what happens to feet when they stand and walk without rest the night through."

He held out his red hands, the tight stretch of white lines, his life line and his heart line colliding in a sharp V across his callused palms.

He said, "This is what happens to human flesh when it cuts into steel. It suffers."

He said, "I want you to have a life that is better than mine. I don't want you to become a machinist like me. I don't want you to live your life with men and boys far stupider than you telling you that you don't belong here, that you are no good for this country, telling you to return to a country you do not have. I want you to have a better life than me. I want you to be better than me."

Xue looked at our father.

Xue said, "What if you are the best man I know how to be?"

Our father shook his head. He didn't want to accept Xue's words. For the first time in his life, he heard the words of a son to his father. He knew what it was like to yearn for a father, to raise a son and burn to make him better than you, and Xue had tried to keep him safe in his fantasies of fathers and sons, but Xue could no longer save our father from himself.

Our father said, "You cannot be me and survive in this country."

Xue said, "Then I cannot survive in this country."

Xue got up. He walked to where Max sat and placed his hand on Max's head. He offered no words, no goodbyes. Xue passed by our father, in the divide between the living room and the dining room. Xue walked into the dark kitchen and opened the cabinet beside the white refrigerator. He pulled out a black garbage bag. He closed the cabinet so lightly it made no sound. Xue didn't turn on the light in the hallway. He simply walked into his room. There was no slamming door.

It was a horrible nightmare, the nightmare we had been dreading, a moment when we believed that our life together as a family would end. Not because of war or soldiers encroaching, but because of the remnants of war inside each of us, the battle we fought to survive in America. Dawb and I ran after Xue. Hlub held to the ends of his shirt and tried to hold him still. Taye and Shell walked in different directions, turned back again, and then stood with their hands over their mouths. Our mother and father watched from the doorway of Xue's room as he stuck a framed photograph of Grandma and him into the garbage bag. In the photograph, there's a twinkle of naughtiness in his eyes; his spiky hair is forced to the side with hair spray. He has a blade of grass in his mouth. On his bookshelf was a photograph of two-year-old Max with his round belly showing from a shirt that was too small. Max's hands were behind his back and his head was cocked to the side. Xue put the picture in the garbage bag, too. He grabbed a few white T-shirts, a pair of jeans, a sweater. There was no waking up from this nightmare.

Xue left that night. Dawb and I stood outside calling for him as he drove away. The taillights of the car disappeared into the dark. In the distance beyond our gaze, we heard the sound of the car riding over the train tracks.

We came inside the house to find our mother sitting on the stairwell with Max in her arms. He hid his face in her neck. Our father was nowhere in sight. The door to our parents' bedroom was closed. Someone had opened the window in Xue's room. A cold wind blew into our house.

Xue stayed away that summer. He stayed at Uncle Hue's house with his children. We knew he was safe. We saw him when we visited Uncle's family. There wasn't much to say. We hoped that our uncle would not mind sheltering our sad brother through the passing season. Our mother wanted to supplement Auntie and Uncle's food budget. Our father said it wasn't necessary. Our mother suggested they call Xue home. Our father refused to make the call.

That summer, our mother spent long hours with her head bent, her hand on the back of her neck, trying to massage the migraines away. Her eyes were red rimmed and continually wet.

I missed my brother. I knew my father did, too. I took walks outside, went in circles around and around our large block, made my way through the long grass on the horse trail that sliced through the small acreage. I picked up sticks and slapped at the tall, windswept grass on either side. I watched the huge grasshoppers take flight, brown bodied, gossamer winged. I comforted myself with the memory of the little boy with round eyes and a big smile, his front teeth too big for his small mouth, excited because the grasshoppers could fly so high in the drying, dying summer grass. I didn't have to look hard to find my father by his chicken coop, see the flashes of the fabric of his shirts among the heavy growth of the aspen trees and the wild bushes at the outskirts of the yard.

As I wandered over our small stretch of Andover, I noticed how green and lush the grass had grown, how long it got each week because Xue was not home to help our father mow our lawn. While I understood the forces at school, I knew what was broken was between my father and Xue, and that the mending had to be theirs.

One day, I found Max in Xue's room. Max was sitting on the bed, staring out the window, his legs crossed. A train was speeding by, its cars a blur of brown and black. Both of Max's hands were in his mouth. He had his tongue between his fingers. He was pulling at it earnestly and carefully. I asked Max what he was doing. He told me that he was trying to die. He missed Xue. He couldn't live with himself.

Max said, "I am angry at my tongue for not having found the words to make Xue feel better, to help him stay."

I pulled Max close. I told him he shouldn't try to kill himself. Didn't he remember the stories about young boys and girls who said they wanted to kill themselves? One never knew where the evil spirits were lurking. What if an evil one heard him and flipped his words, taking the killing out of his hands and doing it for him in an altogether unpleasant way? Did Max really want to chance that kind of death? His fingers loosened on his tongue and they slipped from his mouth.

At dinner, I mentioned what I had found Max doing. The girls told Max never to try that again. Our mother told Max that human beings have no right to take our own lives; we belong to each other. Our father told Max that there was a telephone. If Max wanted Xue to come home, he should call him.

Max called Xue. I don't know what they talked about, but the next day, when our father was at work, Xue came home with the black garbage bag intact, the two photographs still inside.

As a family, we rejoiced quietly. Our mother's migraines got better and the redness in her eyes faded. The girls brought up the phrase "our brother" much more often in their everyday talk of Xue; they referred to Max as "baby." Dawb and I got busy preparing for a new year, eagerly letting go of the worries of the old year. Our father's words and his stories returned. I stopped taking my lonely walks. From the kitchen window above the sink, I watched our father and Xue wander our yard, talking to each other.

The months away had calmed Xue. He listed with a temporary job placement agency along with Uncle Hue's and Uncle Sai's sons. The agency sent him and the boys to a farm factory. They worked with elderly Hmong and Mexican laborers on a factory line processing corn. Xue had been on the job for nearly a month. He did not enjoy the labor but he felt good about it. He came home exhausted each night and had dinner with us before going to sleep. He got up each morning before work and had breakfast with us before leaving each day. Xue's ready laughter reminded us of the meals we shared long ago when he was just a boy. The younger girls, who had adored him, but then grew wary of him in Andover, warmed up to his jokes and presence. Over dinner, they chatted together. Some weekends, they played Monopoly. They told each other to "keep the change."

One day, Xue came home early from work. He told the family that he had quit his job. He wasn't going back there again.

Both our mother and father asked him why.

He said, "Insubordination."

I could see our father begin to shake his head.

My mother said, "Bee, calm down. Let the boy explain."

Our father asked if Xue had an explanation.

Xue said, "I didn't agree with the man in charge. I walked out before he could fire me."

Our father continued shaking his head. He was not satisfied

with Xue's answer. He went to the telephone and dialed Uncle Hue's sons. The cousins told our father what had happened.

The supervisor at the farm had taken to yelling at the elderly Hmong and Mexican workers. The older folk couldn't understand English. On the day that Xue left his job, the supervisor was particularly angry. He couldn't stop yelling at an elderly couple who couldn't keep pace with the assembly line. The wife's arthritis was bad that day. Her husband stood by her, trying to keep up with his own quota and hers. All the boys saw this and muttered in Hmong that it wasn't right. Everybody was uncomfortable.

When the supervisor passed Xue, yelling loudly at the couple, Xue said, "Stop yelling at them. They are doing their best. We will all work faster to make up for their slowness."

The supervisor got angrier really fast.

He asked Xue, "Who do you think you are, boy?"

Xue answered, "Someone who can understand you when you are yelling."

The supervisor's face grew red. He took off his cap, wiped sweaty palms across his pants. He lifted his chin and glared at Xue, daring him to say more.

Xue said, "It is not okay for you to yell at an elderly couple who cannot understand you and who we can all see are trying their best."

The supervisor asked, "Do you want to get fired?"

He added, "Stop it, boy, or I will kick your ass out of here. There's a whole lot more where you come from."

The cousins were scared that Xue would throw a punch. They said they were preparing to hold Xue back. But Xue turned away from the supervisor and walked out of the warehouse. The cousins left their positions and walked out after Xue. They decided that if the man didn't want one of them, he didn't want all of them.

✧

Each day with Xue, we learn a little more of who he will become, beyond being our father's son.

I think often about the wisdom of the Native American man and the words that he spoke: "I am sad to know that there are systems on earth, powerful and mighty systems, that can overlook the coolness of such a young man as Xue. What kind of world are we living in when a man's deeds—the goodness of Xue—cannot translate into a résumé or a job? Xue was sent up to the reservation because he did not fit into the system. I question that system here and now."

Song of Separation

A son wakes up in the early morning.
At the threshold of his house, he says, "Father, show me
    where you have gone."
He walks the dirt path to the garden he must till.
A black-winged bird flies toward a tall tree.
He wonders, "Is this the direction where my father
    could be?"
At the edge of the forest, there is a buzzing bee, perched
    upon a flower whose soft petals glisten in the morning
    light.
The son wanders close and asks, "Father, did this flower
    bloom for you years ago when this was your home?"
In the center of his garden, there is a young deer, head
    bent toward the earth, eating shoots of green rice.
The son quiets his steps and he wants to know, "Is this
    the animal who now carries my father's soul?"

My father knows many things about leaving and being left
behind.

In Laos, my father left the remains of his father.

My older uncles chose my grandfather's burial site in accor-
dance with the laws of feng shui and the advice of an old man
in their village. The old man told them to search for a site that

both attracts water and catches wind. My grandfather was buried in the dip of a mountain's broad back. My uncles believed that the site would bring good fortune and prosperity for his descendants. Neither my uncles nor the old man thought about how hard it would be for those descendants to find their grandfather's grave one day; no one knew then that the Hmong of Xieng Khouang Province would have to leave their homes for their lives.

When he was sixteen years old my father's family fled from the village where he was born and the mountains where my grandfather was buried.

A Communist soldier told my family that a big truck would come for the men in the morning. The trucks had been picking up men and boys from their village for months. Those who had gone on the trucks had not returned. The soldiers said that they were sent to reeducation camps, but the family knew better. All over the mountain villages, people could smell the strong stench of rotten flesh coming from the jungle. Women and girls followed the smell in search of the men they loved. Sometimes the bodies were in a pile. Other times the bodies would be in different spots. Close to my father's village, Grandma and my uncles had found the body of a young boy inches away from his father. He had left finger tracks on the ground where he had been pulled away from his father. He was sliced at the throat. The father had been shot. Most of the time, the bodies were remnants, half eaten by wild animals. What remained was bloated and blue, flesh ballooning from stained, torn clothes. The Hmong of Phou Bia mountain knew that the coming of the trucks meant death. My father's family knew that they had to leave their village before the soldiers arrived with their guns on the big trucks.

My father watched his mother's face by the light of their last fire in the last house he knew as home. Her hair was wrapped in a piece of black fabric, not the traditional deep purple turbans that Hmong women wore at New Year's celebrations but the kind that poor widows of war wore for their husband's burials. Her face flickered in the flames. Her eyes did not move, her mouth did not waver. It was as if her face were set in stone.

My father had never seen his mother run. He could not imagine her running through the jungle, away from the soldiers and the guns.

The only possession of his that my father carried from their home was his prized Hmong rooster. He tucked the rooster underneath his shirt, close to his heart, and held it there for safety. On his back, he carried a heavy sack that Grandma had packed filled with essentials for the family: a large canvas bag filled with rice, a cooking pot, a few dented metal plates, several leaf spoons, salt, dried buffalo jerky, a blanket, a shirt, a pair of pants, and bags of medicinal herbs. At night, my father still dreams of the beat of the chicken's heart against his own, its soft feathers heating up his cold chest.

They were not the only family leaving that night. It was a wonder that the Communist soldiers hadn't yet stationed themselves in the village. News of the family's plans to leave the village before the soldiers arrived had spread to the homes of neighbors and friends, and many had decided to join them in their flight. Some were cooking their final meals in their homes. Others made big fires outside of their homes so they could smoke meat as quickly as possible for the days ahead. A few people took the opportunity to bathe in the river so they could be clean for the run. The village was full of activity as families gathered in front of their houses with their possessions in bamboo baskets, tied in blankets, or secured in tarps, waiting for darkness so they could leave.

With his feet planted on the hard-packed earth of their home, my father wavered between staying and leaving. There was a part of him that wanted to be the one to greet the soldiers in the morning on the big trucks, to stare at them in the morning sun and say, "I will die where my father died." Then there was the part of him that could not forget the look of stone on my grandmother's face.

As the moon watched over the night sky, my father's family led the villagers on foot, through the familiar paths, away from their homes. They heard the cry of night monkeys and the hooting of owls. They saw the glimmer of fireflies in the bushes around them and the glint of stars above their heads where the heavy canopy opened up. At first, the children felt like their flight from home was a game they had never played before. The adults told them to walk as quietly and quickly as their little feet could carry them. The adults told them that there were soldiers coming after them. In order to live, they had to do as they were told. In the beginning, the children played the game with excitement and cooperation, but as the night wore on and exhaustion set in, questions and complaints started, from the youngest to the older ones. They wanted to know where they would sleep, sit, rest, and eat. They wanted to know when it would all end and they could return home. All along the line of villagers there was the sound of adults hushing children with promises they couldn't keep.

"We'll rest as soon as the morning sun comes up."

"We'll eat as soon as the night is over."

"Be good for now. You will be rewarded later."

"Soon. Soon. Soon."

Soon, as the morning light began to filter through the jungle leaves, the sounds of angry pursuit resonated from the mountainsides. Gunshots could be heard. Grenades were thrown.

Villagers scattered in different directions. My father's family, following the order of my older uncles, ran as fast as they could up the mountain slopes. Grandma's sons grabbed her by the hand and dragged her as fast as they could, stumbling with each step, their heavy bags slipping off their shoulders, up the side of a ravine. My father and Uncle Hue saw that some of the nieces and nephews were dazed and confused, standing in the smoke of the falling rocks, looking for their parents, incapable of running, so they grabbed the children closest to them, hoisted them up on their shoulders, on top of the packs, and followed their older brothers and sisters-in-law and their old mother.

The family survived the initial ambush. They resolved to disappear deeper into the jungle and higher into the mountains. They hid in caves during the day. They walked in quick lines at night. On high ground, they looked to the shapes of the mountains as guides. Beneath the towering jungle trees, they kept their hands on each other's backs, so they wouldn't lose anyone.

At first, my father looked up at each mountain they passed. He believed that perhaps they would pass by the mountain where his father was buried. Eventually, one mountain blended into the next, and he stopped looking up. He became more preoccupied with the terrain beneath his feet as the soles of his flip-flops grew thin and the straps broke. His feet bled for days before they grew tough with calluses.

✧

In Thailand, my father left behind his two best friends, our dogs, Choua Long and Aub Seau.

In Ban Vinai Refugee Camp, a place where few got enough to eat, my father found enough food scraps to feed two hungry dogs. For the eight years that my father lived in Thailand, Choua Long and Aub Seau were part of his family.

My father named Choua Long after a Jackie Chan character in a Chinese drama who did not allow his poverty to keep him from challenging the powers that were in place. My father believed that Choua Long was a great dog despite his sad circumstances.

Most of the dogs who found their way into the camp had been abandoned by their Thai owners, and many of them were then left behind when their Hmong owners departed for other countries. Their heads bowed close to the yellow ground, the hungry dogs sniffed their way from one doorway to the next, whimpered at each entry, and awaited their fate. This is how Choua entered our lives.

My father loved Choua Long for choosing to stay in a place where so many were leaving. Lots of Hmong families were leaving the refugee camp for Australia, France, Canada, and the United States of America. Some were killing themselves in the wake of the nightmares from the war. The cries of their loved ones caused vibrations all over the camp. Leaving was all around, and there was nothing to hold Choua Long inside the camp except some belief that love and kindness still lived there. He was a special dog.

By the time I was old enough to recognize Choua Long as ours, he didn't need a little kid pulling on his tail. He spent his days napping beneath the tall trees in the compound. He opened an eye whenever a noise jerked him from sleep. When the sun rose high and grew too hot, when the shadow he rested in grew fat and short, he scrunched to try to fit into it. The thin skin of his belly showed huge ribs underneath—in a different time, a kinder place, he would have been a big dog. Then, I thought him to be a lazy dog. It was only at the sound of my father's voice that Choua Long moved with life. Whenever he heard my father, the highs and lows of an order, a call to come closer, an entreaty for strength—it didn't matter what or why my father called or to whom, Choua Long rose from his slumber. His skin shook, and through leaps and bounds he ended up, inevitably, at my father's side. He did not respond this way to anyone else.

Aub Seau, however, was different.

I was five years old. I did not like animals. Mosquitoes bit. The fruit bats that the Thai soldiers sold to the kids died after only a few days. The chickens in the compound lot all had bald spots that made them look sick. I knew that many of the dogs ate children's poop to stay alive. The only animals I liked were the goldfish that swam in a cement bath full of green lily pads in a distant relative's section of the camp. I marveled at the fish's ability to mirror the color of the sun on the bright days, make the surface of the water shimmer, its golden body slicing through the dark liquid. In my child's eye, minisunrises appeared each time the goldfish came up to the water's surface. It was not important to me that one of the female dogs in our compound was hurt.

I had seen her lying beneath the big tree near the house, first in the shade and then, when the sun shifted in the sky, in the hot sunshine. Her belly was round like a ripe Thai banana and her nipples stood out like little bald grass hills, one after another. Her eyes were closed and her breathing was heavy. She looked thirsty, small bubbles of white foam forming around her mouth. My older cousins hovered over her. They found an old box and filled it with dry grass. Two of the bigger cousins carried her carefully and placed her on top of the grass bed. She didn't struggle. I sat at the edge of the communal bamboo patio, my legs dangling through the rails, waiting for her last breath.

My older cousins helped each other and carried the box right beside the stairs that led up to where I sat, almost right beneath my dangling feet. I watched the dog's exhausted body battle whatever was hurting her from inside. I was concerned that if the dog died right there, its ghost would haunt the patio and the stairs. My imagination conjured up dark nights, the ghostly shadow of a dog with sharp, white fangs and a round belly lurking beneath the bamboo.

I imagined an innocent child, someone close to my age but not me, waking up in the middle of the night, needing to pee, poking her parents in the back to tell them so. The sleepy father says, "Here's a flashlight. You be careful. Go quietly and pee beneath the tall trees close to the house." The obedient child, braver than I was, grabs the flashlight and gets out of bed, unhinges the twine that holds the light bamboo door against the night, and walks across the creaky communal patio. The child follows the flood of her light, walks to the end of the patio, proceeds down the stairs, one plank at a time. Suddenly, terrible pain. A knife cuts into the back of her ankle. She falls. The shadow dog with the fang and round belly trembles over her, its saliva dripping white and foamy on her pale face.

I drew my feet through the rails and sat Buddha-style with them tucked safely underneath me. I averted my gaze from the sick dog. I tried to even out my breathing. I got up quietly and made my way toward the voices of my mother and my aunts talking quietly in their sewing circle by the entrance to the kitchen. A few of my little cousins were sitting in the hammock of their mother's laps, the expanse of fabric from their Thai sarongs providing a small swing. Although I was older than the lap babies, I was my mother's baby, so I crawled into her lap, swung in my little hammock. For the rest of the day, I noticed from a distance the crowds of cousins checking in on the dog, bringing her water and patting her head and her engorged belly.

That night as I drifted toward sleep, I caught a little of the conversation between my mother and father; the word *aub*, the Hmong word for dog, came up again. The drone of my father's steady voice was like the sound of the crickets and night owls, comforting. The scent of the cooling menthol baby powder my mother had patted softly on my neck and under my arms tickled my nose. I yawned. Dogs were not interesting. My lids grew heavy with sleep in the whisper of my mother's and father's voices.

The next day, I got up to an ordinary Ban Vinai Refugee Camp morning. The sun was in the sky. The humidity was high. I could feel the sticky heat under my neck. Dawb had already gotten up and had gone with the cousins to the sewage canal to capture tadpoles. My mother was in the communal kitchen with my aunts, swatting at the black flies that flew around the dishes on the table as they waited for the last of the food to be ready for the morning meal. My father was outside talking with my uncles by the big clay water urns.

I stood at the doorway of our sleeping room, rubbing my eyes and stretching. I called for my father. At the sound of my voice, my father excused himself from the group of uncles and came to get me. He approached me with wet hair from the morning wash and a thin towel wrapped around his neck. I extended my arms for my father to lift me up. I tried to smile in the sunshine, but my father said, "You are grimacing already?"

My father and I had a simple routine. Each morning, he came up to the sleeping quarters at the sound of my voice, lifted me into his arms, carried me across the patio and down the stairs, let me pee beside the big trees in the compound, warned me of the cold water from the huge clay urns, and then led me to the small patch of cement beside the water urns and helped me clean myself. That morning, my father diverged from our routine. Instead of heading toward the big trees where I usually peed or toward the water urns, he walked me to the bin where the female dog had been sleeping. It was crowded with cousins. Some of them, too short to see inside the bin, were on tiptoe while others were lifted onto the shoulders and arms of older cousins.

My father pointed into the bin and said, "Look."

I saw Aub Seau on his first day of life. His was one of many tiny wrinkly faces, eyes peering into the light of morning. I braced myself against my father's hold at the sight of the puppies. Their mother was lying exhausted as the tiny bodies curled around her. Some of the puppies were sleeping deeply, others yawning with outstretched paws, reaching for the warmth of a sun they couldn't see. The little bodies rubbed against each other in shades of brown, gray, and dots of black and white. Many of them were shivering despite the heat and humidity of the morning.

I asked, "Why can't they open their eyes, Father?"

"The little puppies cannot open their eyes because your world is so bright," my father said into my hair.

I don't remember if we picked Aub Seau or if he picked us

by climbing into my father's palm. I was not involved in his name selection. Perhaps it was Dawb who named him Aub Seau, the tiger dog—despite the fact that he didn't look anything like the tigers of my imagination. (We had no books in the camp, no pictures of tigers to reference, so the only tigers I knew were the ones in my head, painted by the words of the adults who told stories of times before.)

Each week, my father measured Aub Seau's strength by his ability to carry me on his back. Aub Seau's hair was so short that I could cling to him only by holding tight to his neck. I remember the thrill and the exhilaration of our short rides, my feeling like I was eternally slipping, but unafraid of hitting the ground because my father's hands were on either side. Aub Seau and I made our way around the small yard of our compound on the yellow dirt made smooth by the feet of animals and humans alike. Beyond my father's shoulders, Aub Seau's were the first and only from which I've seen the world.

On the hot days, my father bathed our dogs by the cement well. He hauled up buckets of water and poured it over the dogs. Choua Long sat patiently as my father scrubbed. Aub Seau was much less mannerly. He jumped in the stream of water from the bucket. During the soaping, he shifted restlessly on his legs and squirmed, turning his head this way and that. His tail went up and down. It was a small battle to wash him. Once cleaned and out of my father's hold, Aub Seau shifted his weight to his back legs, leaped, and started shaking his head, sprinkling water droplets into the air. He was a cloud dog. I ran to feel the falling of his rain. Aub Seau was full of energy and fun and I liked watching him, playing with him, and pretending that he was a water buffalo (the only other animal I knew by sight and sound beyond the dogs and the hungry chickens that pecked the earth dry).

I loved Aub Seau and my father loved Choua Long, but our love could not keep them with us when it was time to leave Ban Vinai Refugee Camp for America. There was no way a family could register its pets as refugees of war. When news of the camp's eventual closing grew strong and hopes of a life for us in Southeast Asia grew weak, our mother and father registered us as asylum seekers. We'd waited for eight years but the end, when it came, was quick.

There was a rush to get ready. There were two large suitcases to fill. There were the relatives who were leaving days before us and those who would follow. The big orange buses drove away from the camp, full of people we loved, day in and day out. Their hungry dogs looked to the empty houses and cried after the trail of dirt dissipating in the distance. At night, they howled and howled at three in the morning.

The night before we departed from the camp, my father did not sleep. The dogs barked from the yard. My father twisted and turned. My mother told him to take deep breaths. He practiced taking deep breaths. They did not work. He got up, dressed, and left our sleeping quarters. I could hear his steps on the creaking of the bamboo patio. I listened and listened, but once my father was outside with the dogs, there was only the silent night and the crickets and the frogs who sang their lonely songs.

The day of our leaving, there was no time for a suitable farewell. All the aunts and uncles and cousins were trying to say goodbye. Each hug, each hold, each rub, each touch was just one more way of connecting. Our dogs, like the rest of our family, nudged closer and closer, the minutes passed, the sun grew high in the sky and then low.

We simply departed with the eyes of our loved ones on us as

we struggled to keep our faces forward, to stem the flow of tears from falling.

A few years after we got to America, a distant relative visited Ban Vinai Refugee Camp. He returned to Minnesota with a video of the nearly empty place we had once called home. My father heard that the relative had footage of dogs wandering around the camp. My father and a long line of uncles asked to borrow the tape. When the video finally made it to our house, we watched it as a family. We paid attention to each hungry dog that passed in front of the camera. None of them were Aub Seau or Choua Long. When my father gave the tape back to the relative, he asked about them. What happened to the beloved dogs after their owners left? The relative told my father what he had seen: truckloads of abandoned dogs were picked up by Thai farmers in old trucks. He had heard that the dogs were taken to different provincial cities where the youngest and most beautiful were sold as pets and the rest killed.

✧

In America, my grandmother left my father.

My father had grown so used to leaving that he was not prepared for Grandma's departure, despite the fact that we all saw it coming.

It was 2002. My grandma had taken a hard fall at Uncle Sai's house in December. She could not get up. The doctors told us that her body was shutting down. They prescribed painkillers and gave us Ensure to feed her. They provided us with a metal hospital bed for her to sleep on. We moved Grandma from Uncle Sai's house to Uncle Eng's because he was more educated, better equipped to read the labels on the medicine bottles and administer her daily care. Near the end, Grandma refused the pills and the liquid nutrition that Uncle Eng offered on a tea-spoon. After two weeks of being in and out of a dark, sweaty coma, waking up at unpredictable intervals to speak of a long journey with people from the past, Grandma passed away on February 18, 2003.

My grandma's parting took two and a half months.

I think about that time often, but only through the haze of my own missing, my yearning to hold on. I could see it through my father's eyes. I could not feel it through his heart. I did not want to because it would force me to reckon not only with my grandmother's mortality but my father's and my own. Perhaps, like me, my father had tried to put off my grandma's demise by not reckoning with it. My father would not give words to her leaving and yet Grandma left.

My grandma had said that there were people who had loved her before us. She reminded us that she had a mother and a father, brothers and sisters, even a husband, my grandfather, waiting for her in the land of the ancestors. Grandma said that her leaving us would be a return to them.

My grandma's last breath was a shallow one. We listened for more, but there were none. The coolness began at her feet and her hands and then traveled toward her chest. The last site of warmth on her body was her heart.

There was a collective cry in the house. The huge family of aunts, uncles, and cousins encircled her body on the bed. The women and the men wailed as the children, hands to mouths, pulled each other close. Many hands reached for Grandma's body and her face. Strands of graying hair were pushed back, a Hmong gesture of love. Her cold feet were massaged, again and again. Uncle Hue held one of her hands. My father held the other.

Time did not stop.

Someone had to report Grandma's death. Dawb did it. A black hearse came for Grandma's body. The two tall men who came in the hearse volunteered to carry Grandma's body out of the house, but my family declined their offer. My father and my uncles carried their mother's body out of the heated house into the cold night. The moon was round and fat, nearly full. The snow glowed in the light of the moon. Our breaths fogged up the air before our faces in little bursts.

We were like a train on the tracks. Grandma's death had ignited a journey. Our extended family gurgled into life. We started the preparations for Grandma's funeral. A date was set. Food was purchased. Sheets of gold- and silver-plated joss paper were folded into boats, spirit money, gold and silver bars. The doors to the family home were thrown open. Friends and strangers streamed in on the cold days and dark nights.

In the month before Grandma's funeral, I recall my father and my uncles dressed in button-up white shirts and black pants. They received guests. They cried with them. They made technical decisions for Grandma's funeral, such as how many cows to kill and what direction her coffin should face. My mother and my aunts wore whatever sweaters they had to keep warm and worked with red, throbbing hands, cooking the endless meals in an outdoor, improvised kitchen. I saw the women through the steam and the smoke of the big pots and pans, standing over the large propane stoves.

Over the course of the three-day funeral for my grandmother, I sat briefly with my father and my different aunts and uncles in stretches of painful time. They were in tears. They stared straight ahead. They walked the length of the funeral home. They sat at the long tables, wiped pieces of white napkins over dry red eyes, stood before Grandma's coffin, crying into open palms. Our eyes and our noses ached like our hearts from the heavy scent of the roses and the lilies, the strong smell of strangers' colognes and perfumes colliding with formaldehyde and death. People came to offer condolences and share memories of Grandma, how she had been a mother to so many of them as well. My father and my aunts and uncles wept.

Years before, Grandma had told my father that when she died, he should go on his knees and ask her for what he wanted most. At the time, my father was sharpening a knife by the sink. It seemed he wasn't listening. He hadn't answered her. But when the moment came for Grandma's body to be carried out to the cemetery for burial, my father went to his knees on the cold ice in the gray parking lot. He bowed his head as my grandmother's body was carried past. Uncle Hue and Uncle Chue helped him up.

Sectioned by my age, my relationship to my grandmother as her grandchild, surrounded by older and younger grandchildren, it was enough that I was where I should be: a student of grief, learning about loss.

After we buried my grandmother, we spent days and nights at Uncle Eng's house with the relatives trying to live life in a place where death had visited. We slept on the floors in the living room and bedrooms. The only spaces free from bodies in the crowded nights were the two bathrooms and the kitchen. On soft blankets, we shared thin pillows and stories as we looked to the darkened ceiling.

One night, one of my cousins closest in age and circumstance told me of a story she was working on in her head. It was a Chinese drama with many parts. The men and women fought with swords and magic. They flew on the tops of the bamboo groves, dived deep into the caverns beyond the foam of waterfall. The heroes and heroines found special plants that brought the dead back to life; they loved each other beyond thousands of years. My cousin was excited. She wanted to turn it into a book. I tried to follow her story, but I was hearing another voice, my grandmother's, tell me a different tale, the one she had shared about the days after her mother's death many, many years ago, in faraway Laos, on a high mountain-top, in the place where Grandma said her heart dwelled, Hmong Mountain.

✧

Grandma was only a young girl, about ten years old, when her mother died. It was the night after her burial, and my grand-mother and her three younger siblings were staying in the house of an uncle. She had no idea where her father was that night. The four of them were sleeping on a guest bed in the main part of the house. The night fire had dwindled down to embers. There was a small hole in the thatched roof, placed there for the smoke of the fire to escape. The younger children were asleep, the two boys against the wall, the baby, a little girl no more than six or seven months at the time, was cuddled close to Grandma, whimpering. Grandma said the shadows of the night shifted; it started as a darkening of the air above them, air that turned into the shape of a hand, a hand that grew first up high in the ceiling, and then bigger and fiercer as it made its way down toward the children in the bed. At first Grandma was scared, but the embers from the fire strengthened in the waft of a cold current, and she could see that the hand reaching for them was her mother's. The fingers, straight and strong, came closer and closer. Grandma blinked to make sure she was awake.

When she felt the hand and its cool wave before her face, she whispered, "Mother, please go where you are supposed to go. Don't wake the children up. Don't scare them." At her words, the hand halted, a moment of indecision, and then it slowly retreated, all the way back to the ceiling, and out the hole, a shadow in the dark of night, disappearing with the coming of the morning light.

$\diamondsuit$

Grandma's long life, Grandma's stories, came flooding at me in those early days after her death. I did not give voice to them or write them down, but I paid close attention. They were stories from her childhood, from her early years with my grandfather, from the years she toiled taking care of her children, my aunts and uncles and my father. Unlike many of the adults around me, my grandma did not speak much about the war or the years in it. Many of her stories were of life in an earlier time; she was the only person in my family who had lived long enough to have come to a lifetime's worth of stories before the guns and bullets severed our ties with peace. My grandma had survived the war in Laos, the years of waiting in Thailand, and the poverty and racism of America; she had lived to be an old woman who died of natural causes. She became in this simple way my first American hero, a survivor and a keeper of stories.

As I was mourning the loss of my American hero, my father was feeling, for the first time, the reality of being an orphan. Although he had always articulated his life in those terms—and at times so convincingly that I had taken for granted the love and the work my grandma had invested in her children—

my father learned after her death what life as an orphan was truly like. His older brothers and sisters aged overnight. He could see how the lines in his own face deepened and the skin on his lids grew thin and sagged.

When my grandmother left my father, all the beautiful words that he had borrowed from neighbors and friends to comfort his heart disappeared, and there were no more songs to sing.

Dreams and Nightmares

It is the same dream. It is the same nightmare.

My mother and I are on our way to the garden. I am young, maybe three or four, and she holds my hand firmly in hers. Her gait is uneven so I mirror it with my walk. First, one step to the right, a small bend in the knees, and then one to the left, another bend in the knees. I see the familiar tree and the beloved rock. It is a fat, stout tree; its leaves are heavy like an uneven cloud of green atop the thick trunk. The rock is only a rock but it is the rock that my mother sits on to hold me in her lap on our visit to the garden every day. My mother tells me that it is the rock she sat on to nurse me when I was a baby.

In the dream, we are happy. I can smell the fresh morning dew on the grass and feel a slight wetness to the leaves from the bushes as they touch my shoulders along the path. The sun is bright. The morning sky is a clear, light blue with patches of white cloud trailing along the horizon, evaporating slowly in the growing heat of the day.

In the nightmare, I know what will happen. There's the sound of metal slicing air. Up high, I see what looks like a rocket speeding across the blue, coming closer to my mother and me. Just as we are approaching the tree and the rock, the rocket falls in front of us. There is the sound of wood splintering and rock exploding. The air is a fog of debris. I lose my mother. I hear her frantic voice yelling my name, "Bee! Bee! Bee!"

The last word I can make out in the noise is "Run!"

I run from the smoke. My hands are in the air. Both palms wide open. I want to call back to my mother but the debris has entered my mouth. I try to wet my mouth with my tongue. All I feel is something jagged. Rocks? Teeth? I do not know.

I wake up from the dream and the nightmare. My hands are shaking uncontrollably. In the palm of my right hand I can feel a remnant of rock embedded. I look in the gray dawn streaming in through the Minnesota night but I see nothing. I feel my right hand with my left, but I find only hard flesh, torn and mended by machines and time. I cannot stop the shaking in my hands. I cannot dislodge the feeling of the rock that has pierced my flesh even as I massage and massage my throbbing palm.

At the dining table, in the light of morning, my children watch me. They notice the shaking of my right hand on the table beside my plate. They do not say anything. I tell them about the dream and the nightmare.

I tell them, "It is only a rock, but it is the rock that my mother sat on to nurse me. You cannot see it but I can feel the rock in my hand."

I close my palms, willing the fingers of my right hand to cover the rock of memory protruding from my flesh.

❖

After Grandma passed away, our father stopped singing. At first we didn't notice. We were busy dealing with our own grief, and then we were busy growing up and getting older.

Dawb was graduating from law school. I was off to writing school. Xue was caught up in not belonging. Sib Hlub, Shell, and Taye were in middle school and high school—tumultuous years of bad makeup, lots of laughter, headphones on and off, Hmong and English colliding in midsentence. Our mother was busy exploring the world with Max, our baby, and meeting the challenges of each child.

In the early months after Grandma's death, our father drove in circles on his way to and from work. He said he passed the right exits on the highway but took the ramps to the wrong exits. Somehow he read the time in the car as eight o'clock when it was just five, causing a panic. He thought the light on the street was red when it was green. Cars honked at him. He stopped at the sides of the roads. He turned on the emergency lights. He sat there playing with the signal turns. The way to work and the way back home stretched from its normal twenty-five minutes to thirty, forty, fifty minutes.

We knew he missed Grandma. We asked if he did.

He said, "Yes."

We didn't know what else to say. We said, "We miss her, too."

He said, "Yes."

The months turned into a year and then the year turned into five. The absence of our father's songs became our daily lives, caught up in a past we did not believe we could retrieve, lost to a time and place where and when our father lived in the presence of his mother's love.

Dawb graduated from law school. I graduated from writing school. Xue found a small path in the forest of strangers to walk toward us again. Sib Hlub began her college journey. Shell and Taye made their way through the public school system. Max learned how to sit, how to stand, how to walk, how to run, how to talk, and how to listen.

There was nothing Max loved more than listening to our father's stories. Our father, certain that Max was to be his youngest and worried that his second son may have come too late in his life, scared that his child might live a life yearning for a father like he had, worked to pass on the pieces of our history through stories. He told Max the old tales he had told each of us and others we'd never heard, lighthearted, funny stories about Zab the Liar, whose farts and poops and lies overthrew devious kingdoms and conquered coldhearted princesses. Cuddled in our father's arms, Max listened to story upon story of how the Hmong people had lived in Laos, in Thailand, and in America, and how we had dreamed in these countries of places beyond.

Max's favorite story was of a true incident that happened to one of our distant relatives in Laos. He loved it so much and asked for it so often that when our father wasn't around, we took to telling his story via our individual voices:

"It was the late 1940s. The incident took place in the high mountains of Phou Bia, in Xieng Khouang Province, close to where our family comes from.

"Yor was a young man at the time. His father had died when he was just a baby. His mother had raised him by herself. Yor and his mother lived in a small hut far from the nearest village, close to their rice and vegetable fields. Because it was only the two of them, they could not afford to lose the time walking to and from their fields like bigger families.

"His mother adored him and worked endlessly to give him everything that he needed and many things that he wanted. If he wanted a brand-new spinning top, she would walk far into the woods, find the sturdiest tree, and proceed to chop it down, even if it took her from sunrise to sunset, so he could have a spinning top made from the best wood. If he wanted a new outfit in a certain design, she would sit in the bright, merciless sun day in and day out, with her needle and thread in hand, to make the exact pattern he had envisioned. When Yor grew into a young man, he became unhappy; he found that the thing he wanted most his mother could not give him: the friendship and companionship of those his age.

"All day long, Yor would work at his mother's side in their fields, but each night he grew restless and would leave her alone in the hut. He would make the two- to three-hour journey by foot to the surrounding villages to chat with the other young men, and make visits to the young women who laughed softly from behind split-bamboo walls.

"His mother worried about him through the long nights. She could not sleep because she knew that the French were in Laos and they often sent contingents of men around the mountain villages to collect taxes and cause mayhem. She could not sleep because she knew there were large animals that traveled through the dark of night, preying on vulnerable flesh.

"Yor's mother asked and then pleaded with him not to go out so often at night. At first, he merely looked at her and shrugged a nonchalant shoulder, and when night fell he proceeded to do exactly as she had asked him not to. In time, he became frustrated with her requests. When she started to speak, each time dusk fell, he would look at her and growl. No words, just raw anger from his throat. She grew exasperated and then scared.

"One night, as Yor was walking out of the hut, his mother called to his retreating back, 'Yor, Yor, you do not listen to me at all. I am your mother but you do not hear me as your mother. You look at me as if I am a nagging woman, asking you to do things that would be bad for your health and your life!' In the wake of her rising voice, she could see that he was quickening his steps away from her. In a desperate fall to the ground, she looked at the surrounding wilderness and said, 'Yor's father, wherever you are, I am calling on you to teach our son a much-needed lesson. He will not listen to me. Please talk to your son and make him understand that the life he lives is more precious than my own. It is for his safety that I cannot sleep.'

"Yor heard his mother's words but he did not hesitate. He walked, hurried, to the village and got there just as darkness fell heavy and thick. The mountain stars glistened. He was surrounded by the sounds of night insects and the laughter of young friends, and the night passed quickly for Yor. Before he registered the coming of day, he recognized the crow of the rooster and he knew that it was time for him to return so he could attend to the work of the fields.

"Yor was tired from his night of fun and talk. He walked half-asleep in the gray light of early morning. The grass was wet with dew and soaked the bottoms of his wide-legged Hmong pants. The mountain air was cool. A brisk wind blew, causing the trees to sway and leaves to rustle. He felt goose bumps on his arms rise. He had walked about an hour away from the village when he first felt the inklings of hot air behind his back. At first, he welcomed the warmth, and then the thought occurred to him: how could such a warm breeze blow through the mountains before the sun was up?

"Yor turned around quickly. He saw nothing but the little overgrown path in the dense jungle brush. After a few wary steps backward, he turned again, straightened his shoulders, placed his hand on the Hmong knife he carried at his waist, and walked on. The faster he walked, the stronger he felt the warmth on his back. As his own breathing quickened, so did the warmth at his back. In and out the air went, like someone or something was breathing on him.

"Yor ran the rest of the way home. At some point, he lost both of his flip-flops. Still, he did not look behind him. When he saw the smoke rising from the little hut and the morning sun begin its eastern ascent, he could not contain himself. He called out, 'Mother, open the door for me. Help me! Something is after me!'

"His mother rushed to the door at the sound of his voice. She watched as Yor ran to her. She saw nothing behind him. At the doorway, he had to bend over to catch his breath. His mother was full of worry. She said, 'What's wrong? What's wrong, my son?'

"When Yor calmed his breathing and was able to see nothing but wide, familiar open space behind him, he explained to her the sensation of someone or something breathing on his back. She listened but it did not occur to her that this could be anything but his exhaustion from the night's activities in the village.

"Yor and his mother spent the day weeding their garden, bent close to the earth, beneath the tall stalks of rice.

"When the sun began its descent, both mother and son noticed that the late-afternoon insects had disappeared from sight and that there were no cries of wild birds cutting through the sky. An eerie silence stretched across the wilderness. They did not confer with each other. Instead both hurried to attend to the evening chores and eat a meager dinner of rice with water and sliced ginger dipped in salt.

"After the evening meal, as Yor was preparing to leave for the village, they both heard what they described as a growl that sounded like this: 'Yaorwwwws, Yaorwwwws, Yaorwwwws.' It seemed the sound was coming closer and closer to the little hut.

"Yor and his mother looked at each other. Yor said, 'Mother, I don't think I am going to go to the village tonight, after all.' His mother nodded. They worked quickly in unison. They went outside and gathered their entire firewood stock and piled it beside their fire ring. As night descended, Yor and his mother secured their split-bamboo door to the frame and waited.

"They did not have to wait long. The sound arrived in the wake of the closed door, and heated breath entered through the split-bamboo walls in gusts of steam. The growl was outside their door; the sound had the echo of thunder. 'Yaorwwwws, Yaorwwwws, Yaorwwwws!'

"Yor grabbed the knife at his waist and pointed it in the air. His mother hid behind his back. The door swung inward, the twine rope they had secured it with stretched taut. Yor and his mother could see the broad striped body of a tiger standing up, its front paws hitting their bamboo door, its eyes glistening. Yor's mother recognized something familiar in the glint of the tiger's eyes, dark and luminous, lit by an inner flame. She cried out, 'Oh, my son's father, I beg you: leave my son and me alone. I know I asked you to come and help me talk to him. I did not mean for you to come and eat us both. I beg you, please go away.'

"The door swung back out slowly, but the huffing and puffing did not cease and the steamy breath of the tiger continued to enter the hut. The tiger's breath smelled of rotten meat and the undertone of strong Hmong liquor, which no regular tiger's breath would contain. Only a tiger compelled to act by the spirit of a Hmong man would have had the smell of Hmong liquor on its breath.

"The whole night long, Yor and his mother cowered together close to their fire ring. The tiger spent the night walking around their little hut. Its steps thudded on the ground. They could hear its breathing, in and out, a small rumble from its cavernous chest. Yor and his mother dared not speak a sound. They followed the glint of the tiger's eyes through the bamboo walls. They took turns feeding dry logs into the fire as they waited for day to come and hoped for mercy from the wild force they had unleashed.

"When the shadows of the night slowly began to lighten, they heard once more the growl of the tiger: 'Yaorwwws, Yaorwwws, Yaorwwws . . .' As the sun rose higher and its heat grew stronger, it seemed to them the sound of the tiger's growl weakened. The stench of rotten flesh faded slowly. The night had taken its toll on Yor and his mother, and alas they could not keep their eyes open any longer.

"When Yor's mother woke him up, it was afternoon. The sound of day was around them. There were no growls or movements from outside. Together, the two of them made their way to the door. They peeked out into the sunshine. Yor slowly unhinged the door to find nothing but open air and sunny sky. When they looked down, they saw tiger paws the size of big watermelons on the ground. They followed the trail of paw prints around their home, little islands in the dirt, indentations where sharp claws had been.

"After that night, Yor never left his mother alone again to venture into the nearby villages to seek the company of the young. By the time of the harvest, Yor's mother had saved up enough money to make a dowry payment for a respectable Hmong girl, and Yor was married.

"According to Yor, the story was a reminder of the power of the enraged father, something he had never had the opportunity to witness or learn from."

Max loved the story. In school, he told his friends that his father worked with machines and stories. I told Max that our father was also a song poet. Max did not believe me. He had never heard our father sing.

◇

The loss of my father's poetry dawned on me on a beautiful April day. I was driving my father's truck. Outside, there was a light drizzle. The smell of wet earth entered through the open windows. It was sixty degrees, the warmest day we'd experienced in Minnesota since early October. The snow was gone. The grass was beginning to show green along the highway. The heavy winter had left behind salted roads that were full of potholes. It was impossible to avoid the holes without the danger of swerving into other cars. I pressed the CD button.

I was surprised when a voice, clear and strong, came through, loud. It was a CD of Hmong song poetry. A woman's voice told the story of how love was born between a maiden from the valley of the wind and a man destined to live where the mountains meet the clouds. I listened to the CD for the forty-minute drive from St. Paul to Andover, refamiliarizing myself with the poetic form that my father loved.

In my father's car, I listened to the melodious rise and fall of my language. With the poetry around me, it was easy to believe—as my father had done when his songs had come easily—that the entire world was a garden of meaning. I felt my father's voice calling out to me from the rhymed stanzas of the song on the CD. The woman's voice in the car and my father's voice in my heart together yearned, pleaded, begged, and cried for the rushing river to slow down, for the shifting clouds to halt on their trajectory across the sky, for the moments to converge once more, so that feelings could be reawakened.

When the car came to a stop in front of our brown house, when my fingers turned off the ignition, I could hear for the first time the silence in our lives, the places where my father's songs had been, and feel the desire to call them forth.

✧

For my father, the birth of poetry began in the sounds of words coming together. It was those first early words of comfort and care he had heard and hungered for that inspired his growth in poetry. Through most of his life, poetry had been his friend, a blanket against the cold, a fire to keep his family warm, his gift to his community. Grandma's death had saddened him and his poetry had halted, but we believed he would eventually sing again. None of us thought he would lose the ability to do so.

✧

All my father's life, he had battled an ongoing ear infection— as a boy and a man. My grandma's medicinal concoctions had kept it at bay, but when she died the infection went out of control. The doctors prescribed antibiotics but to no avail. When the drugs ran their course, the fevers and chills started once more. After many doctor's visits, he got a referral to an ear specialist.

The prognosis was dismal. The ear, nose, and throat doctor told my father that the infection had gone untreated for too long and that it had grown deep into the bones behind his left ear. The doctor said that the only treatment option for my father was surgery. In order to heal my father, the doctor would have to remove the infection by hollowing out the bones behind his left ear, where the infection was worse.

My grandma had always taught my father that metal in flesh was not a good thing. In her world, it was the unexpected stab of a sharp Hmong knife, it was a garden hoe slammed into an unwary foot, it was a bullet into flesh. My father hesitated over the doctor's words. He asked his children what we thought. We reminded him gently that we didn't live in Grandma's world anymore. More precisely, she didn't live with us anymore in the world we called home.

Dawb and I asked the specialist questions about the magnitude of the surgery, the recovery process, and the odds in our father's favor. The doctor told us it would be a small operation and that the surgery would take just a few hours. There would be no hospital stay. The doctor said he would do two things: remove some tissue from our father's temple to replace the missing parts of his eardrum and then make a cut behind the left ear, take a drill, and drill out the infection. While he couldn't guarantee the complete success of the operation, he was confident it was our father's best chance for taking care of the infection and preserving his hearing over time. Dawb and I interpreted the doctor's words for our father. We told him that we believed in the doctor's words. He said he believed in ours. The surgery was scheduled. The operation failed.

At a follow-up, two weeks later, the doctor said sorry. While he was successful in taking out the infection, he hadn't anticipated that the drill would be so loud. He explained that there was so little room for doctors to practice the surgery these days with the popularity and effectiveness of antibiotics that young doctors who want to specialize in ear, nose, and throat go to Alaska in search of indigenous folk to try the surgery on as part of their training. There was nothing more he could do. The doctor said that my father's left ear would now be completely useless. The only sounds he would hear would have to be via his right ear.

I asked my father what he heard from his left ear. He said that day and night, the only sound he heard was the ghost of an ocean he'd never visited, its waves washing in and out. When Dawb was in college she had taken a trip to Africa. On a beach by the Indian Ocean, she had purchased a big, pink shell with a smooth, lacquered surface. She thought she could carry the sound of the ocean to our parents. At home, she had held the shell to our father's ears. He told me that while he did not feel the cool of the shell, its sound was what accompanied him now.

The loss of hearing in his left ear created changes in our father. At first, I noticed this only in public spaces. At family picnics, funerals, and weddings, men and women who approached our father from his left side could not draw his attention. In a crowded room, if people talked to him from his right side, the volume of our father's voice in response was often too loud.

Slowly, the loss of his hearing changed the dynamics of our home life. Calling for our father became a challenge unless we were in the same room. Similarly, he could no longer talk to us unless he was close enough to hear. We saved the seat closest to the television for him so he could hear the news. Instead of looking directly at the screen, our father turned his right ear, watched the images from the sides of his eyes. On the telephone, with the receiver to his right ear, the voices of our uncles on speakerphone, our father struggled to multitask as he'd always done in the past.

Beyond our house, our father struggled quietly on his own. On the highway, the sound of a siren coming from the left meant nothing until the lights were flashing before his sight. At work, he took off the earplugs he used to wear to make sure that his right ear could notify him of the beeps of the machines, the alarms in the factory. Slowly, our father started searching the world around him in ways we had never seen, trying to trace the song of the birds, the call of neighborhood children. He turned in circles, trying to locate the sound's whereabouts in a surprised, scared manner. It gave him an old man's startled appearance.

We suggested things for him to try, like reading lips. He complied only to realize that it was impossibly hard because we belong to a language dictated by tones. There were few hearing aid options for him. The one that might work involved a permanent installation, another surgery, an implanted device to amplify the hearing from his right ear around his head. Our father was not ready for more surgeries.

Instead, he started asking people to speak up, to speak louder, to his right ear. Whereas once he had taught all his children that one needed to turn up the volume of one's hearing in the presence of important words, not ask the speaker to just speak louder, now our father had lost his status as a good listener.

With the loss of his hearing, the way our father spoke changed. It began with where he placed emphasis on certain words, and then he lost the clarity of his pronunciation over other words. The way he heard the Hmong language, the language of his heart, had changed forever and it affected the way he spoke it. Our father knew he would never be able to sing his songs the same way he had in the past.

✧

Thus, there were no songs for Max to hear. Max did not get to meet our father as a song poet, and yet the man he got to meet, he loved.

✧

The beautiful April day was gone. Once more, the sky was gray. The air was cold. The greening grass was covered with white flakes. The wind blew biting bits of snow at my father and me as we walked across the clinic's parking lot.

The ear specialist had just apologized: "I'm sorry. Your left ear is now completely useless. You have your right ear for a while. Enjoy it. As we age, these things go."

My father had just said, "Thank you for trying to help."

My father and I walked together, our hands in our respective pockets, to his parked truck. The world felt heavy. This was our life, the spring we had been waiting for. My father got into the passenger's side and I walked to the driver's.

In the car, I pressed Play on the CD player. Now I heard the voice of a Hmong man. The volume was loud. I didn't flinch. I tuned out the volume and focused on the words. He sang a song about sickness and aging, about a man dying and leaving the woman who taught him how to love. He lamented the aging of the human heart and not just his body, the scars on one, heavy on the other. I wanted to press Stop but my father seemed to be listening.

I alternated my gaze between the road and my father. I saw how he sat straight but his face turned toward the window on his side. He raised his right hand, and with his knuckles he knocked gently on the glass of the window. He paused. He listened. He knocked again, once, twice, three times. My father expelled air from his lungs, breath he had been holding. My father raised his hands to the sides of his face. His hands gently cupped his ears and made an armor of skin and bone to protect what was left.

◇

I said softly, "I am so sorry, Daddy. I wanted you to continue hearing the world with me for much longer." I didn't say I wanted to hear his songs again, to tell him that it didn't matter if he didn't sound the same, so long as it was his voice and his words, that my ears would hear the heart that beats there.

I was afraid to look at my father, afraid to see that he had not heard me, or worse yet, that I yearned for something that couldn't happen, was wishing for an impossible return to the man who had taught me how to love words and value them.

The minutes it took us to drive home grew long and heavy. I lost track of the poetry in the song as I focused on my father's silence.

I parked the truck in the driveway of our brown house. My mother's potted plants were dried stalks covered by dirty white snow. The forsythia bush looked dead.

As we got out of the car, my father turned to me and said quietly, "I've not heard the world the way you do for a long time now."

We walked to the front door of our house, looked into the front window, saw nothing but my mother's plants vying for sunshine that didn't exist in the gray day. Instead of just opening the door, I rang the doorbell. I heard the scurry of Max's feet running to the door. The door opened.

Max greeted us with a smile, his dark eyes glistening. My father went on his knees and opened his arms. Max leaped into them.

Max said, "I've waited all day for you to come home so you can tell me a story, Daddy."

Return to Laos (Duet)

On the high mountains, we turn back to take one last
 look:
The roosters, the pigs, the cows, and the horses cry and
 wander aimlessly.
The wild fields yield their ghostly harvests.

Kalia

Our mother and father voted for their first American president
on November 4, 2008. The voting members of the family went
to the YMCA in Andover, Minnesota, to cast our ballots. We
all knew whom we would be voting for: Barack Obama. Our
mother and father were nervous as we approached the long ban-
quet tables; they had just gotten their citizenship earlier that
year. The senior citizen volunteers were matter-of-fact as they
found our names on the long lists. A few of the men who came
in after us glared because we were interpreting for our mother
and father, but we pretended we didn't see their disapproval.

When Barack Obama won the election, my family cried.
Like much of the nation, we believed that while racism existed

in this country, there was hope and promise in the election of an African American president. We had tears streaming down our faces along with Jesse Jackson and the rest of the old civil rights activists on television.

When President Obama said in his acceptance speech, "If there is anyone out there who still doubts that America is a place where all things are possible; who still wonders if the dream of our founders is alive in our time; who still questions the power of our democracy, tonight is your answer," our father looked at Max and said, "He is your president."

In the days after, Max walked around the house with a cape around his neck, his arms swinging by his side, fearlessly. Each time he passed Grandma's photo, he paused and said, "She makes my heart strong like Superman." Each time there was a mention of Barack Obama or his image on television, Max declared, "That is my president."

Thoughts of Laos and Thailand were drifting farther and farther away for my family. We rarely watched Chinese or Bollywood movies dubbed in Thai anymore. We had discovered Hollywood and it was taking more and more of our leisure time and dollars. While we still ate mostly Hmong food, we were also beginning to make our own spaghetti dinners. Along with gingery Hmong sausages, we had started grilling bratwursts— to be eaten not with rice and water, dipped in spicy chili sauce, but on a hot dog bun with ketchup and mustard. The children had started referring to Laos and Thailand as the old country. Our mother and father talked of it less and less.

When we were younger, our father used to tell us that one day when we were all grown up, he and our mother would return to Laos. He talked of the high mountains and the fresh streams flowing strong. He told us of the multitude of songbirds and the wild flowering trees. He said that it would only take fifty dollars a month from each of his children for him to live in Laos like a wealthy, respected man. It was where he wanted to die, he said: the place where he wanted to be buried.

Each time our father spoke of a return to Laos, our mother talked of how the country had changed. She reminded him of what they had heard on Radio Free Asia: the Hmong were prohibited from entering territory still considered rebellious by the Laotian government. She said he would not get to return to the villages he knew, and that many of the people he loved were gone. Her own mother was gone. The grandma we never knew passed away in 1993, more than twenty years after parting with our mother in the jungles of Laos. It was clear that our mother was afraid of returning to the country of her birth in the absence of her mother.

Our father hesitated. A visit to Laos would be no good without our mother. More important, he realized that he had been in America for as long as he had been in Laos and Thailand combined. One country had raised a lonely boy into a young man. Another had aged him with waiting and fear. Now, in America, at long last he had accepted that there was no such thing as a safe country, and that he was destined to live and to die as a poor man. In each country he had lost something of himself. He had come to believe that there would be no salvaging of the past, no return to a time before, no father or mother waiting to be found. Loss was a thing that defied borders, allegiances, claimed each and every soul that sought shelter and light in a thing as troublesome as land and belonging.

In late December 2009, thirty-one years after fleeing from the country, our mother and father had an opportunity to return to Laos. Earlier that year, Dawb and her husband,

Robert, had moved to Cambodia and she was expecting her first child. She would give birth to her baby in Thailand and she wanted our mother and father to be with her. Dawb and her husband bought plane tickets for them and for Max. Hlub was in the midst of her freshman year at college. It was winter break and she was anxious about never having been abroad. Born and raised in America but studying about the rest of the world, she yearned for foreign experience. I got her a plane ticket so she could accompany our mother and father and Max.

Once the tickets were purchased, our mother started dreaming about her mother and the last time they had been together in 1978, shortly after she had married my father. In the dreams things were just as they had been. She would be walking with her mother to the field or gathering wild plants from the jungle. In her dreams, she did not think about waking up or worry about us, her children. She became her mother's daughter again and the future was a distant place rich with possibilities. In the days leading up to the trip, she did not speak of how much she missed her mother or lament about how late the visit was in the coming. My mother lost herself to imagined reunions.

My father was anxious and nervous. He said he had to save money to give to Uncle Shong's children when he met them. He was concerned about the Communist government and its treatment of Hmong Americans. He remembered the names of Hmong men and women from America who had gone missing in Laos. He was apprehensive about Dawb giving birth. He worried that she wouldn't have the strength to push a baby through to life. He grew morose with thoughts of missing us, the children in America, and despite our assurances that I was twenty-nine years old and that I could take care of the house and the three teenagers at home, his eyes were afraid for the adventure to come.

We tried to cheer him up and bolster his excitement. He had always said that the sky he lived under had fallen on him and the earth he walked on had thrown him off. I told him, "This is your chance, Daddy, to see that the sky is still holding and that the earth is intact."

We wanted him to be brave.

Bee

My children wanted me to be brave. They did not understand that I have been running from the nightmare of what happened in Laos since I left. Or that there were things waiting for me in Thailand, little boys and lost dogs, that I knew I could never return to. They did not understand that the bravery they asked of me I never had in Laos or Thailand, and I could not have it on returning to these countries.

At the airport, Chue and I fought tears as we pulled Kalia, Xue, Shell, and Taylor close and held them for a moment. We knew we weren't abandoning them. We knew that they had aunts and uncles who were a mere telephone call away, but we had never traveled so far without our children. All four of them waved us into the long line for security check with big smiles on their young faces.

Standing in the line of men and women, some of them with red passports in their hands and others with green, but most with the blue American passport that Chue, Hlub, Max, and I carried, I felt a communion with the strangers. In 1987, when we had first arrived in America, we carried no passports. We were refugees of war. We, along with all the other families, had carried big plastic bags full of paperwork saying that we didn't have passports or citizenship. Now I felt the stiffness of the passport in my hands. I opened up the front cover with its gold seal and the words "United States of America." I saw the page that read: "The Secretary of State of the United States of America hereby requests all whom it may concern to permit the citizen/national of the United States named herein to pass without delay or hindrance and in case of need to give all lawful aid and protection." I looked at the way I had signed my name at the bottom, the small letters, all connected, like Lao and Thai and English script all at once. I saw in it a brief glimpse of the story of my life.

On the plane, I sat with Max in my arms. He was the same age as Kalia was when we had come to America over twenty years ago. Unlike her, he was not afraid of being in the clouds. He could hardly wait for the plane to take off. His excitement made my own grow. I looked at Chue beside me; she sat straight in her seat, her eyes looking ahead. She looked younger than I had seen her in years.

It took us three flights and over twenty-four hours to return to the side of the world where we had been born. Chue and I shifted our bodies every few hours, trying to find comfort in the chairs and stretching our aching backs and necks. Up high in the sky, surrounded by the darkness of night, I lost myself to thoughts of my journey away from Laos and Thailand. My life played before my closed lids like a movie: I was a young toddler trying to cross the threshold of my house into the bright sunshine; I heard the voice of my father comforting me, telling me not to cry because my short legs were not long enough; I remembered the loneliness of my boyhood and teenage years, how hard it was to learn how to defend myself and those I cared for, first against the people around me and then against the soldiers with the guns who came from the folds of the dark jungle; I saw Chue, young and beautiful and uninterested, filled with much promise and potential, and myself, full of yearning, then we were married and our life happened, one moment at a time, and it got harder and harder from there, with each passing child, with each place we sought shelter in, each year we made it through, the year my mother died, the stillness of her body in her coffin, her face gray to the eyes, cold to the touch, and I felt each song I had and had not sung. I saw it all and I was as helpless in reflection as I had been in experience. Memories assaulted me on my return to Thailand and I was defenseless.

It was a relief when the pilot announced our arrival in Bangkok. Hlub and Max were sound asleep. Chue woke them up gently. When it was our turn to stand up and walk the aisle, I felt my legs shake beneath my weight. In the airport, the sound of Thai voices surrounded me. To my left, it was a buzz. To my right, I made out bits and pieces of conversation. I had missed the language. I had missed the sight of dark-headed people my height. The breath went out of my chest slowly and I could feel myself relaxing.

Chue and I thought we remembered the Thai heat, but we were not prepared for the smell of diesel and the furnace of hot air that bellowed its fiery breath at us as we exited the sliding glass doors of the airport with Dawb, Hlub, and Max. Horns sounded. Men waved at us from different directions. It was a new chaos for us, so different from Minnesota and so far from our experience of Thailand.

At the curb, there were lines of taxicabs waiting to pick up travelers. Dawb approached a man with a shirt pocket full of receipts and pens. She greeted him in Thai, "*Sawatdee ka*," and then she spoke in English. When he shook his head and raised a hand to slow her down, she inserted a few more words of Thai, a language she had picked up in the last few months, words that she remembered from her short time in school when we lived in Ban Vinai Refugee Camp. The driver shook his head. He did not understand her. She turned to us, her mother and father, and said, "Mom and Dad, please help. Tell the driver where we are going and ask him how much he will charge. It is better to agree on a fare now than wait for it to surprise us."

Chue said, "Bee, go," and I did. I spoke carefully because the words felt rusty on my tongue, but natural, too, because at no point in my talk did I feel at a loss about where to proceed next. In English, I always wonder, unsure of the next sequence of words in the translation process. In Thai, I did not have the same hesitance. The driver was excited by my ability to speak Thai. He apologized for thinking I was a foreigner. He welcomed us back to this side of the world. He called me a friend. He made me happy.

The taxi driver and I talked all the way to the apartment building where Dawb and her husband had rented a studio apartment near theirs for our stay in Bangkok. Stationed in Cambodia, they were only in Bangkok to have the baby. The apartment complex was close to the hospital where Dawb would be giving birth. The driver pointed out changes in the country in the last twenty-five years for me to admire. I didn't tell him that I had only been in Bangkok on my way out of Thailand, or that my time in Thailand had been restricted to the four hundred acres of the refugee camp. It was the first casual conversation with a stranger I had had in many years.

Neither Chue nor I had ever been on a vacation. We did not know what to do with the free time. The last time we had days to spend doing nothing was back in Ban Vinai Refugee Camp and that had felt like a punishment. Now we found ourselves surrounded by our three children, free to do nothing beyond the weekly hospital appointments, the city stretching out in all directions around us. Hesitant to spend money we didn't have, we kept to the food stalls and restaurants around the neighborhood, went where Dawb took us, and while Chue, Hlub, and Max were excited by the sights and sounds of Bangkok, I realized I did not know how to enjoy a vacation.

✧

The whole time we were in Thailand, I had been thinking about Laos. My heart was hankering for the country on the other side of the Mekong River. The spicy and sweet of each Thai dish I tasted brought to mind the simplicity of the grilled bamboo shoots dipped in salt I had known as a child, and the thick coconut richness of red and green curries gave way to a yearning for the clear broth of chicken soup with herbs. But more important than the tingling on my tongue, I knew that Chue yearned to see her brothers and sisters—as much as she feared meeting them without the presence of her mother. There were pieces of us that we had left in Laos, and after all these long years, we knew that we had to return to collect them for our journey forward.

Ten days after our arrival in Bangkok, Dawb made arrangements for Hlub, Max, Chue, and me to go to Laos for a week. Her doctor had assured us that she would be fine in the time we were away. The night before we left for Laos, I could not sleep. I listened to the humming of the small air conditioner unit in the room. I couldn't find a comfortable position on the thin mattress. I kicked off the towel-like cover. I drifted in and out of sleep, restless as the gray clouds floating past the round moon. I got up and opened the door to the small patio of our room. Once I slid it across, I felt the heat and humidity of Thailand reach out to me. I closed the door quietly behind me. I stood on the small balcony, my hands on the railing, and I saw fireflies flitter to and fro across the dark corners of the courtyard, small floating sparks in the shadows of bushes and trees. The hot wind blew its nightly breath. The city talked its loud talk of honking horns, zooming motorcycles, tinkling bells, and from somewhere I heard the lonely sound of traditional Thai instruments reminiscent of the Hmong *qeej* drift toward me.

I missed my people in a way that I had never missed. I missed Laos. I missed my fatherless youth. It wasn't only my father, or my mother; it was Laos that had orphaned me in my journey. Separated by decades of time, the leaves of my heart have yearned for a return. Laos was ravaged by war and its aftermath as I had been by life. I knew the old villages would be gone. I believed the majestic mountains would stand. Through the years there had been moments when I believed I would return to Laos only on the wings of death. In death, I would meet again the land that had given me life. I stood on the dark balcony, feeling the flow of liquid fall down my cheek. I felt the roughness of my hands on my weathered face.

Kalia

It was nighttime in Minnesota. The house was sleeping under a blanket of fresh fallen snow. Taylor and I were asleep in the bedroom we shared downstairs. My cell phone rang at two in the morning. I reached one hand out to the small nightstand and felt around for the buzzing phone. I unhooked it from its charger and held its small screen to my face. In the dark, the words "Unknown Number" jumped at me with each frantic ring. I knew that my mother and father were leaving for Laos. Perhaps they were there?

Hlub's urgent voice jarred me from sleep: "We are in Laos but they won't let Daddy enter the country. I don't know what's happening. They are holding my father behind."

I said, "What's going on?"

She answered, "Mom, Max, and I all cleared customs but they stopped Daddy. They've taken him to the side of the customs area. He is talking to them in Lao. The woman keeps shaking her head. She has a gun. Her hand is on her gun."

"Have you called Dawb?"

"No. I'm calling you first."

"I am too far away. I want you to hang up, call Dawb, and she will tell you what to do, okay?"

"Okay."

Hlub hung up.

The next hour was long. I could no longer sleep. I left the room with my cell phone in my hand. The air downstairs was cold. Winter was slipping in through the old windows. I moved to the next floor. I turned on my laptop and Googled "US Embassy in Laos." I looked at the screen. They wouldn't kill my father. They can't kill my father. I Googled "Hmong Americans missing in Laos." Google immediately came up with about 1,640,000 results. The first site was a blog entry from Tuesday, September 4, 2007, titled "Three Hmong Americans Missing in Laos." The men were from St. Paul, Minnesota; they had been visiting relatives in Laos; they were arrested by Lao authorities and all disappeared. The second was an Associated Press article titled "Hmong American still missing after vanishing en route to Laos." Charlie Vang, from Minneapolis, age forty-five.

When my cell phone rang again, it was Dawb. Her voice was calm. She was using her professional voice, the one with which she dealt with irate clients and frustrated attorneys.

She said, "Mom, Dad, Max, and Hlub are waiting for their one-way flights back to Thailand. They are fine."

"What happened?"

Dawb told me the story in clipped chronology. The family flew into Luang Prabang Airport. Our mother, Max, and Hlub made it through customs with no problems, but when it was our father's turn, the officials stopped the line. They asked to make a photocopy of his passport. Two of the uniformed individuals, a man and a woman, took the passport into a back office while our father waited for them at the side of the line. When they returned, they told him he couldn't enter Laos. He asked what the problem was but one of the women in uniform said there was no problem, that our mother, Max, and Hlub could go forward into the country if they wished, but she added, "We will not guarantee *your* safety if you leave this airport."

Our father asked to speak with the family. The woman conceded. Our father told our mother that she could take the children and go through the gate; her brothers were waiting for her on the other side. She started to cry and Hlub became angry. She approached the woman in uniform and asked to speak to her supervisor. The woman placed her hand on the gun at her belt. Our father went over to stop Hlub, telling her, "We are no longer in America. You can't do that here."

Our mother continued to cry. The officials lost patience and said that if the family did not want to enter the country, then they should all leave. They walked our father to the counter and told him that the tickets they came to the country with were no longer effective; they had to buy new one-way flights back to Thailand. They increased the fare. When our father hesitated, the woman in uniform told him, "We forced you out of our country once, do you want us to do it again?"

✧

The only image we have of our mother and father in Laos is a photograph Hlub took as they boarded the plane back to Thailand from the Luang Prabang Airport. Our father is holding Max's hand and they are stepping onto a small plane with its door open and stairs down. He is looking ahead. Max is looking up at him. In the photo, the wind is blowing our mother's hair into her face. She is holding a piece of tissue. Her eyes are downcast and her shoulders are low. Her face is broken. The blue sky above is massive.

Bee

In Thailand, Dawb waited for us at the airport. Her belly, which had already seemed huge that morning when we left her, appeared even larger on her small frame. Dawb had reported the incident to the US Embassy. She told us not to worry. She led our way out of the sliding doors of the airport into nighttime Bangkok.

In the rented studio, Chue called her brothers and told them she was sorry. I could hear them responding to her words, at first calm and then faltering; I could not make out what they were saying. I felt the room grow hot as Chue started crying. I went to stand out on the balcony. Max followed me. We looked down at the pool. Max had no words for me and I had none for him.

Chue came out quietly to tell me that it was my turn to call Uncle Shong's children and tell them that I would not be visiting. She stayed out with Max, looking at the tall buildings in the distance. I dialed the long line of numbers on the page I had carried with me from America. A man's voice picked up after a few rings. There was one phone in their village. He said he would have one of his children go get Shong's oldest son. I waited the few minutes it took for a voice to appear on the other line.

It was a young man's voice that said, "Hello."

I told him, "This is your father's youngest brother, Bee."

I told him what happened at the airport in Luang Prabang. I told him I would wire the money I had brought for him and his brother and sister. As I said these things, I was calm, but the calm wavered. "Laos is a stupid country," I said. "I might never get so close to you all again. I am so sorry I could not come. My heart has made the journey a thousand times, but my body cannot follow."

He was solemn, my son from a deceased father. He had no memories of me. I had not been good about sending pictures all these years. I had seen photographs of him and his brother and sister and their families. Still, in a crowd, I would not be able to pick them apart from strangers. On the phone, I felt my heart breaking for the loss of Shong all over again. The son said he understood. He, too, was sorry. We hung up once our apologies were offered, the dead quiet of distance between us.

At dinner, Dawb said, "Mom and Dad, I want you both to go climb a high mountain in northern Thailand. I hear that from its top, you can see into Laos."

Chue and I agreed.

Dawb secured a guide to take Chue, Max, Hlub, and me up

to Phu Chi Fa mountain in Chiang Rai. Our guide was a slender young man with dark hair that curled about his shoulders. He picked us up in a compact car with no air-conditioning. We drove out of Bangkok with the windows open. At first the sounds and sights from the city held our attention and then it was just the greens along the highway, the miles and miles of banana trees, some of them with green stalks of bananas hanging heavy. The air cooled as we moved farther away from the city. It was dusk by the time we made it to Chiang Rai. We spent the night in a small inn with flickering lights.

Before dawn, the guide knocked at our door and we prepared for our climb up Phu Chi Fa mountain. It was cold and dark. The stars glistened from up high. We shivered in our T-shirts and shorts as we made our way to the car. The beams from the headlights showed us nothing but road as we made our way into the darkness.

When the guide parked the car and told us that we were at the mountain's base, we stepped out of the car. All around, the sounds of frogs and crickets grew loud at our presence. The leaves on the trees rustled in the wind. The guide took us to a small opening in the wall of thick trees that marked the beginning of the trail up the mountain and told us to follow him. He told us to tell him when we needed help or if we felt like we could no longer continue the climb. I was worried about the children and Chue's and my ability to follow the slim figure of our guide in the dark, but it was too late to turn back. The stubborn heart of youth clings even in the body of the aging.

Mount Phu Chi Fa was high and steep. At first both of us remembered the past, when our muscles were strong and sturdy, when mountains had been the place where we had learned to walk and then run, but the exertion of the climb interfered with the beauty of memory. After the first thirty minutes, all we could do was focus on our steps so we wouldn't tumble along the steep route or fall over tree roots and jagged mountain rocks. Chue and I had tried to keep our breathing even, but as the minutes shifted toward sunrise, we lost control of the hot spasms pushing through our tight chests for oxygen.

Chue's trembling hands reached out for mine and I found myself pulling her along. The children, more nimble than either of us, kept close to the guide. For me, the mountain became a series of unsure steps, one after the other, my hand holding to Chue's smaller, softer hand and pulling on her to follow. I could tell that Chue was running on sheer stubbornness. Occasionally, I found myself using her hand as a brace on the uneven ground. Somewhere on the climb up, I realized that she was keeping me going.

I wondered if Chue was thinking about our run through the jungle those many years ago, when the threat of death pushed us forward, when we were too eager and too young to see the eventuality of aging, before we started to understand what time could do to our bodies and our bond, long before we realized that we were moving toward death, each and every day we had together.

When the guide said "This is the top of the mountain," I allowed my feet to stop moving. Chue struggled for breath beside me. She leaned against me. We stood together and saw that the dark had disappeared. We were in a gray-tinted world.

It had not occurred to us that there would be others on the high mountain, but groups of quiet people stood around the mountaintop. We looked up at the sky and saw the stubborn stars that clung to the day. The air was cool and clean. Our breathing evened out. A hushed stillness held the crowd.

Chue and I did not let go of each other. It had been a long time since we had held hands.

When the gray was tinged with touches of purple and a golden sheen began to glow in the east, I allowed Chue's hand to fall out of my hold and walked a few steps away from her. I crouched down on my knees, close to the mountain terrain, and placed my hands on the earth. I felt the hardness of the rocky surface on my knee. I felt the cool wetness of the early morning on the ground.

The sun appearing on the horizon was a shining point reaching in different directions. Out of the mist of morning, I made out a twist and turn, a shadow like a river, the one we had crossed into Thailand, low beneath the mountains. The Mekong River stretched its long body far into the distance. I scanned the mountains of Laos, but I did not know how to find what I was looking for, the place where my father was buried. I knew that Chue would not find the faces of her brothers and sisters in the still forms around us. We were at an impasse. We could not return to the past. We did not know the way to the future. We stood in the moment.

I talked to my father. I told him that I had returned.

Hlub and Max stood together facing the sunrise. They did not care about our moment. They stood in theirs, and this made me happy, freed me from the constriction in my chest.

I asked my father to keep my children safe.

✧

We came back from the mountaintop in time for Dawb to deliver our first grandchild, a little boy we named Phoojywg. In Hmong his name means "friendship." As I tied a cotton string around his small wrist to bless his birth and looked into the murky depths of eyes that appeared to be a marble of brown and green, I said, "May you learn how to be friends with life, Little One."

✧

On the plane back to America, Max looked at me and said, "Let's go home." Up high in the clouds, I found myself missing the hold of the earth.

Album Notes

Niamhostxiav—
We've come here as strangers,
Our sons have learned their letters, and
Our daughters have learned their voice.
But their mothers and fathers miss, we miss.
Miss the act of carrying water and the motion of
    harvesting wild greens,
Miss how the paj dia birds fly in their flock.

Ninety-eight differing flowers bloom, and
Seventy-eight insects cry in their varied voices.
We can hear the nkauj kim yaj hlauj birds cry in the wind.

The cloud flowers fall upon the harvest of cloud fruits.
Up high on our mountainous homes.

The mothers and fathers whisper sorrow among
    themselves,
We whisper of missing each and every little thing.
We whisper: How do we live in this land as strangers
    beneath the foreign sky until the day we die?

Every night the specialists on television predicted that the
economy would get better. They had numbers showing a
decrease in the unemployment rates. President Obama said he

had plans. I was hopeful. Chue had been let go from her job because she had taken medical leave. Her many years as a file clerk, the repetitious motions, raising her hands up high to put heavy mortgage files on the tall shelves, had taken their toll. She had needed carpal tunnel surgery in her hands and rotator cuff surgery on her right shoulder. It was not healing well. We got a letter in the mail saying that the company she worked for had given her job to someone else. Although I didn't know how we would make do with only me working, I told Chue that so long as I had a job, we would be okay.

At work, our supervisor was having me and fourteen of my fellow Hmong coworkers run more and more machines, preparing canning and drilling tools for the big oil-digging operations, on the evening shift. He said that things were picking up, and if we wanted to keep our jobs, we had to work harder, faster, smarter. There was no intelligence in running the heavy machines, just alertness, all the time, energy, even when our eyes grew tired and our hands started shaking. We couldn't ease up on the work, stretch our sore muscles, or close our dry eyes. I felt tremendous pressure because I could no longer hear out of my left ear, and with all the noise from the machines my right ear wasn't holding up well. Still, my friends and I persisted. We were men without options. Many of us had worked over a decade at the company. We knew we would not be able to find other work. We didn't have other skills. More critical, we were all too old to start anew elsewhere.

One of our oldest coworkers, Nhia, had developed bad carpal tunnel. The muscles in his hands had grown weak. He was being asked to run four machines. I couldn't help him because I was the last guy on the line, the polisher. Every piece of tool had to pass by me. But one of the younger guys who could speak

English asked our supervisor if he could help Nhia by running one more machine so that Nhia could run one less. The supervisor said "Fuck you" and walked away.

During the break, the men and I talked about what was happening at the company. We knew that this time the pressure was on Nhia but it could be any one of us. I myself had had carpal tunnel in both hands and had undergone surgery to keep the pain under control. But of course I did the same work, so the same symptoms were coming back. At night, I could no longer pull the covers over me; sometimes my hands caused me so much pain that it woke me from sleep. I didn't say any of this to the men. All I said was, "We are friends. We have to love each other. If we don't, there's no one here who would love us."

We did not expect to be treated like the white men we worked with. None of us got opportunities to train on the fancier machines. Many of us were in positions where the pay was capped. When production slowed, we were often the first to be sent home without pay. At a company barbecue to reward us for our hard work and excellent production, we, not the other people, were asked to eat the hot dogs that fell on the ground. We wanted to have a conversation with the management team about the real danger we were in, running so many machines at once, not about the way management treated us in comparison to our white coworkers.

At the end of the break, we agreed to let the younger men who could speak English talk to the supervisor and request a team meeting. We knew we needed to talk. We would be stupid if we didn't speak up and something dangerous happened to any one of us.

At the end of the shift, as we were clocking out, the younger men told each of us that the supervisor said we could talk tomorrow as a group.

I drove home that night underneath a waning moon. I needed gas but I didn't stop at a gas station. The price per gallon was $3.42. I had no money in my wallet. I knew I should not use the bank card.

The house was quiet. Everyone had gone to bed already. It was past midnight. Chue had left a small bowl of rice and a plate of blanched mustard greens on the table for me. Although I was hungry, I didn't feel like eating. I showered. I tried to sleep. Chue slept on her side, on the shoulder that didn't hurt, turned away from me. My hands hurt. I got up and left the bedroom. In the kitchen, there were a few spotted bananas. I had one. I walked to the living room. I turned on the television. It was a news channel: Syria was going further into civil war; the US military death toll in Afghanistan had reached two thousand. I sat in front of the television until my eyes closed. Chue woke me up sometime before dawn when she realized I was not beside her.

I was tired the next day, but it was nothing different from so many other days. I got ready for work, putting on my uniform and my safety-toe boots. I said goodbye to my children. Chue wanted to know why I was going to work early. I told her about the conversation with the supervisor. Chue approved. She hated that I didn't speak up for myself at work. Chue felt bad about not working. She worried about me. Chue knew about the carbide particles in the air and the dangers of operating heavy machinery and working with hard metals. Like me, she had come to accept it; still, running multiple machines felt illegal to her. She urged me to speak up, even if I had to use one of my friends as an interpreter. I told her I would if it became necessary. She said that she would be by the phone, waiting for me to call at break time.

Most of the men had arrived early. We asked the young ones to check with the supervisor to see when the conversation would be. We were tense but calm. We were quiet as we waited. We all looked tired beneath the bright factory lights. When the two young men came back shaking their heads at each other, we knew something was wrong. When we could see the supervisor walking behind them, we didn't know what to expect.

The supervisor did not wear a uniform like us. He did not have on the blue polyester shirt with his name and position on it and the blue worker pants. A tall man, he towered behind the two Hmong men walking quickly toward us. There was no time for them to interpret. There was no need.

The supervisor said, "Guys, if you don't like the way things are operating, leave."

We understood his words. The young men who could speak English tried to explain to him that we were not giving up our jobs. They said that we only wanted to talk. The supervisor shook his head. He would not talk with us. There would be no conversation. He ordered each man to his station.

My feet would not move. I thought about Chue not having a job. I thought about my younger children at home who needed more time to go to school: Xue, Hlub, Shell, Taye, and Max. I thought about Dawb just having had a baby and Kalia still struggling to build her career. I thought about Chue waiting for me by the phone. I thought about my mother dying. I thought about my older brothers who never had a chance to work in America. I thought about Hue with his own business in America. I thought about the things I had spent most of my life thinking about: fate, destiny, life and death. I did not heed the orders to go to my station. I found the heart of me that was Xue, my rebellious son, my unhappy child in America, my struggling child who knew he did not fit in and did not try to.

All of us stayed in place.

We said, "We are going to get our tools from the lockers. We are going home. We will return when the company is willing to talk with us."

We had lived in America for a long time. We had seen the movies and heard the news about workers like us: Mexican workers and Chinese workers, African American workers, and women and children making a stand until the conversations were had. While many of us did not speak English fluently because at work we were not expected to talk to others, only to the machines, we understood enough. Perhaps hoping that the supervisor would have the conversation with us if we gave him another opportunity to pay a little respect, from one human being to another, we repeated what we had said: "We are leaving if we cannot talk to management about what is going on here."

The supervisor had never seen us stand up for ourselves. He had yelled at all of us throughout the years. He had gotten angry, slammed tables, said "Fuck you." He looked at us, his face registering his surprise.

We waited for him to find suitable words and actions. The round clock on the white wall ticked away the minutes. The supervisor's bafflement turned to anger as his face grew red. He said, "Before you walk out of here, think about your children."

He did not understand us at all. He did not know why men like us stayed at places like this. He did not know the way the human heart worked—at least, not ours. He didn't know that we had been thinking about our children all this time. We had not run through wars, waited in captivity, only to come to this country to work in such factories and have men like him yell at us and mistreat us year in and year out because we had not been thinking about our children. We had taught them we could survive, we had taught them how to work hard; we thought we were teaching them the important lessons. Had we forgotten in our exhaustion to teach them what we were worth? What they were worth? We would bow no longer, bend our heads no more. We were thinking about our children. We were thinking about how we, their fathers and brothers, had to teach them that they were worth fighting for.

I clenched my fist. The burning was no longer in my hands. It was in my heart. The embers I had been banking for so long grew fierce and fire erupted—toward the men in power who dictated how we had to survive. I led the men out of the room. We gathered our toolboxes from the lockers. We left the company.

In the days after, we hoped that the company would call. We grew scared being with our wives and children. We saw the circles grow dark beneath the eyes of our wives. We saw the questions in the gazes of our children as the clock ticked away and we had nowhere to go for work. The days grew so long. The refrigerators emptied. We were scared our families would go hungry.

Dawb wrote a letter to the company on our behalf, listing our grievances and requesting a formal meeting with management.

Before the letter even reached the company, a week after we walked out, each of us got notification from the company saying we had willfully and voluntarily left our jobs. If we wanted our jobs, we had to report to work immediately. No conversation. Nothing.

We despaired. On and off the phone, in conversations with each other and with our wives and children, we weighed our options. We had none. The question we kept coming back to was whether we were men or animals. Did we have a right to ask for a conversation like human beings when we knew we were being abused? Did we want our children to see us as victims, not of war this time but of money? We could not return to work under the terms of the letter, as if we had just walked out for no reason at all. We made a group decision not to return.

The hard times, the American depression, hit us badly. We could not get unemployment help from the county because the company said we had quit. Many of us had carried health insurance for our families. With the loss of our jobs, we lost our health insurance. Each day I watched my diabetic, high blood pressure, and high cholesterol pills disappear and eventually the bottles grew empty. I did not tell the children because I did not want them to worry. I wanted to be strong. I was not. I leaned on Chue, who told me there was no way I could have continued the work under those conditions. I leaned on my brothers, who called and talked to me of Asian politics and the best song poets they were listening to on the Hmong radio stations. I leaned on my children, who told me, "Do not be afraid. Everything will be okay. We will not let anything hurt you."

◇

On Highway 51, headed toward St. Paul, listening to a discussion about probable war and the dangers of nuclear weapons on the radio, Max wants to know, "If there was a time machine, and you could go to the future or the past, where would you go?" He smiles, stretches his palm toward Rosedale Mall, and says, "Look at what human intelligence has built." He says, "Human beings have had the power to kill each other for a long time now, to explode the world, but we haven't. People keep on giving birth to little boys like me, people keep telling us to walk toward the future, the beautiful future. You tell me that everything will be okay, Daddy."

◇

I don't work anymore. Chue and I gave up the house in Andover. We took out the money in my 401(k) account and pension plan. We moved to a house on a hill with the help of our children. It is nothing like the mountains where I was born, but it is high ground in Minnesota. Chue and I have a house with only three bedrooms, not enough for all the children to have their own, but our children know how to share. We live in a clearing, surrounded by woods. A lone, unpaved drive leads up to our house. An empty pole with a tattered rope flies where once there may have been an American flag. In its place, there is the wide, open sky.

My mother would have loved this house, this hill.

I think of her often here. I imagine her walking at the edge of the clearing, right at the tree line with her old sickle in her hand, hacking away at the overgrown bushes and the pesky tree branches. She would have liked walking the quiet woods here, looking for mushrooms, for wild berries, for American equivalents to the healing plants and trees she knew in the mountains of Laos and Thailand. I see her walking with the old black hat she'd gotten from a church basement when we first got to America. She would wear the soft, old canvas shoes that Chue and the girls had gotten her from Kmart. She would wear her black skirt with the red flowers and green leaves and perhaps her favorite polyester shirt, the purple one with the black vines growing wild. I imagine my mother enjoying this phase of my life with me, a stretch closer to the end than the beginning. I think she would be proud of me.

My Hmong chickens scratch at the dirt and the short grass. There are forty, fifty of them. The roosters are in cages, not made of bamboo, of course, but chicken wire I've fashioned in the manner of bamboo domes. The hens lead their chicks. Some of them hide in the cool shade of the pine trees, while others sit at the base of the trees, on the fallen needles. The sight of the chickens makes me happy. They help me remember my father and the ropes he had once upon a time, in the shadows of memory, made for me as he sat by a fire.

I can hear the big German shepherd barking from the back of the house. Xue calls him Sherlock. He was expensive, shipped from some other state, the cost of a small used car. I had objected to it, but to no avail. We don't have the money, I had said. In the end, when the initial anger had burned its course, Chue had reminded me that having money is not why or how people have dogs. She didn't need to say more. My heart fills with love and loss at the memory of my time with Choua Long and Aub Seau.

Uncle Shong, would he be proud of me? Of the man I have been? I don't know, but I think about it as I carry out my actions, big and small. The memory of his gentle wisdom guides me.

Max runs outside with a stick he wields like a sword, followed by Dawb's young boys, Phoojywg and Lajlim, each holding a similar sword. They are fighting dragons beneath the sunshine. I don't need to hear them to know they are on a quest to find treasure, a very important mission to find turkey feathers to put on the house so that we can fly to different places in the world; they are off to build a time machine to take us all to the future.

Inside the house, I know Chue is home with Dawb and Kalia and their baby girls, Shengyeng and Txheeyees, and their husbands, tall, white men whom I cannot have long conversations with but who I hope will build strong lives with my daughters. Shell, Hlub, and Taylor are away at college. In a few more weeks, they will return home for a small break before setting out again in search of their dreams.

I tell them, "When one dreams in the right direction, the dream never dies, one never wakes, it always only grows bigger and bigger."

Chue and I have no money. I raise chickens. She tends her garden. The children grow up more each day and we grow older.

I have no idea when I will run out of time, but each breath I breathe, each song I hear, gives my heart something to sing about—silent, silent songs to enter into the world.

Acknowledgments

I asked my father how he became a song poet. He told me that my grandmother was busy with many mouths to feed. When he was young, he used to go from the house of one neighbor to the next, collecting the beautiful things they had to say to each other. Alone, he whispered the words to himself for comfort. One day, the words escaped on a sigh and a song was born. I told him that this could be the beginning of a book. He laughed. He said maybe it was the ending, and then he said, "Who would read a book about a man like me when there are books about presidents, men like Barack Obama, written by themselves?"

My stubborn heart wanted to prove him wrong, and it had grown strong because of the readers of *The Latehomecomer: A Hmong Family Memoir.* Because many readers told me that they wanted to read more from me, about the men and women who are in my life, they gave me the strength to write *The Song Poet.*

Aaron Rudolf Miller Hokanson, you read over each and every page before I did, and urged me to continue writing even when life dealt us the heavy blows. Thank you for the family and the friends you gifted me with when I married you. Mom Susan and Dad Rudy, your blessing means so much to me and the life Aaron and I are building together.

Baby Jules, I think of you. Losing a baby is something I never imagined and loving one in the process is something I will never forget. I find in the gift of you perspective and the courage that makes life continue.

Shengyeng Coraline Hokanson-Yang, each time I hold you close I enter your bubble of softness, the gift of your scent. You allow me the opportunity to practice the lessons I've learned from Chue Moua, my mother, who offers me warmth even when I don't know I'm cold, food when I forget I'm hungry, and always a shelter in the cocoon of her heart. My daughter and my mother, my hope is to love you both the way I have been loved.

Thayeng Leland Hokanson-Yang and Yuepheng Langston Hokanson-Yang, in the Hmong culture, we say that to welcome life, you must travel to the gate of death. In delivering you both to the world, my heart stopped beating and my breath fell away. When I woke up to the clamor of people around me, calling my name, it was the sound of your cries that I searched for first. One day, I hope you both will pick up this book and find in it pieces of the story and the people you come from, the people you've journeyed far to be with.

Thank you, Coffee House Press, for allowing me room to risk on the page with *The Latehomecomer* and for helping me make the journey into the life of a writer.

Thank you, Bill Clegg, for hearing a young writer read her words and for letting them wiggle their way into your memory so that she could enter into the realm of your expertise and reach further in her aspirations. You make me believe that so much more is possible for the stories I am living to tell.

Thank you, Riva Hocherman, for your patience, your kindness, and the care you've taken with my father's story and my words, and for helping them grow stronger in your presence. I am so happy that I get to learn about how you read and that I get to become a more conscientious writer because of the notes you write me.

Thank you, Hlob Shong, Hlob Nhia, Hlob Chue, Hlob Sai, Hlob Palee, Phauj Ya, Hlob Eng, Phauj Ka, and Hlob Hue. Your love sustained and sustains my father.

Dawb, Xue, Hlub, Shell, Taye, and Max, thank you for your courage of heart, your trust and faith in allowing your lives to help me map out the terrain of our family for a bigger world.

Robert, I cherish that you disagree with all of us on every political and economic argument and agree only on the importance of love and generosity where people are concerned.

Phoojywg, you give me strange birds to look at on days when I have no energy to see.

Lajlim, I will go with you into the woods to play with the baby wolf even if his mother has red eyes and knife teeth and says, "Come."

For my father: It is your poetry and your songs that feed my hunger for language and love. I know I belong to an imperfect man who struggles to love me as perfectly as he knows how. I am proud to be your daughter, to carry in my heart your wealth of emotion and heartache, your quest for meaning in life. Your songs, sung and unsung, guide me in each story I encounter.

About the Author

KAO KALIA YANG is the author of *The Latehomecomer: A Hmong Family Memoir*, which was a finalist for the PEN/John Kenneth Galbraith Award and the Asian American Literary Award, and received the 2009 Minnesota Book Award. Her work has been published in *Longreads* and the *Virginia Quarterly Review*. Yang, who has taught at Columbia University and Concordia University, St. Paul, among other places, lives in Minnesota.